The Case of Peter Rabbit

CHILDREN'S LITERATURE AND CULTURE
VOLUME 7
GARLAND REFERENCE LIBRARY OF THE HUMANITIES
VOLUME 2115

CHILDREN'S LITERATURE AND CULTURE

JACK ZIPES, *Series Editor*

THE CASE OF PETER RABBIT
CHANGING CONDITIONS
OF LITERATURE FOR CHILDREN

MARGARET MACKEY

GARLAND PUBLISHING, INC.
A MEMBER OF THE TAYLOR & FRANCIS GROUP
NEW YORK AND LONDON
1998

Library of Congress Cataloging-in-Publication Data

Mackey, Margaret.
    The case of Peter Rabbit : changing conditions of literature for
children / by Margaret Mackey.
        p.   cm. — (Garland reference library of the humanities ; v.
2115. Children's literature and culture ; v. 7)
    Includes bibliographical references (p.   ) and index.
    ISBN 0-8153-3094-4 (hard cover) (alk. paper)
    ISBN 0-8153-3264-5 (paperback)
    1. Potter, Beatrix, 1866–1943. Tale of Peter Rabbit.   2. Children's
literature—Publishing—Technological innovations—History—20th century.
3. Children's literature—Marketing—History—20th century.   4. Children's
stories, English—History and criticism.   5. Children—Books and reading—
History—20th century.   6. Authors and readers—History—20th century.
7. Potter Beatrix, 1866–1943—Adaptations.   8. Peter Rabbit (Fictitious
character) 9. Rabbits in literature. 10. Rabbits in art. I. Title. II. Series:
Garland reference library of the humanities ; v. 2115. III. Series: Garland
reference library of the humanities. Children's literature and culture ; v. 7.
PR6031.O72T335   1998
809'.89282—dc21   98-6480
                                                                 CIP

Printed on acid-free, 250-year-life paper
Manufactured in the United States of America

Everything is to be found in *Peter Rabbit.*

Malcolm Lowry, *Under the Volcano,* p. 178

Contents

Acknowledgments

It is not possible to acquire and work with scores of versions of a single story without developing a certain obsessiveness. Many people helped me with what sometimes felt like an unending challenge, to find and assess the implications of a representative sample of the huge world opus of *The Tale of Peter Rabbit*. People gave or loaned books and artifacts; they sent newspaper cuttings and souvenirs; they discussed particular texts with me.

The Tale of Peter Rabbit is both an international and a specifically English text. The fact that I did this work in Canada and was able to make several visits to the United States during the time of this project gave me access to large numbers of American texts which would have been difficult to obtain if I had been living in Britain. At the same time, however, there is no doubt that Beatrix Potter is more widely known and more broadly marketed in the United Kingdom than anywhere else. My debt to Jenifer Allaway who acted as my British eyes and ears, who acquired specific books and general information for me, who took every long-distance request as a personal challenge, and who along with her husband Richard made me welcome whenever I could get to Britain, is enormous.

My friends and colleagues in Edmonton were also assiduous in supplying Peter Rabbit presents of all kinds, and contributed substantially to a lengthy and ongoing discussion over a period of two years. Thanks, alphabetically, to Anna Altmann, Joyce Bainbridge, Karen Day, Gail de Vos, Evelyn Ellerman, Merle Harris, Jan and Gary Horwood, Margaret Iveson, Ken Jacknicke, jan jagodzinski, Ingrid Johnston, Rebecca Luce-Kapler, Tom Kieren, Janet and Sunny Marche, Elaine Masur, Jill McClay, Bruce and Anna McCurdy, Lillian Macpherson, Joe Norris, Hope Olson, John and Bev Oster, Pat Payne,

Teya Rosenberg and Elaine Simmt—and many others. Special thanks to Ann Manson for lending her mother's 1908 pirate edition of *Peter Rabbit* for the cover. Few researchers can be blessed with such a supportive academic community; both the Department of Secondary Education and the School of Library and Information Studies at the University of Alberta provided ongoing encouragement. At times it seemed as if half the city of Edmonton was on alert for Peter Rabbit. My next-door neighbors phoned to tell me the animation was showing on CBC television; my sister-in-law's friend found a Peter Rabbit organic cook book at a garage sale; my husband's work colleague in the United States sent a newspaper cutting. My parents also took a great interest in the project and of course I owe my original acquaintance with Peter Rabbit to them, a relationship that in retrospect seems delightfully uncomplicated.

Long-distance assistance came from a number of sources. Nancy and Aidan Chambers provided very helpful advice on copyright questions, as did Judy Taylor. Geoff Fox and other members of the editorial boards of *Children's Literature in Education* supplied general and ongoing support. Suzanne Levesque of Calgary generously offered computer back-up and contributed her considerable expertise in online searches on the subject of Pearson. I would also like to thank Jack Zipes and Marie Ellen Larcada of Garland Publishing for their help throughout this process.

Financially, this work was supported by a postdoctoral research grant from the Social Sciences and Humanities Research Council of Canada and by a grant to support work on literacy and fiction reading in an age of multimedia from the Alberta Advisory Committee for Educational Studies. I am indebted to both these agencies.

My greatest debt, of course, is to my family. They tolerated my obsessiveness (though we did have some family discussions about my husband's recommendation that we all acquire lapel buttons reading "Arm Mr. McGregor!"). My daughter Beth was responsible for finding some of the most extraordinary examples in this study, which would be much the poorer without her eye for spotting Peter Rabbit in the most unlikely places. My daughter Sarah served as my guide to exploring many of the subtleties of different computer texts and made a major contribution to my thinking on the subject of computers and literacy. My husband Terry (who has disliked Peter Rabbit intensely from early childhood, a perspective that was very valuable to me if not to him) was heroic in his support for a project that sometimes seemed as if it would never come to an end, and kept an eye on the international and financial news services for information about Peter, Potter and Pearson. I could not have done any of this work without the help of all three of them. I thank them for that and, more importantly, for all the other ways they enrich my life.

My obligations are many, but, of course, the responsibility for the information, the opinions and the errors in this work is mine alone.

COPYRIGHTS

There are also official acknowledgments to be made. The majority of publishers refused permission for me to make use of their images of Peter Rabbit and I am correspondingly all the more grateful to the following who generously agreed to let their pictures appear in this book.

From *The Tale of Peter Rabbit* by Beatrix Potter. Illustrations (c) 1985 by Lulu Delacre. Published by Julian Messner, an imprint of Silver Burdett Press, Simon and Schuster Elementary. Used by permission.

The Complete Tales of Peter Rabbit and Other Favorite Stories, Running Press, Courage Books, 1986. Illustrations copyright (c) Charles Santore 1986.

Reprinted by permission of the publisher, from Harry Bornstein, Karen L. Saulnier and Lillian B. Hamilton. *The Tale of Peter Rabbit Coloring Book* as told in Signed English, p. 39. Washington, DC: Gallaudet University Press.

Reprinted with the permission of Atheneum Books for Young Readers, an imprint of Simon and Schuster Children's Publishing Division from *Dear Peter Rabbit* by Alma Flor Ada, illustrated by Leslie Tryon. Text copyright (c) 1994 Alma Flor Ada. Illustrations copyright (c) 1994 Leslie Tryon.

Reprinted with the permission of William Heinemann Ltd. from *The Jolly Pocket Postman.* Copyright (c) Janet and Allan Ahlberg 1995.

From *The Parables of Peter Rabbit: Friends.* Video cover illustration by Jerry Hopper (c) 1994. Reproduced by permission of Brentwood Music Publishing, Inc.

Introduction

Print has always been seen as an agent of social change; children learning to read have gained access to a source of potential power. Now print itself is under siege and children are learning to read amid a welter of expanding technologies and different media and increasing commercial pressures.

Not very long ago, reading represented a child's first independent access to the delights of story and information. Radio, television and film all operated on a schedule determined by someone else, and the pleasures of the record player required adult supervision in order to minimize damage to discs and stylus. Today, however, a toddler may learn to manipulate video and audio cassette, CD-ROM and computer mouse, long before tackling the complexities of print.

Commercial as well as technological changes affect the ways in which children engage with fictions. Children's books and toys have been associated from the very beginning; John Newbery offered a free ball or pincushion with copies of the first book to be marketed specifically for children in 1744 (Carpenter and Prichard, 1984, p. 375). However, it is only very recently that a family's discretionary spending has included substantial expenditure on children's recreation. Children's stories have long been recast into other forms (ranging from paper dolls to major stage presentations), but the scale of such transformations has now expanded beyond recognition. Authors or commercial groups who successfully engage children's fictional imaginations may ramify that imaginative commitment into multiple versions and multiplying profits. Children may now meet their favorite characters and their favorite plots over and over again, even without rereading. We have only begun to explore some of the consequences for how they learn to think about fiction.

The market for children's literature is a specialized one but there are good reasons for looking at it carefully. Jan Susina (1993) offers one of them:

> [P]erhaps children's literature should be viewed as a test case for all literary texts in that children's books are more a more open and obvious mix of artistic, educational, and commercial ideologies. From John Newbery to Chris Whittle's "Channel One," children's media continues to be a market-driven commodity produced by the culture industry and influenced to a large degree by parents and educators who make selections for children. To make sense of children's texts, critics are obligated to look beyond the texts themselves to those cultural and social forces that help produce and generate their sales. (p. vii)

The way in which the pressures and potentials of children's literature reflect the larger cultural mix of Western societies is certainly a fruitful area for study. Margaret Meek (1990) suggests that the further importance of children's literature lies in the way it impinges on the development of literature in the future.

> [L]iterature for children may be seen as the significant model, the cultural paradigm of subsequent literature in *the experience of the reader*. Children's literature is undeniably the first literary experience, where the reader's experiences of what literature *is* are laid down. Books in childhood initiate children into literature; they inaugurate certain kinds of literary competencies. (p. 168)

If children's first encounters with texts inaugurate what they come to expect of literature, and if their expectations later translate into both a vague climate of receptivity to certain forms of art and also a measurable propensity to spend money on one kind of text rather than another, then many people should be interested in the importance of children's literature.

John Gray (1995) expresses it differently:

> [W]hat is most essential in each of us is what is most accidental. Our parents, the first language we speak, our memories—these are not

only unchosen by us, they create the very selves that do all our later choosing. (p. 5)

Gray does not specifically mention the first tales we are told as babies and toddlers, but it is not hard to make a case that our early encounters with story will also mark our future understanding, both of the societies described in stories and also of how stories work in themselves and become part of the way we align ourselves with the world we perceive around us.

Storytelling, of course, does not occur in a social or economic vacuum, and the ways in which children meet books and other versions of narrative are currently altering very rapidly. Tom Engelhardt (1991) has suggested that contemporary market forces have reduced the distinctiveness which once attached to the act of reading:

For even the youngest readers, the "book" has, in a sense, been freed from the page and can now be encountered in an almost unending variety of audio, video, play, and fashion formats. In the same sense, the habits of reading, listening, viewing, playing, dressing, and buying have come more and more to resemble one another. (p. 58)

At the same time, he suggests, the massed quantity of material aimed at children represents a kind of threat in itself.

What is at issue here is not whether a child will somehow be damaged by a book, any book, or whether there aren't wonderful children's books amidst the thousands of new titles churned out yearly . . . What is at issue is the *mass itself,* and whether the habit of reading in the context of such a mass may not represent something other than the simple development of a wonderful lifelong practice. Certainly, the entry into children's time of a full-blown commercial apparatus and an ever-larger cast of adults bent on selling Product to the child have also meant the entry into childhood of a new dependency. Previously, it was assumed that dependency on parents would end in some form of independence at adulthood. In this newer world of commercial planning for children, however, early brand loyalty means a lifetime adventure in dependence. This, it seems to me, is what the "habit" of reading is coming to mean in children's books—and the only exit

increasingly being offered from such a world is into infantilized
bestselling genres for adults. (p. 62)

I do not entirely share Engelhardt's generalized pessimism, but I
am grateful to him for making the point that reading is not necessarily
some kind of formless and generic Good Thing. Literacy can be a
domesticating force as well as a source of power. Engelhardt's concern
also emphasizes how much we need to be alert to the changing
framework within which children are being exposed to the idea of
narrative fiction. Even when we are vaguely aware of shifting
marketing strategies, it is very easy to underestimate the scale of what
is happening in the world of children's books and their associated texts,
toys and domestic accouterments.

THE TALE OF PETER RABBIT

Engelhardt is certainly right to emphasize the mass nature of the
children's book market. Any investigation of this mass will quickly
become overwhelming. In order to keep some sense of focus and
proportion, it makes sense to concentrate on a single text as we explore
some of the complexities of contemporary conditions of literature for
children. Just as geologists can learn a great deal about the ground
beneath us by taking a single core sample, so we may explore many
contemporary issues of children and their stories through a study of a
single text.

The example I have chosen is one which, at first glance, might
seem to belong to another, simpler era. *The Tale of Peter Rabbit* by
Beatrix Potter was first published in 1902 and has held a central spot in
the conventional canon of children's literature ever since. Its publishers,
the company of Frederick Warne, have for decades pronounced their
determination to respect the heritage of Potter's artistic achievements. It
would seem logical to look on *Peter Rabbit* as one secure icon in the
maelstrom of contemporary marketing developments.

In fact, however, right from its initial appearance, *The Tale of
Peter Rabbit* has been plundered to sponsor an ever-expanding
collection of consumables and collectibles. Potter herself, as early as
1903, was exploring the potential for manufacturing a Peter Rabbit doll.
During her lifetime, artifacts multiplied, from coloring books to
wallpaper to slippers. She left the copyright of the books to the firm of

Frederick Warne, and, since her death in 1943, the company has been assiduous in promoting her work in a variety of media.

The treatment of *The Tale of Peter Rabbit* over the years supplies a miniature example of factors and forces at work in the world of children's literature as in other forms of publishing. A study of the history of *Peter Rabbit* offers a focus for exploring many important questions about developments in the artistic, technological and commercial frameworks of literature. Questions of ownership, of esthetics, of reception, of copyright, of adaptations and of scale, all need to be considered.

OWNERSHIP

The small company of Frederick Warne could stand as a model of the days when publishing was a profession for gentlemen, often kept in the family. Beatrix Potter's association with her publishers was certainly personal; for a brief period before his untimely death in 1905, she was actually engaged to Norman Warne. For many years after her death, the company guarded her works carefully.

In 1983, however, Frederick Warne was purchased by the larger company of Penguin, in a decade when publishing houses were bought and sold by ever larger businesses. Penguin is a branch of the international conglomerate Pearson, which also owns all or part of a number of other publishing and broadcasting enterprises. These include the *Financial Times* of London, *The Economist*, a number of local and regional newspapers in Britain and Europe, the educational publishers Longman (largely based in Britain with extensive African branches) and Addison-Wesley (largely based in the United States), the more general publisher Penguin, and the purveyors of cheap supermarket books for children, Ladybird. In the years since 1983, Pearson has also moved into television. The conglomerate is part of the consortium which bid successfully to establish Britain's fifth terrestrial television channel (Enchin, 1995, p. B2). It has been associated with Thames Television and the British satellite organization BSkyB, and is currently involved in negotiations with the BBC over international distribution of World Service programs. Recently Pearson purchased a company (Software Toolwords, renamed Mindscape) which specializes in software development and particularly in CD-ROMs.

Pearson has also held extensive stakes in various parts of the oil-drilling business and has owned smaller companies such as the Royal Doulton China Company (though in recent moves to divest itself of businesses which do not relate to the media industries it has sold most businesses which do not directly pertain to its three main areas of information, education and entertainment). One extraneous interest remains in its substantial investment-banking holdings, notably in the international firm of Lazard Brothers (Lazard Frères in France and the United States). The company is heavily involved in the entertainment industry in Britain (and to a lesser degree in Europe) as the owner of such attractions as Madame Tussaud's Waxworks and the Alton Towers theme park.

The effects of Pearson ownership on *The Tale of Peter Rabbit* have been manifold, and tracing the impact of that purchase illuminates more general issues of contemporary publishing. As part of a much larger group, Frederick Warne gained the ability to draw on substantial sums of money to invest in promoting its bestselling product. The first sign of this higher level of investment came in 1987 with the expensive reissue of all of Potter's little books (she produced a total of 23) with their watercolor illustrations "re-originated." What this meant was that Warne returned to the original paintings, made new transparencies, and used newer forms of reproduction to guarantee a fresh faithfulness to Potter's original work. Coincidentally, it also offered the company the opportunity to recopyright the illustrations. This was particularly helpful since Potter's work was due to go out of copyright in 1993, 50 years after her death.

The second sign of massive investment came with the authorized animations of the Potter stories, produced to commemorate the 100th anniversary of the author's original illustrated letter to a small friend in which Peter Rabbit made his first appearance. This centennial also fell in 1993. The first video appeared on BBC television in December 1992, followed by an American premiere in March 1993, and sales of the home video were instantly substantial. The animations (which, according to Warne's front-cover advertisement in The Bookseller of October 9, 1992, cost a record £5.5 million to produce) led to a flood of related print and audio material and a resurgence in marketing products based on the original texts.

A third manifestation of high investment came late in 1995. Mindscape, Pearson's newly acquired software company, began to market a range of *Peter Rabbit* CD-ROMs. *The Adventures of Peter Rabbit and Benjamin Bunny* and *Peter Rabbit's Math Garden* (known as *Peter Rabbit's Number Garden* in the United Kingdom) combine entertainment, instruction and new ways of encountering texts. Clearly the potential for substantial further examples of reworked Potter material is enormous.

There have been other signs that Potter's work was under new ownership, and these do not necessarily reflect huge investment. In 1987 there was considerable uproar in the British media as Ladybird Books (also, of course, owned by Pearson) published "simplified" versions of *The Tale of Peter Rabbit* and *The Tale of Squirrel Nutkin*. These rewrites eliminated many of Potter's more daring and demanding phrases and replaced her watercolor paintings with photographs of stuffed animals. The critical and public reaction to this bowdlerization of classic texts was outraged and vociferous.

ISSUES OF ESTHETICS

In fact, as Brian Alderson pointed out in *The Times*, there was an ongoing precedent for interference with *The Tale of Peter Rabbit*. In 1902, the company of Frederick Warne made a major strategic error when it failed to register the book for copyright protection in the United States. American publishers were quick to pirate the work; in 1904 Henry Altemus & Co. brought out an edition based on Warne's fourth printing (Linder, 1971, p. 109). Potter often lamented the substantial loss of earnings which this mistake had cost her.

Potter's financial and artistic loss, however, now supplies us with a much more interesting and complex esthetic case study. In addition to the artistic heritage so carefully controlled by Frederick Warne, and in addition to the contemporary proliferation of materials based on the animated rendition of that heritage, we also may look at American versions which are much less strictly confined to Potter's own words and images (especially images). The American editions, including a computer program for beginning readers, offer some insight into questions of what makes a story recognizable.

In this welter of versions, adaptations and recastings, we may find ways of exploring just what it is about *The Tale of Peter Rabbit* which survives so many transmogrifications. Is there something in the original words and pictures which is essential and invariably lost with any interference? Are there more durable aspects of the story which shine through regardless of the means of expression? How many elements of *The Tale of Peter Rabbit* can be subtracted or altered before its identity wavers?

ISSUES OF RECEPTION

There are questions about the reception of a highly adapted text as well. What is the impact on cultural reference points if one reader's image of a cultural icon such as Peter Rabbit is extremely different from another's? What is the impact of newer and coarser versions of old stories? How do young readers respond to a subtle text when they have previously met it in a crude and unsubtle adaptation? Does even asking such questions hark back to a frame of values now obsolete?

Perhaps some of the most important questions relate to issues of what children learn to understand about the role of stories in society. If children perceive that one of the key functions of stories is to help them make decisions and organize their lives as consumers (do they want to collect Peter Rabbit or Mighty Morphin' Power Rangers?), how does that affect the relationship between them, their stories and the world they inhabit?

QUESTIONS OF COPYRIGHT

None of these questions is entirely new but, in the contemporary world of children's literature, their significance increases. It seems very clear that the proliferation of versions is not going to go away in the immediate future. Stockbrokers and investors, analyzing Pearson's prospects, do not mince their words about the importance of making varied use of copyright materials. In a 1995 report on Pearson, M. Beilby *et al.* of S.G. Warburg Securities are frank in their assessments: "Pearson's core business is the ownership and generation of copyright. It is a beneficiary of new delivery systems, especially the CD-ROM" (n.p.). "The prospect of secure growth from copyright exploitation outweighs market concerns over recent acquisitions" (n.p.). Pearson, says this report,

> has been transformed from a multi-faceted conglomerate into a more
> focused developer and exploiter of copyright and content . . . The
> business focus therefore is the generation and exploitation of

copyright and the operation of high growth delivery systems. Pearson is increasingly becoming a business that is driven by its back catalogue. Prima facie this should prove to be a high multiple business long term. (n.p.)

Pearson is only one company, albeit a large one, but its ownership of Penguin, and hence of all the Puffin copyright material, makes these statements powerful auguries for the immediate future of children's book and materials marketing. The arrival of the new Penguin CEO, Michael Lynton, underlines the potential in this direction. Lynton previously worked in a variety of capacities for Walt Disney, and departing Chief Executive Peter Mayer said, "Pearson and Penguin are lucky to have found someone with such broad experience of books and brand management" ("Michael Lynton," 1996, n.p.).

It seems clear that the current state of children's publishing and marketing, with potential for considerable future development in CD-ROM and computer material, calls for a contemporary esthetics of versions. The new facts of ownership, with most publishing firms now part of one international conglomerate or another, also suggest the potential for change in how literature is presented to children. We need to find ways of taking account of the role of the marketplace in framing children's developing understanding of narrative and of fiction. *The Tale of Peter Rabbit* offers one productive route into the exploration of such territory.

VARIANT VERSIONS AND COMMODITIES

The story of Peter Rabbit exists in a large number of variant versions. Almost every one of these versions provides interesting insight into many of the possibilities in reworking and marketing texts for children. There are *Peter Rabbit*s which draw on traditional variations: pop-ups, lift-the-flap books, toy theaters (see Lewis, 1995, pp. 183–188). There are new tellings which draw on modern technology: videos, audiocassettes, CD-ROMs, a computer program, Internet sites. Different authors have produced stories loosely linked to Potter's book which demonstrate postmodern sensitivity and intertextuality. Warne and their collaborators and competitors have produced a large collection of activity books and a monthly educational magazine.

The market in merchandise and artifacts is almost unbelievably enormous, with some products aimed at children, others at adults. The range of commodities is staggering: stuffed animals, crib toys and mobiles, puppets and board games, baby clothes and dishes, china figurines, clocks and music-box collectibles, expensive hand-knitted sweaters and a book of knitting patterns, ready-made children's clothes and bolts of cotton fabric printed with Potter characters, tea, jam, toothbrushes and soap, placemats and coasters, wall stencils and stickers, paper towels, even a Peter Rabbit cake sold by branches of Sainsbury's supermarket in Britain. At least two major toy shops, F.A.O. Schwarz in the United States and Hamley's in London, have whole sections of the store specially signposted and earmarked exclusively for Potter-related toys and other merchandise. In the Lake District of Britain, where most of Potter's stories are set, and in Covent Garden in London, entire shops are devoted to selling Potter materials.

Most of these products are approved by Warne and produced by a variety of companies operating around the world, licensed by a firm called Copyrights. The pirate market is also substantial and while it mostly flourishes in North America, I did find isolated examples of noncopyright materials in Britain as well. Some of these unauthorized versions of the story of Peter Rabbit attenuate the association almost to invisibility. One of the most extraordinary examples is an animation called *The New Adventures of Peter Rabbit* which comes with its own spin-off package of book and audio-tape versions. Sony Wonder, the producers of this animation, claim a link with Beatrix Potter's classic text, but the cartoon alters just about every essential aspect of the original story. Peter is given a set of buck teeth, an American accent, a fourth sister Hopsy, an entirely changed character, a large set of allies, comical sidekicks and enemies, and an entirely new plot. Another amazing retelling casts Peter Rabbit as a Christian preacher, singing songs about God and Jesus on home videos. This Peter is a human-scale puppet, like Barney the Dinosaur, and he sings and dances with a group of four children and a set of animated vegetables.

ISSUES OF SCALE

Collectively the variants allow for some perspective on a contemporary phenomenon. David Lewis (May, 1995) has usefully pointed out that books, related toys and other kinds of merchandise have a long history of association. Nevertheless, the sheer scale of what has happened to Peter Rabbit is breathtaking in its own right; such an explosion in reworking and commodifying represents a qualitatively new development in the relationship between children and their stories.

In the course of this project, I have worked with a limited budget. I decided almost from the outset that I would buy none of the associated merchandise and that I would acquire print or multimedia versions only if they offered some new perspective on the issue of reworking. Even operating within these limits, I find I have two large boxes containing approximately 100 variant texts in a variety of media, not to mention a Sainsbury's cake box and a special order form for Potter figurines from a package of Kellogg's cereal. Having explored a range of shops in cities in Canada, the United States and Britain, I have notes and prices concerning more than 200 different Peter Rabbit-related texts and objects, defining this category very strictly and overlooking all the mass of material which relates to other Potter characters. And my search has by no means been comprehensive or exhaustive.

If *The Tale of Peter Rabbit* were a single, isolated example of "exploitation of copyright," it would still be an interesting story but not necessarily one of vital importance. However, though I would like to think that the Potter phenomenon represents the upper end of the spectrum of possible marketing initiatives, it is only one case among many, with the range of fiction-based collectibles for juveniles growing every day. Similarly, there is long history of stage presentations and other reworkings of children's stories, and the 20th century contributes its own substantial list of film, audio and now computer versions of books.

However, it is only very recently that domestic video and audio machinery and the cheap availability of numerous video and audio productions have given even toddlers more or less simultaneous access to a variety of versions. A two-year-old can now easily be a connoisseur of variant texts, and there is clearly a great deal of money to be made in marketing such variants to the parents of the smallest consumers. Computer texts are still relatively expensive, but their prices are falling and parents' perception of the desirability of computer literacy drives their sales even at today's relatively high prices.

This is not a national or even a Western issue. I pursued my Potter inquiries in three English-speaking countries; however, Peter Rabbit, like many other fictional characters, does not stop at national or linguistic borders. Japanese tour buses are causing problems of overcrowding at Potter museums and shops in the Lake District of England (Darnton, 1995, p. A4). The Internet contains a number of sites for Peter Rabbit and Beatrix Potter and while many of these are marketing ploys of one kind or another, they indicate another way in which national boundaries are becoming irrelevant. Pearson's own official Peter Rabbit Home Page gives a list of addresses to contact if you want to order Potter stories in various languages; 31 countries are listed.

The idea of exploring "conditions of literature for children" by means of a single text is a fairly grand and ambitious notion. In fact, I began work on this project with the simple and relatively modest idea of exploring the multimedia versions of a single text. What I found was that this particular text led me to ask much larger questions. The implications of what is happening to *The Tale of Peter Rabbit* are both daunting and fascinating. What follows is an account of what I discovered and what my findings imply for contemporary children.

THE CASE OF PETER RABBIT

The Story of Peter Rabbit, Chicago: The Reilly and Britton Company, 1908.
Illustration by John R. Neill.

CHAPTER 1

Peter Rabbit: Potter's Story

On my table lie 35 books of *The Tale of Peter Rabbit*. Each is different in some important way. There are other versions of the book on the market, but this sample is reasonably representative. This collection does not include any kind of activity book, a different form of text to which I will turn later. All 35 of these books are simply bound sets of words and pictures purporting to tell the story of Peter Rabbit. Some of them are authorized by Frederick Warne; others are not. Some of them include Potter's own words and pictures, although not all of these feature Potter's own words and pictures arranged on the page in the form and design she originally dictated. Some of the books include Potter's own words and someone else's pictures; others include Potter's own pictures and someone else's words. Eleven books contain the story both retold and reillustrated. Surely, in such a range of versions, there are discoveries to be made about how we may define and talk about a textual work of art in our time.

THE ORIGINAL TEXT

Three of my copies are editions of the little book produced by Potter. To all intents and purposes, this is now a stabilized text. Potter's first telling of the story came in a letter to a friend, followed by a privately published edition and then by the first of many printings produced by Frederick Warne. Early print runs led to some changes, but by the fifth printing the text and pictures were recognizable as we know them today and the text has not changed since 1903. (Linder, 1971, pp. 108–109)

My three copies of this text are very similar but not identical. The quality of production in the artwork varies, but otherwise the most significant differences among them probably lie on the copyright pages.

The copy which was bought for my children, probably in 1981, is undated and simply asserts the copyright ("in all countries signatory to the Berne Convention") of Frederick Warne. The 1987 version is more aggressive. It establishes copyright of the text and original illustrations as of the first publication date, 1902, and goes on to declare a separate copyright for the new reproductions, dated 1987. Unusually for a copyright page, it includes a paragraph asserting the virtues of the new edition:

> The reproductions in this book have been made using the most modern electronic scanning methods from entirely new transparencies of Beatrix Potter's original watercolors. They enable Beatrix Potter's skill as an artist to be appreciated as never before, not even during her own lifetime. (p. 6)

I bought the third small-text version in the United States. It is a Dover Edition paperback which purports to be an "unabridged republication of the work first published in 1903" (p. 2). By 1903, the published text had more or less stabilized into the version familiar today. It is not clear whether Dover's edition is a reproduction of the Warne 1903 copy or of the American pirate edition. There is no mention of Frederick Warne anywhere in the Dover copy.

The colors in the Dover version are very dark and sludgy compared to either of the other two editions. The print is very marginally larger and the arrangement of words on the page is therefore not quite identical, though the differences are extremely slight. The actual ordering of words and pictures is exactly the same.

To my eye, the two Warne editions are identical except for the increased subtlety and detail of the illustrations in the newer production. Brian Alderson (1987), however, suggests that the new reproductions fall short of the standards established in the first editions of the Potter books.

> It has been an honorable, and expensive, undertaking and the results compare very favorably with the often wayward reproductions that figured in post-war editions of the books. Many pictures now emerge with a spirited freshness . . . How far the plates measure up to the author's intentions is less easy to assess . . . I have been able to compare all the 23 books with their first editions (all of which were

supervised by Beatrix Potter) and the new "authorized" series often falls short of the standards established there. Time and again plates appear to be too lightly tinted so that detail is lost (Lakeland landscapes are a blur; peeping faces fade into the background) or natural appearances alter (blackbirds look like thrushes; bluebells turn mauve). In addition there has been a regular move to enlarge the pictures—which may, in fact, bring them closer to their original size, but which causes them to swamp the books' small pages (nor does poor positioning on the page help here). (June 1987, p. 63)

It is important to note that every reproduction of a text may carry some costs. For this study, however, I shall not develop any detailed comparisons but simply refer to the 1987 production with the "re-originated" pictures, as representing the original text.

THE TALE OF PETER RABBIT

There are at least three distinctive elements of the picture book considered as art form: the gutter which divides the two pages of any opening, the demands of the page turn, and the convention that words and pictures will work together in some complementary way. Other aspects of the book (text, pictures, overall design) can be judged by criteria established in other genres.

These six general topics can aid us in reaching judgement on a particular picture book. Potter's work bears investigation under all six headings.

Text

The content of the story of Peter Rabbit is fairly slight. Peter is forbidden by his mother to enter Mr. McGregor's garden, since his father was put in a pie by Mrs. McGregor. He disobeys this injunction and stuffs himself with vegetables to the point of feeling sick. At this point, he encounters the dreaded Mr. McGregor and a terrible chase ensues. Sparrows, a mouse, and a cat are all unable to help him. Eventually, Peter escapes and arrives home with a stomach-ache. His mother doses him with camomile tea, but his more obedient sisters have bread and milk and blackberries for their supper.

The telling of the story is considerably more distinctive than the plot outline. Potter's language is spare and ironic. On the surface, she is clearly on the side of law and order; Peter's misdeeds are punished by his terror in the garden and by his stomach-ache and unsympathetic treatment that night. But the detached tone with which Potter describes Peter's disobedience actually functions to raise the question of just whose side she is on.

All the ambiguities of the word "brisk" may be applied to this story: the pace of the telling is sharp and lively; the author's matter-of-fact attitude suggests that Mrs. Rabbit's strictures about the garden never had a chance with a young rapscallion like Peter. And yet, the wording, while spare and polished, is more than just "brisk;" it is supple and elegant, without a superfluous syllable. Potter claimed that when in doubt about her style she turned to her Bible which encouraged her to cut and simplify.

> My usual way of writing is to scribble, and cut out, and write it again and again. The shorter and plainer the better. And read the Bible (un-revised version and Old Testament) if I feel my style wants chastening. (quoted in Lane, 1968, p.135)

Much has been written about Potter's refusal to write down to her young readers; the sentence usually quoted as the telling example from *The Tale of Peter Rabbit* is this one:

> Peter gave himself up for lost, and shed big tears; but his sobs were overheard by some friendly sparrows, who flew to him in great excitement, and implored him to exert himself. (p. 33)

Similarly, in terms of the content, Potter pulls no punches; Mr. Rabbit's horrible fate is made clear on the second page of the story. Again the word "brisk" comes to mind, yet the wording is delicate as well as robust. "Your father had an accident there," says Mrs. Rabbit; "he was put in a pie by Mrs. McGregor" (p. 10). The euphemism of the word "accident" is sharply negated by the subsequent explanation, but even in the final phrase the use of the passive voice and the humor of the incongruity mitigate the appalling facts, if only slightly.

In the original letter to Noel Moore, the reference to Peter's father and the pie does not appear. By contrast, in both the privately published text and in Warne's very first edition, the horror was more graphically conveyed than in the version we have come to know. The remark about

Peter's father originally had its own page, complete with a picture of Mrs. McGregor serving a handsome pie (*Linder, 1971,* Plate 4). These early versions also enlarged on Peter's sensations while lost in the garden. After the mouse fails to help him, the story continued,

> Then he tried to find his way straight across the garden, but he became more and more puzzled. There surely never *was* such a garden for cabbages! Hundreds and hundreds of them; and Peter was not tall enough to see over them, and felt too sick to eat them. It was just like a very bad dream! (*Linder, 1971,* p. 52)

A further section, later deleted, was even more gothic:

> He went towards the tool-shed again, but suddenly there was a most peculiar noise—scr-r-ritch, scratch, scratch, scritch. Peter scuttered underneath the bushes. Then someone began to sing, "Three blind mice, three blind mice!" It sounded disagreeable to Peter; it made him feel as though his own tail were going to be cut off: his fur stood on end. (*Linder, 1971,* p. 53)

The text in these early editions also contains further details about Peter's mother, interpolated upon his return to the fir-tree. Most of these eventually appeared in *The Tale of Benjamin Bunny* and emphasize the hardship of her working life.

The deletions were made for reasons which demonstrate that even an original work of art has to work within the constraints of its methods of production. Warne specified that they could afford a total of 30 color illustrations plus the frontispiece, so Potter had to remove 11 pictures from the privately printed edition which included mainly black and white pictures. Sometimes she transferred the corresponding text to another page; sometimes she deleted the text altogether. Further cuts were made after the fourth edition had been printed in 1903, in order to make room for colored endpapers which, among other functions, advertised other titles in the series of little books.

Insofar as Potter approved all the changes, the text we use today may be considered her final best opinion on *The Tale of Peter Rabbit.* Nevertheless, today's version is really the fourth production of this story, preceded by the letter to Noel Moore, the privately printed book, and the very early editions from Frederick Warne. There were some slight changes made and revoked over subsequent editions, but effectively today's version has been available since 1903. To keep this study readable, that 1903 text, in its 1987 incarnation, is the one I shall refer to as the "original" *Peter Rabbit*, in order to distinguish it from all its imitators.

In the 1903 text, as in its predecessors, Potter provides an authoritative, though not intrusive, narrative voice. Her editorial comments are direct: "good little bunnies," "very naughty." The narrative "I" appears only twice (pp. 30 and 56), but the feeling of a story under the control of the storyteller is always present.

The story of Peter Rabbit raises real questions of great significance for young readers. Peter disobeys his mother without a moment's hesitation, and her powers of punishment appear to be limited to the dose of camomile tea. Her response to the loss of the jacket and shoes is confined to "wondering" (p. 54). The threat represented by Mr. McGregor, however, is enormous. Peter, running and hiding in the garden, is in a state of very real jeopardy; he and his young readers are entitled to be truly terrified. Potter does not belabor this point, but she does not camouflage it either. Peter, both as a rabbit and as a child, lives in a world where some options are closed to him, but all choices have consequences. His dawning awareness of his own mortality is not made explicit anywhere in the book but it does dominate the story.

Contemporary sensibilities have raised questions about gender in this story. The good girls and the bad boy are stereotypes which have a lingering afterlife even in our own enlightened times. The tearaway son of the widowed mother is another highly conventional figure. Mrs. Rabbit's difficulties with Peter are clear to see, but Potter does not take sides. Peter takes foolish risks out in the world, but home is still safe and his mother is there to look after him.

However the details of this story suit us today, it is clear that *The Tale of Peter Rabbit* tells a story and raises issues that are not trivial, and that resonate with small children who must also work out the limits of obedience, assertion and consequences.

Pictures

The small watercolors which also tell the story of Peter Rabbit are as distinctive as the prose. Potter's delicate lines and washes are instantly recognizable. While the stories reflect her acuity about human foibles, her pictures are famous for the care with which she portrays recognizable animal demeanor, despite the clothes and the upright postures.

Overall, the pictures communicate a strongly unified effect. There is no sharp framing of the pictures but none of them floats unanchored in space. If the background does not provide linkage for the figures in the foreground, Potter substitutes a light grey background shading so that no figure is unconnected from the others. Even the picture of Peter slipping into the watering can (p. 36), which is the closest to free-standing, is grounded by a very pale grey shadow.

The little vignettes are irregularly shaped. Many of them are some form of rough rectangle or oval. Often details of the drawing break the boundary of this shape, which is, in any case, rather nebulously established. Mr. McGregor's outline rises above the background on page 24, for example; Peter and Mr. McGregor are both silhouetted against the white page in the next drawing on page 27, although a grey wash connects their feet. Peter and the watering can on page 36 create their own outline. In other cases, smaller details break the frame, such as it is; the rake handle obtrudes past the background wash on page 39; Peter's ears do the same on the next page, as does the mouse's tail on page 44.

The home scenes, with two exceptions, are firmly anchored in a relatively regular shape, some form of rectangle with rounded corners. One exception is the frontispiece which shows Mrs. Rabbit dosing Peter with the camomile tea. The other exception is the second picture within the main body of the story. Mrs. Rabbit is issuing her warning about Mrs. McGregor's garden. Flopsy, Mopsy and Cotton-tail are receiving their baskets and their instructions with equal docility; Peter, with his back turned and his whiskers on the alert, is clearly entertaining rebel thoughts. The picture serves almost as a form of technical foreshadowing; we are not surprised, later on, to find the cosy ovals and rectangles disappearing. This picture makes a similar contribution to the plot; there is nothing in the words to suggest problems to come (except the well-known convention that a character in a book would not issue such a warning for nothing), but the picture makes it plain that Flopsy, Mopsy, Cotton-tail and Peter are not all cut out of the same cloth.

The decision to produce the pictures in color is (as we will often find in this study) one marked by questions of judgement, technology and price. Potter's own privately printed book contained largely black-and-white drawings, partly because of price considerations, partly because of her fears about the technological difficulty of color reproduction and partly because she thought the colors might be repetitive over so many drawings, consisting as they did mainly of "rabbit brown and green." (Linder, 1971, p. 21) Warne insisted on color but this decision meant that the number of illustrations must be reduced. Potter wanted to use a three-color printing process used by Hentschel and there was much negotiating over costs and royalties as a consequence. Warne's 1987 reorigination of the pictures is simply one more stage in an ongoing process.

Openings and Gutters

Potter's use of the gutter is straightforward and conventional; on any double-page opening there is one page of text and one page of picture. In *The Tale of Peter Rabbit*, the pictures alternate without exception between the right page and the left page of the opening.

One aspect of the book that sets it apart is the exquisite visual balance between text and picture. The gutter is used almost as an equilibrium-setter. Text and picture are each set slightly towards the top of the page, and the blocks of text contribute much the same weight to the page as the opposing watercolor vignette. The sense of control and regularity thus created is considerable, and may indeed contribute its own weightiness to help answer the question, "Whose side is Potter really on anyway?" Visually, law and order rule across the gutter. A set of words is associated with a particular picture in an utterly stable way.

Page Turns

The page-turning requirement of a picture book contributes a great deal to the overall impact of the text. On a page full of print, it is just about impossible to dictate that the eye must not flick on ahead and spoil the surprise. When the next words and pictures are hidden over the page, the author may be much more definite in announcing surprises. Furthermore, the page turn takes time, builds in obligatory pauses in the reading. Its contribution to the rhythm and pacing of a text is enormous. No amount of punctuating and paragraphing can be as absolute as the built-in break (brake?) of a page turn.

Beatrix Potter, working at a relatively early stage in the evolution of the picture book, shows a command of the page turn which has rarely been bettered. The page breaks serve many narrative and poetic purposes. The good behavior of Flopsy, Mopsy and Cotton-tail is established (pp. 16–17); the potential for contrast lingers for the time of the page turn before we see Peter heading straight for Mr. McGregor's garden (pp. 18–19). Peter's feast on the vegetables (pp. 20–21) lingers for a moment while the page is turned, time enough for the consequence of feeling rather sick to set in on pages 22–23. Mr. McGregor himself, appearing on the very next page (pp. 24–25), comes as a complete surprise to the reader as well as to Peter; the page turn in this case has acted as a shield. When Peter hides in the watering can (pp. 36–37), the delayed mention of the water appears at the end of the page, setting up suspense over the consequences to Peter, and this time the page turn delays resolution. By the end of the book, we are not surprised to find the last two openings (pp. 56–59) returning to the symmetry of contrast between Peter and his sisters. To those who have read the story aloud over and over again, the timing of these pauses becomes an integral part of the story and its performative impact. The story is shaped around the bursts of text and the delays.

And yet, some of these page breaks were based on contingent rather than absolute artistic decisions. When Warne decreed color and also said that 11 drawings would have to go, Potter was obliged to repaginate much of her text. She could play with the limits of convention and form, but some of the limits of technical reproduction were non-negotiable. Such limitations are part and parcel of almost any form of art which is publicly distributed.

Design

Size, shape, arrangement of words and pictures on the page, choice of typeface and arrangement of lines of print, all these design details contribute to the overall impact of a picture book. The element from this list which is most immediately associated with Potter's books, of course, is size. The little books, which Potter insisted should be the right size for small hands, are as distinctive for their dimensions as for many other ingredients. Libraries and bookshops often locate them separately and very early on in the book's publishing history, special bookshelves were marketed for the Peter Rabbit stories.

Other design elements also contribute to the overall effect, and another distinctive element in *The Tale of Peter Rabbit* is the use of white space. Margins are generous, especially at top and bottom. The amount of text varies from page to page, a fact which provides yet more reassurance that the page turns were chosen for esthetic impact rather than because the author ran out of room. The effect is one of spaciousness and stability. A particular set of words and a particular picture are juxtaposed on purpose. The words end at a given point because the next words belong to the next picture. No matter how contingently the original decision was made, more than 90 years of fixity have made their mark. The effect is subtle but psychologically real: each opening is *under control*.

Integration of Pictures and Text

One of the conventional distinctions between a picture book and a story with illustrations is that, in the picture book, both words and pictures are essential to the telling of the story. The pictures are not simply an additional embellishment; they share with the words the task of conveying the import of the story.

On this level, *The Tale of Peter Rabbit* is a triumphant success. The illustration of Peter and his sisters on page 11 conveys far more about character and potential plot development than any word in the text. At the opposite end of the spectrum, words and picture on pages 42–43 work quite differently. The rabbit in the illustration could be merely disconsolate; from the text we know that Peter was in a state of extreme terror and confusion. On pages 46–47, where Peter sees the cat, text and picture combine to create a *tour de force* of reticence; neither is explicit about the sinister potential of the cat, but the sense of menace is clearly conveyed.

All the elements of this little book combine to create a commentary on an issue of vital importance to small children: the importance and limits of order and stability versus the importance and risks of disobedience and self-assertion. The overwhelming achievement of the book is its ultimate ambiguity on this topic. The reticences of the text (Peter had a stomach-ache, but he also had the feast and Potter never makes any explicit judgement on his behavior), the potential for anarchy in the frame-breaking pictures versus the containing stability of the surrounding white space and page boundaries, the security of the rhythms of words and page turns, all combine to support a bounded and limited consideration of the important idea that risks have consequences.

CHAPTER 2

Peter Rabbit:
Ways of Recasting

There are many, many variant texts of *The Tale of Peter Rabbit* in print at any one time. The firm of Frederick Warne has made substantial efforts to keep control over reproductions of the image, but, at least in North America, the battle has clearly been lost. Warne continues to issue warnings, however; in 1993 the company placed a stern advertisement in *The Bookseller*, the publication of the British book marketing trade. "Peter Rabbit packs a powerful punch," admonishes the headline, and the advertisement goes on to spell out the consequences for those who ignore Warne's copyright status. This advertisement is so remarkable it is worth quoting in full.

> For 90 years Frederick Warne, publisher of **The Original Peter Rabbit Books (TM)** by Beatrix Potter has been caring for **Peter Rabbit (TM)**, **Jemima Puddle-Duck (TM)**, **Tom Kitten (TM)**, and the many other famous characters created by Beatrix Potter. From the first toy Peter Rabbit in 1903, Frederick Warne has built up a large licensing program worldwide, successfully merchandising high quality products featuring the **Beatrix Potter (TM)** artwork and characters supported by a substantial body of copyrights, trademarks and trade usage.

> Today, as part of the Penguin Group of companies, Frederick Warne continues to develop its international publishing and licensing program in conjunction with its associate companies, licensees and world-wide merchandising agents, The Copyrights Company Limited. Over the years, this program has attracted imitators and infringers, all of which Frederick Warne has successfully pursued through legal

action in this country and overseas. Frederick Warne takes very seriously its responsibility to look after and protect the integrity of the **Beatrix Potter (TM)** property, and will always take action against any person, firm or company producing or selling any product depicting a character or artwork which has not been licensed by Frederick Warne.

Authorized **BEATRIX POTTER (TM)** products bear **THE WORLD OF BEATRIX POTTER (TM)** or **THE WORLD OF PETER RABBIT (TM)** logos. Look for these logos or ask your supplier for proof that their product is an authorized **BEATRIX POTTER (TM)** product licensed by Frederick Warne. Do not buy goods infringing Frederick Warne's rights, as to do so will involve you in expensive legal action. (*Bookseller* 12 March 1993, p. 65)

It is all enough to make one start thinking of Warne as a verb rather than a proper noun! Nevertheless, in North America at least, the genie is out of the bottle. I had no trouble, either in Canada or the United States, in locating and buying many recastings of *The Tale of Peter Rabbit*. Even in Britain, I found two examples of texts which seemed to me to flout copyright: a miniature version of Charles Santore's reillustrated Tales of Peter Rabbit and Sony's extraordinary video animation, The New Adventures of Peter Rabbit, which claims an association with Beatrix Potter on its cover.

Warne's admonishment is doubtless unabated in its legal implications, but the force of its moral and esthetic rhetoric is considerably diminished by the fact that I also had no trouble in finding numerous recastings of Peter Rabbit bearing the Warne imprimatur. By my count, *leaving out* all the hardback and paperback editions of Potter's original little books, the Canadian Fall 1995 catalogue for F. Warne & Co. contains no fewer than 196 Potter-related entries; the Ladybird catalogue, whose productions all require Warne consent, offers another 32, and there are further Warne-authorized titles available in Puffin.

I propose to organize my discussions of the recast texts on esthetic rather than legal terms, and to group my explorations of variant texts of *Peter Rabbit* according to their degree of divergence from the original work. The levels of contrast between the work of Potter and that of her imitators offer many kinds of illumination on the original as well as the variants.

A complexity which arises in discussing such books is the degree to which it is possible to treat them on their own merits. In the very terms of their creation, their existence is parasitic on a previously existing work of art. Anyone who wanted simply to tell, in whatever medium, a story about a rabbit stealing vegetables from a farmer's garden, could produce a different story; there is nothing preemptive about the plot of *Peter Rabbit*. These stories are all adaptations; to what extent should we discuss them with reference to the original and to what degree should we attempt to take them on their own terms? The answer to that question is complex.

At the same time, it is easy to fall into the trap of taking Warne's legal and financial assessment too literally. Reworking a previously existing story is a legitimate artistic enterprise, which has existed as far back as we have records. Copyright questions and esthetic questions should not be confused.

As always with issues of artistic judgement, there would seem to be an irreducible element of subjective esthetics at work. Clarifying the basis of such subjectivity is part of the challenge of dealing with multiple versions of a story. It is possible to divide the *Peter Rabbit* texts and artifacts into two categories, those which create the effect of having been produced to exploit a willing market and turn a profit, and those which strike the observer as taking the original story as a set of limitations and boundaries to a genuine act of reimagining. Not everyone will agree on each example (as will become clear when we look at the 1992 animation), but at least such a distinction makes it easier to discuss the explosion of linked materials which marks many fictional enterprises nowadays.

POTTER'S OWN WORDS AND PICTURES RECAST

In my pile of books about Peter Rabbit, the closest form of variant is one which preserves Potter's own words and pictures. For example, there is a set of miniature volumes (*The Original Peter Rabbit Miniature Collection*) which reproduces the original text in such tiny form that its appeal would appear to be to the collector rather than to the reader. Warne has also issued more than one form of Potter compendium which reworks the little pages as panels on a larger page; an example is *The Complete Adventures of Peter Rabbit*, produced by Warne and then by Puffin. Many of Potter's subtle touches of design and layout are instantly lost in this arrangement; and the story reads differently when it is one of a collection of stories or a chapter in a book. The sense of the story as a complete, unique and satisfying unit is altered with the loss of the book's own covers.

I want to explore three individual publications in this section. One would appear to be a pirate edition, copyrighted by Ottenheimer Publishers in 1993. My copy says, "This book is for resale in the United States only," but I bought it on a bargain bookshelf in Canada. The second is the Puffin paperback, published in association with Frederick Warne in 1991. The third is entitled *Scenes from The Tale of Peter Rabbit*, published by Warne in 1989; it contains five three-dimensional cut-out pictures from the book, tagged with quotations from the story. At the back of the book, cunningly sealed with a Velcro sticker, the entire text is reproduced along with some line drawings from the privately printed edition. The book can be folded back and the covers tied together to produce a carousel effect.

The first of these three books, the Ottenheimer edition, is much larger than the original and square. It contains the same text on a smaller number of pages, and eliminates some of the pictures.

It would be tedious simply to use the reissues as a checklist of what is superior about the original book, but in this case the comparison is hard to avoid. The larger pages take longer sections of text, so that in many cases two pages are collapsed into one, and one of the pictures is sacrificed. The choice of which picture to drop has not been made very intelligently. The second picture in the original book, the one which sets Peter apart from his sisters and shows him primed for mischief, has been eliminated in favor of the next one which shows Mrs. Rabbit buttoning his coat. The illustration which, perhaps above all others, has come to stand for the archetypal image of Peter Rabbit, the one of him eating the radishes, has disappeared in favor of the one where he is beginning to feel sick. The picture of the sparrows actually appears a page before their arrival in the text. And so on. The sense of dislocation to a reader familiar with the original is pervasive. The loss of rhythm is perceptible; it is difficult to reestablish the gaps created by the lost page turns even if (or perhaps especially if) you know where they fall.

In short, this version is simply an example of diminishment and loss. The text is not abridged but the pictures are, and there is no hint of this fact anywhere on the book's apparatus. This book probably provides the most straightforward case for judgement of the entire list;

although, superficially, it is one of the closest to the original, it is a clear example of reduction, of subtraction, of inferiority. The Puffin book avoids many of these pitfalls. It contains the Potter text, word for word, and none of the pictures is missing. Nevertheless, there are some significant changes. For one thing, the book is much larger than Potter's original. Any question of whether there can be a specific esthetics of scale is answered by a comparison of this version with the original. The impact of the pictures is altogether different when they are expanded to a much larger page. Furthermore, the pictures vary in scale among themselves. Some almost fill the page with only a small white margin around the edges. Some take the top or bottom two-thirds of the page with a few lines of print above or below. Others are much smaller and are set one or two into a page with print surrounding them.

In the original version, the set size of all the pictures makes it much easier to establish some sense of distance and focus. If Peter Rabbit is small, it means he is some distance away and we can make our esthetic and psychological judgements accordingly. With the variable size of pictures, this effect is entirely lost; indeed, we have much less interest in such issues because we have lost the establishing and sustaining framework which makes such observations possible.

The typeface is much larger than Potter's as well, and set in a more luxurious surround of white space. Again, however, the variable relationship between the size of the type and the size of the pictures sets up a dynamic in the reader's relationship to the text which is entirely missing in the original version. The page turns are also different, of course; though the text and its accompanying picture remain contiguous (unlike some of the pirate editions), there are two ways in which the effect is altered. One is that only a few openings contain just one picture and its text; turning these pages is like meeting an old friend. The effect of Potter's page design is instantly lost when pictures are combined on an opening; even the first page includes two pictures. The sedate rhythm is lost along with the secure relationship between text and picture.

Even in a relatively faithful recasting such as this Puffin edition, it is hard to avoid the question of why anyone felt the need to bother with an adaptation of a book which works perfectly well in its own terms. The motivation behind the carousel version seems clearer; here the impulse is not narrative at all but decorative. The book cover tells us,

"This charming version of Beatrix Potter's best-loved tale is both a book to read and a delightful room decoration." The cut-out pictures layer foreground and background, sometimes building up details from more than one picture. The final effect, while pretty, is surely too delicate for small children to handle without very strict supervision. The text is nothing more than captions, direct quotes from the book but largely incomprehensible without reference to the entire story. The cover blurb assures us, "This exquisite presentation of a Beatrix Potter world-in-miniature will enchant readers of all ages," but it seems clear that the appeal here, as in many other cases of Potter material, is to the adult rather than the child.

POTTER'S PICTURES AND DIFFERENT WORDS

A number of texts make use of some of Potter's pictures but retell the story. A sample of three will give some idea of what happens in such a case; two are published by Warne, the other by Ottenheimer Publishers.

Warne's first offering is the board book, *Meet Peter Rabbit*, which puts the name of Beatrix Potter on the front cover. There is no sign of any other writer's name and the book describes itself as "A very first board book to introduce babies to *The Tale of Peter Rabbit*." It is sold separately and also as part of a package with a stuffed rabbit (at a considerably higher price).

The book contains five pictures, with a sixth on the cover. Each is framed by an inked line, outside of which is a pale blue border. The text is minimal to the point of barely mentioning Mr. McGregor. In its entirety, it reads as follows:

> Peter Rabbit lives with his mothers and sisters under the root of a big fir-tree.
>
> Peter wears a blue coat with brass buttons for going out. His sisters, Flopsy, Mopsy and Cotton-tail have pink cloaks.
>
> Flopsy, Mopsy and Cotton-tail are having bread and milk and blackberries for supper.
>
> Naughty Peter likes to eat lettuces and radishes from Mr. McGregor's garden.
>
> But he doesn't like his mother's medicine! (n.p.)

This rendition of the story is almost completely pointless. It does provide cues for a mother to make soothing noises, perhaps, as she turns the pages with her baby, but it is entirely beyond the comprehension of any baby small enough to need a board book, and it is utterly unsatisfying otherwise.

My second example in this category is a pop-up book, retold by Elsa Knight Bruno and published in the United States by Ottenheimer. Printed in Hong Kong and hand-assembled in China, it is, at first glance, rather pretty and appealing. As a satisfying story, however, it runs into some problems. Elsa Knight Bruno has an approach to page turns which is diametrically opposed to Beatrix Potter's. In a total of six openings, she runs the sentence over the page in no fewer than three of them. This approach certainly alters the pacing of the story. The fact that pop-up books call for a certain amount of leisurely admiration of the visual and technical effects, however, introduces an element of conflict between text and pictures. The sense of incoherence is increased by a close exploration of the pictures. This pop-up book provides the first of many examples of reworkings of the story where the conventions of the new medium and the demands of the original story are incompatible. In this case, as in many others, the conventions of the medium appear to have won hands down. The pop-up pictures straddle the gutter, as is necessary if they are to spring up as the page opens. The fact that the pictures must therefore be grouped in the middle of the page opening alters the flow between the different individual pictures which have been assembled for each montage. The producers of the pictures (who get no credit) have chosen, in five examples out of six, to move the eye from lower left to upper right to follow the action of the story. The effect is to lead the eye from the bottom of the page to the top, which feels counterintuitive to anyone used to reading English and used to following action from the top of a page to the bottom. Unfortunately, in the only example which runs from top to bottom, two pictures have been reversed, so that on the bottom left-hand page we see Peter escaping from the sieve with his jacket abandoned behind him, while on the bottom right-hand page we see him caught in the gooseberry net, still wearing the jacket.

These may be small details, but they did noticeably interfere with my close investigation of the pop-ups and I was left with a sense of chronological incoherence in the picture arrangement. A child with a less developed sense of the conventions of how the eye sweeps over the page in an English language book might be less challenged by this arrangement than I was, but, on the other hand, that child would be, at best, failing to gain further mastery over conventional page arrangements, and, at worst, learning or reinforcing "rules" which will be unhelpful in the long run.

The third example is in some ways the most ingenious. The book is called *Where's Peter Rabbit?: A Lift-the-Flap Book.* This book is rather cleverly assembled, making use of Potter's original pictures and layering them under the disguise of paper flaps. The text is close to Potter's, but ruthlessly altered where it is necessary to fit the format.

The book works along the following lines. The first opening contains this text:

> Once upon a time there were four little Rabbits, and their names were Flopsy, Mopsy, Cotton-tail and Peter. They lived with their Mother in a **sand-bank**, under the root of a tree. (n.p.)

The highlighted word is "sand-bank;" the picture shows a detail of Potter's fir-tree with the rabbit-hole pictured on a liftable flap. When the flap is lifted, underneath we see a second Potter picture, of Mrs. Rabbit warning her children.

It is not always possible for the designers to use a Potter picture underneath the flap. Mrs. Rabbit's basket on the second opening, for example, conceals the five current buns and the cake, which are not mentioned in the text. Perhaps the most unsatisfying addition, at least from an adult point of view, comes in the picture of Peter being administered the camomile tea; pulling back the flap of the bed-covers, we see a cowering rabbit resisting his medicine; my own preference for the eloquence of the ears representing the invisible resistance is pronounced. Overall, however, the designer, Colin Twinn, has fulfilled his mandate with some intelligence.

The text has been altered to suit a particular purpose as well. With one exception, the highlighted word comes in the last sentence on the page, an arrangement that allows child and adult reader to pause for flap-lifting and discussion without undue interference in the rhythm of the reading. This particular pressure does not improve the text *qua* text, but it does allow for a coherent approach to this particular kind of interaction.

Whether you like such tampering with a text is a separate question. In this case, I must at least allow that the designers have made the necessary compromises between the original book and the technical demands of the new format with rather more grace and economy than in many other examples.

CHAPTER 3

Reillustrating Potter's Words

Many books, especially those published in the United States, keep Potter's words and reillustrate them. Many of my examples have been published since 1985, but *The Tale of Peter Rabbit Animated!* (in many ways the most remarkable and bizarre of the lot) was published as long ago as 1943, the year of Potter's death. I also have a miniature Little Little Golden Book "Little Little Golden Book" version, first published in 1958, republished in 1970, and reissued in its present tiny size in 1993.

Given the copyright history, it is not surprising that all of the books I propose to discuss in this section are American in origin. Six picture books all give Potter credit for the text and all assert on the cover that the book has been "illustrated" rather than "reillustrated" by the artist in question. The books differ in how they acknowledge the provenance and frame the reading of the story. The Scholastic edition, illustrated by David McPhail, suggests on the back cover that *The Tale of Peter Rabbit* is an "easy-to-read folktale" and quotes Bruno Bettelheim: "Nothing in all of children's literature can be as enriching and satisfying to children and adults alike as the folk fairy tale." *The Complete Tales of Peter Rabbit and other Favorite Stories*, illustrated by Charles Santore, talks about the stories as "beloved by generations of children." This book, retitled *Tales of Peter Rabbit*, is also published in a miniature and truncated version, which, to my surprise, I found for sale in Britain. The Rabbit Ears version, which comes as a boxed set with a cassette recording (there is also a videotape animation of this version) describes itself on the back as an example of "Family Classics from the Stars" On the front of the box, apart from the title the greatest prominence is given to the name of Meryl Streep, who is the narrator. Beatrix Potter as author shares equal billing with Lyle Mays, who wrote

The Tale of Peter Rabbit and Other Stories by Beatrix Potter. Illustrations by Lulu Delacre.

the music for the video and audio version, and David Jorgensen, who provided the illustrations.

Three other books, A Little Golden Book illustrated by Cyndy Szekeres, a Little Little Golden Book illustrated by Adriana Mazza Saviozzi, and a publication of Julian Messner illustrated by Lulu Delacre and containing several stories, all credit Potter with the text but give no hint that *The Tale of Peter Rabbit* has any existence outside of this particular version. Depending on your point of view, Delacre either mitigates or compounds this oversight by her dedication: "To Beatrix Potter, for being an example and an inspiration."

Leaving aside for the moment the two older versions, the Little Little Golden Book of 1958 and the 1943 edition, *The Tale of Peter Rabbit Animated!*, let us look at the contemporary efforts to re-present Peter Rabbit. It is difficult to find a way to organize discussion of their merits and drawbacks. Simply plodding through them one by one would be repetitive; on the other hand, generalizing is difficult and probably counterproductive. Whatever their merits as books in their own rights, it is necessary to consider the importance of reception, of the fact that these books are in the world and being read by real people. There are children and parents, presumably, to whom each of these versions actually is *The Tale of Peter Rabbit*. With such a plethora of reproductions and imitations, the issue of what readers understand about a particular title or character, or about the world of books in general, becomes ever more complicated.

THE REILLUSTRATED PICTURE-BOOK VERSIONS

In order to focus my account of how the reillustrated versions work, I propose to make some general points and then explore how one Potter picture fared with her imitators.

Most of these versions show some form of cosy domestic clutter (up to and including a powder puff for Mrs. Rabbit in the Little Golden Book) and/or cute old-fashioned clothing for the rabbits. What is utterly lost in this kind of transformation is any sense of economy of effect; backgrounds are generally busy and loaded with detail.

The balance between picture and text is different in each case. The number of sentences on a page varies from version to version, affecting both the rhythm and the relationship between words and pictures. Where the text is compressed tightly onto the pages, picture and relevant text may become separated. The shaping of the text is considerably altered when the words are differently clustered and the loss of pauses created by the page turns at particular climactic points is noticeable.

It also makes a difference to the impact of the page when pictures bleed off all four sides or cross the gutter and bleed off the opposite page as well. In some cases, the print is overlaid on the background wash.

In my view, none of these effects is as delicate as Potter's original approach. Absence of delicacy is not necessarily a drawback in itself but, in this case, it does mean that the overall effect of reticence is missing. The effect of miniaturization has also disappeared in the larger pages and the final impact of each of these books is much heavier and denser than Potter's original. This leads to a different kind of emphasis on the words, almost by a form of osmosis. The combined effects of more words on the page and of heavier drawings makes the story feel less honed, even though the wording is still the same.

In each of these books, the opening picture sets up a story quite different from the original and from the others. The way we develop expectations from the early illustrations in a picture book is an underexplored topic, but my comparison of the different versions of the same text suggests that such expectations are important even if we are vague about what details actually ground our feelings. The first picture may convey spareness or clutter, austerity or cosiness, lightness or heaviness of touch; these and undoubtedly many other factors all make an immediate impact and must surely affect how we attend to the book as a whole.

It may be argued that these books deserve to be judged outside of the context of constant reference to Potter's original book. This argument has some considerable merit, but there are two confounding factors which need to be taken into account. One is that these pictures are part of a larger unit which includes Potter's own words, so she cannot disappear from the scene altogether. The second point is that the artists themselves seem to be unable to overlook the impact of Potter's own pictures.

Peter in the Shed

Potter's picture of Peter and Mr. McGregor in the tool-shed (page 39 in the original text) provides a very interesting example of how imagination and technique work within and against constraints. Mr. McGregor, in the background and partially obscured by a pillar, is turning over pots; in the foreground we see the watering can with Peter's ears protruding from it. In choosing to paint the shed from this angle, Potter had to find a way to show her young readers where Peter is hiding; a top view of the watering can, for example, could have him crouched in the bottom with his ears laid flat, but that kind of information would be invisible from the angle she selected. The appearance of Peter's ears, therefore, is to some extent dictated by the needs of the picture as a whole and its role in the communicative force of the story. However, Potter has made use of these constraints and triumphed over them. When I was a little girl, this was always my favorite picture in the book. Probably I was flattered by knowing that I knew more than either Peter or Mr. McGregor about what was going on. Certainly I never doubted that Peter thought he was safely hidden. Those ears, at once vulnerable and yet insecurely insouciant, are eloquent of far more than the technical need to describe where Peter hides.

The text makes no mention of the fact that Peter is not as thoroughly invisible as he seems to think. In the event, he is betrayed by a sneeze and the protruding ears have no plot significance whatsoever.

And yet, of six illustrators (excluding the "animator" whose approach is so bizarre as to require special attention), five show some version of Peter protruding from the watering can; the sixth, Delacre, has no picture set inside the tool-shed. Each of these illustrators had the option of a top view; clearly, in their reimagining of the story, they refer to details that were purely pictorial in the original. The effect is one of a curious kind of auto-referentiality. The illustrations recall another illustration, the original illustration of the same story, rather than feeding into and expanding onto the text in the organic way that should attend an original picture book. Potter's shed picture shows something which is missing from the text, and that unspoken information seems to affect how the later illustrators "see" *The Tale of Peter Rabbit*.

Once upon a time
there were four little Rabbits,
and their names were—
Flopsy, Mopsy, Cotton-tail, and Peter.

They lived with their mother in a sand-bank,
underneath the root of a very big fir-tree.

The Complete Tales of Peter Rabbit and Other Favorite Stories.
Illustrations by Charles Santore.

I am, of course, paying these artists the compliment of assuming that they genuinely intended to reimagine and were not simply out to reproduce a cute effect. Whatever their motives, it seems clear that the impact of *The Tale of Peter Rabbit* is expressed in a combination of words and pictures working together. My ultimate reaction was to wonder how you could acknowledge this interrelationship in an exercise that necessarily replaces one ingredient, the pictures.

SOME GENERAL COMMENTS

Of all the different forms of text of Peter Rabbit, the reillustrations of Potter's own words are the group I find hardest to assess and to discuss. Potter's words were written to combine with her pictures; their rhythms and placings are precisely aligned. If you remove a piece of a jigsaw puzzle and replace it with another piece, you are constrained in the shape of your replacement. The issue of reillustrating Potter is not quite so clear-cut, but the metaphor is helpful in describing some of the difficulties.

Nothing in Potter's texts decrees a particular illustration or a particular perspective on an incident. That being the case, it is surprising to note how many *doppelgänger* effects appear in the reillustrations. Delacre and Szekeres, in their separate pictures of Peter sitting in the wheelbarrow looking towards the gate, strongly recall Potter's illustration; the similarities of perspective are startling. Santore and McPhail each produce a picture of Peter squeezing under the gate into the garden which is expressed in their own idiom but unmistakably reminiscent of Potter's version.

Jorgensen's pictures are the least connected to Potter's. His is a special case for a different reason, to which I shall be returning later. His book is part of a multimedia reinterpretation of *The Tale of Peter Rabbit*; there are video and audio versions of this rendition as well. What Jorgensen demonstrates is that a more substantial readdressing of the illustrations is possible; the decisions of the other five artists to re-produce elements of Potter's composition and perspective were not essential. It is possible to think of them as a form of homage to Potter's distinctive vision, or as a form of laziness, or as a form of not daring to meddle too much with what has already been definitively established. The whole issue is clearly a very complex one.

These reinterpretations would seem to incorporate a story that has already been told pictorially. The visual ghost of Potter's Peter, as it were, still lingers around some of these pages.

THE CHAPTER BOOK

Dover Publications has produced a collection of "Children's Thrift Classics" which features twelve Potter stories collected in a chapter book. Unlike most of the Warne collections, which tend to include most or all of the colored pictures, this book provides a few small black and white drawings. The illustrator is Pat Stewart, but the title page acknowledges that the pictures are "based upon watercolors by the author." There are five little drawings, very closely allied to the Potter pictures, inserted in the seven pages of text. The effect is very strongly that of an illustrated chapter book; the picture book framework is altered beyond recognition.

The most noticeable impact on the text is that the forward momentum of the story is much more strongly emphasized without the breaks of numerous pictures and page turns. The text, in fact, stands up very well to this relatively radical reformatting, and the shape and interest of the story is maintained (though most readers who know the original will lament the loss of the illustrations). This version of the text is matched only by the audiocassettes for its heavily verbal orientation. It is far more unpretentious than many of the other, more lavish reillustrated versions, but, for my taste, works far more successfully.

THE GROSSET AND DUNLOP BOOK

A final word for the 1943 book, *The Tale of Peter Rabbit Animated!*, illustrated by Julian Wehr. Well might the producers include an exclamation mark in the title. This book, produced in garish colors on cheap paper contains Potter's wording with a number of regular illustrations and also with four special pages which can be activated by a moving tab controlling a set of activities. The first one of these movable pages is my favorite, demonstrating as it does that when the need to reimagine meets the need to conform to a particular technology, imagination can take a real beating. The tab controls Mrs. Rabbit's wagging head at the far end of the rabbit hole, and in the living room, the four rabbit children engage in activities which also obligingly go back and forth. Peter rides a rocking horse, one sister scrubs clothes on a washboard, and the remaining two sisters saw logs over a sawhorse. The text is Potter's text but the preposterous effect of the pictures is almost surreal.

Novelty value was probably all this edition ever had to offer, although now the drawings may have acquired a patina of nostalgia for those who can recall the cheap books of the 1940s. The overall effect of the whole, however, is quite plainly ludicrous. It is well worth reminding ourselves that the idea of making money out of such liberties with a cherished text is not the invention of our own era.

CHAPTER 4

The Story Retold and Reillustrated

Many versions of the story use neither Potter's own words or Potter's own pictures. What is it about these books that makes us call them *Peter Rabbit* at all?

In contrast to some of the precedents in other children's classics (I am thinking of Disney's Pooh and also of the television version of *The Wind in the Willows* featuring animated puppets), Peter Rabbit, for the most part, lives a fairly limited and restrained life, largely confined to the limits of Potter's original plot. Certainly most of the retellings do not venture far beyond the parameters of the original, either verbally or pictorially.

THE BOARD BOOKS

Frederick Warne has produced a tiny board book called *Peter Rabbit and his Friends*, part of a series of *Beatrix Potter(TM) Mini Board Books*. It includes not only the Rabbit family but also characters from other Potter stories. The illustrations of this book come from the animations, and the text is basic and repetitive: "This is . . .," "Here is . . ." The book acts almost as an introduction to Potter's larger set of characters, an idea borne out by the exhortation on the back cover, "Look out for other titles in this series." With this approach, of course, Warne is operating on the basis of a long-set precedent; Potter's own story of Peter Rabbit as we now know it was truncated in order to make room for endpapers advertising other characters from her books.

Golden Books have also produced a board book, but this one has a more narrative thrust. Labelled a Golden Take-a-Look Book, this story has holes in each page through which the reader may view scenes from the previous or subsequent page. The basic story is told in a few lines, with sparrows, cat and mouse all deleted. The illustrations, by Jody Wheeler, are cute and cuddly. The blurb on the back cover of this version, addressed to parents, is very keen to point out the educational virtues of this text:

WHAT'S IN THE HOLE?

When you encourage your child to find the hole on each page of this book and say what's inside it, you are also helping your little one learn to *look closely* at the page. This activity is a very important step in beginning to read.

And to add to the enjoyment of reading *The Tale of Peter Rabbit*, you can encourage your child to "retell" the story while you turn the pages.

Another lively retelling occurs in *Peter Rabbit*, a Lift-a-Flap board book illustrated by Wendy Edelson. The reader raising the flap discovers not only a picture but also the concluding words to the sentence or the answer to a question in the main text. The impact on the reading experience is distinctive and I found it quite appealing.

A Tiny Tale of Peter Rabbit, a Chubby Board Book, tampers with the story in a different way, truncating the establishing scenes of the book and starting straight into the plot:

Flopsy, Mopsy, and Cotton-tail, all good little bunnies, went down the lane to gather blackberries one day.

Naughty Peter Rabbit went straight to Mr. McGregor's garden, where bunnies are *not* allowed. (n.p.)

THE LITTLE RAINBOW BOOK

The Tale of Peter Rabbit, retold by Sarah Toast and illustrated by Pat Schoonover and published by Publications International of Illinois in 1995, could be described as a straight copy. The pictures are direct imitations of Potter's, fluffier and more textured but identical in pose and perspective. The text is a "simplification;" everything distinctive has been removed and what remains is a skeleton. Sarah Toast uses Potter's words as far as it suits her and then switches to her own without compunction. The results are risible:

"Now my dears," said Mrs. Rabbit one morning, "you may go down the lane or into the fields, but don't go into Mr. McGregor's garden! He does not like little bunnies." (n.p.)

On the opposite page we see Peter with his back turned to his three sisters, registering some form of rebellion against his mother's words. His expression retains some of the shock and challenge which enliven Potter's drawing, but it is difficult to account for this reaction in his mother's newly banal words. The effect of overall incongruity is enhanced by the decorative flourish at the top and bottom of each picture which centers on a gnawed carrot.

Some of Toast's small alterations are incomprehensible. Potter wrote, for example, "After a time he began to wander about, going lippity—lippity—not very fast, and looking all round" (p. 42). Toast's version of this sentence is, "Peter wandered about, not going very fast, going lippity, lippity" (n.p.). Perhaps she thinks that young readers need to have their sentences composed always in standard order, perhaps she thinks that by putting the explanation, "not very fast" ahead of the "new" word, lippity, she is making life easier. What results, however, is a sentence whose distinctive rhythm has become broken-backed and counterproductive.

Toast also makes one other inexplicable change. Instead of ending with Flopsy, Mopsy, Cotton-tail and the blackberries, she puts them on the second-last page and closes as follows:

Mr. McGregor found Peter's little jacket in the gooseberry net and his little shoes among the cabbage and potatoes. He hung them up, making a scarecrow to keep the blackbirds out of his garden. (n.p.)

Again, the writer's absence of ear is lamentable. Furthermore, it is arguable that this rearrangement alters the whole balance of the story. Flopsy, Mopsy and Cotton-tail feasting on blackberries which Peter is too sick to enjoy is a form of justice which leaves room for some ambiguity about the author's position in all this. To end with Mr. McGregor, to suggest that the final balance is closed by Mr. McGregor acquiring a scarecrow, is to tip the scales in favor of conventional law and order in a way which undermines much of the subversive charm of the story. And yet it is an alteration which appears in a number of versions.

THE 1987 LADYBIRD BOOK

In 1987, there was uproar in the British media as Ladybird Books, with the approval of Frederick Warne, produced a simplified version of *The Tale of Peter Rabbit*, rewritten in "simple" language and reillustrated with photographs of stuffed animals. News articles, feature articles, editorials, letters to the editor, all recorded public outrage at the operation. The response of the media raises some interesting questions about what makes a story itself, as it were. What kind of existence does Peter Rabbit have away from his own particular words and pictures? What can you subtract from the story while leaving it recognizable?

Alan Hamilton's article in *The Times* of London raises some interesting answers to that question.

> The whole reason for Peter Rabbit being warned against going in the garden, as lovers of Beatrix Potter will be instantly aware, was that his father ended up in Mrs McGregor's pie.
>
> But a new edition of *The Tale of Peter Rabbit*, published by Ladybird books, omits all reference to this vital key to the whole narrative as it does any mention of the mouse, the cat or the goldfish pond. It is *Hamlet* without the ghost, *Othello* without the handkerchief. (1987, p. 5)

Hamilton also objects to the loss of the watercolors and the absence of particular words and phrases. This objection is also raised by an editorial in *The Guardian*.

> Ladybird's true intentions are betrayed by its illustrations. Where Beatrix Potter's Peter is pure rabbit, and her Nutkin pure squirrel, Ladybird's equivalents are cuddly toys. And the language of the stories has been altered to match. ("Revised Peter Rabbit," 1987, p. 14)

The Guardian editorial applies many uncomplimentary labels to the Ladybird process: cloth-eared, insensitive, lumbering, prosaic, ruthless levelling-down. Brian Alderson, writing in *The Times*, talks about "the language of Noddyland" (September, 1987, p. 16).

Sally Floyer, a Warne publisher, defended the decision.

This is a way to introduce Beatrix Potter to a whole new market, particularly to people who never go into bookshops. Peter Rabbit will be in supermarkets, and in many other retail outlets. (Hamilton, 1987, p. 5)

However, even within the Warne network, there was not unanimity. Judy Taylor, the author of a number of books about Beatrix Potter, was hired by Warne in 1981 to act as their consultant on Beatrix Potter. In the September 25, 1987, issue of *Publishers Weekly* she was interviewed about the new reproductions of Potter's pictures, and described her role in guarding Potter's legacy.

"I'm the artistic adviser," she says. "No one can reproduce anything with the Beatrix Potter characters without going through four or five approval stages and I represent Warne." (Fakih, 1987, p. 25)

A month later, *Publishers Weekly* was reporting her resignation, in the wake of the Ladybird publications.

Judy Taylor, who . . . acted as Warne's artistic adviser on any Beatrix Potter merchandising, has resigned her position. "I would find my role very difficult," she stated in early October, "knowing that Warne had licensed these vulgar new versions, when it was necessary to be so strict on the merchandising side." She added that it was a publishing decision she found incompatible with Warne's guardianship of the stories. (Jennifer Taylor, 1987, p. 26)

Judy Taylor spoke for herself in a letter to *The Bookseller* on 9 October 1987.

I have been asked by more people than I care to count this past week whether, in my position as consultant to Frederick Warne on the Beatrix Potter merchandise, I have been responsible in any way for the Ladybird versions of *Peter Rabbit* and *Squirrel Nutkin*. I should like to put on record that I am in no way responsible for them, was not consulted about them and find them distasteful and unnecessary. I have resigned from over-seeing the merchandise. (p. 1517)

What of the book itself? It is perhaps not surprising that an out-of-print Ladybird book takes a little time to track down, and as a consequence I had read a great deal about this version before I clapped eyes on the book itself. Knowing that the cat and the mouse had been stripped from the story, I had hoped that what remained might represent a kind of core *Peter Rabbit*, that it might show us what is absolutely essential about the story in order for us to recognize it as *The Tale of Peter Rabbit*. My hopes were far too exalted for what Ladybird has actually accomplished with this text. Although they have removed the characters of the cat and the mouse (possibly because they would involve making extra puppets, another potential example of technical priorities driving artistic decisions), they have filled up the story with dilutions of what was already present. Consider this page of waffle:

> Mrs Rabbit made sure that Flopsy, Mopsy, Cotton-tail and Peter were wearing their warm clothes. She waved them goodbye as they went out to play. Then she put on her bonnet and shawl and set off to the baker's. She wanted to buy a loaf of bread and some buns. (n.p.)

The text plods on in this dreary way throughout the whole book. Any distinctiveness of narrative voice is lost altogether. Robert D. Hale calls it "television-talk" (1988, p. 100), and while it is possible to detect a kind of snobbery in such a description, it is hard to defend the rewriting. For example, Potter wrote:

> And rushed into the tool-shed and jumped into a can. It would have been a beautiful thing to hide in, if it had not had so much water in it. Mr. McGregor was quite sure that Peter was somewhere in the tool-shed, perhaps hidden underneath a flower-pot. He began to turn them over carefully, looking under each.
>
> Presently Peter sneezed—"Kertyschoo!" Mr. McGregor was after him in no time. (pp. 37–38)

David Hately writes this instead:

> When he got inside the shed, Peter hid in a watering can. Mr. McGregor couldn't find him anywhere! But the watering can had water in it, and suddenly Peter felt a sneeze coming on. *Ker-tyschoo!* went the sneeze. *Ker-tyschoooo!* (n.p.)

Clearly the motivation is to lay out every fact plainly so that no child could possibly wonder for a moment about the linear development of events. But a child who learns about reading on this kind of diet will find almost any other form of text more interesting than print, and rightly so. Hale, objecting to the "so-called simplification of language," points out,

> Aside from being appallingly patronizing, it ignores what is already there. Simplicity is the goal of genius, of which Beatrix Potter had a special variety. Simplifying genuine simplicity is stupidity. (1988, p. 101)

The photographs of the stuffed animals which replace Potter's paintings are certainly a change from the original pictures. According to Roy Smith, Ladybird's art director, the puppets, created by Stan and Vera Veasey, achieved Ladybird's objective. "'They had a different approach and that was what we wanted,' he said" (Walker, 1987, p. 7).

I have, at times during this work, been tempted to think that the first requirement of a reworking of a text in a different medium must be the powerful reimagining of the story within the constraints of the original story and also within the constraints of the new medium. The 1987 Ladybird *Peter Rabbit* tests that theory and, in some ways, tests it to destruction. It may well be a necessary condition but it is not a sufficient condition in and of itself. No matter how comprehensive the reimagining, there must also be some way of assessing the final artistic effect. In the case of these puppets, the final effect is disastrous, yet the Veaseys took a lot of trouble with their stuffed animals.

> "We had three attempts at Peter Rabbit," she said. "We rejected the first because its ears were too far apart. The second one wasn't chubby enough and its face was too angular." (Walker, 1987, p. 7)

Unfortunately, the third attempt isn't right either. In several pictures, including the one on the front cover, Peter's head is noticeably lopsided.

The wider problem is something more general, however. One of the key appeals of Potter's original work is the ambiguity about Peter's role: Is he a rabbit or is he a boy? This debate is not simply stifled, it is mocked in the answer which this book supplies: "Neither; he's a stuffed toy!" It is difficult to convey in words the reductiveness of that visual transformation.

My second-hand Ladybird book has a child's name written inside but otherwise it is in immaculate condition and I am not surprised. There is nothing in this text to make me want to look again. The story is uninteresting and the pictures are not even cuddly.

THE 1988 AMERICAN LADYBIRD EDITION

In 1988, Ladybird Books of Maine issued an American version of the 1987 Ladybird. A comparison between the two versions is instructive. Once again, we can see the importance of page size and shape. The American version is much larger and more nearly square in shape, allowing for larger type, more white space surrounding the text, and a more generous layout for the pictures. The effect of reducing the crowding on the page, while not exactly rendering the stuffed animals pleasing in any esthetic sense, does at least give the reader some breathing space.

The alterations in the text are less easy to understand. David Hately has made numerous small changes. None of them actively amounts to a real improvement and in most cases they simply seem gratuitous. Compare, for example, the two versions of Mrs. Rabbit's warning. Here is the 1987 version:

> One day they were allowed to play outside. "Stay near home," said their mother. "Please don't go to Mr McGregor's garden."
>
> "Why not?' asked Peter.
>
> "Because he doesn't like rabbits," answered Mrs Rabbit. "He will try to catch you." (n.p.)

And here is the 1988 version:

> One day their mother let them play outside.
>
> "Stay close to home," she said. "And don't go near Mr. McGregor's garden."
>
> "Why not?' asked Peter.
>
> "Because he doesn't like rabbits," Peter's mother answered. "He will try to catch you." (n.p.)

Such a level of alteration appears to me to be entirely inexplicable. I explored the option that the American edition was being sensitive about Mrs. Rabbit's marital status, but she is called Mrs. Rabbit on many other occasions during the book, so that is not the answer. Neither example is a remarkable improvement on the other; throughout both versions of the book the rhythm remains choppy and unsatisfactory, whatever small changes are inserted. As with so many other aspects of this whole enterprise, the abiding question remains, "Why would anyone bother?"

THE 1992 LADYBIRD EDITION

The current Ladybird version, with a different simplified text, uses stills from the animated television and video version which was first broadcast in 1992.

I do not much like the drawings for the animations; I find them crude and flat compared to Potter's original subtle artwork. Nevertheless, this Ladybird edition has some interest, since its hybrid existence owes some allegiance to both the Potter book and the television animation. The pictures are not good pictures but the layout is lively (if rather crowded) and the pages have more energy, partly perhaps because they do not have to be aligned with the original Potter text.

This is not to give any particular credit to the 1992 Ladybird text. After the 1987 uproar, the editors have salvaged more of the vintage Potter lines: the "lippity lippity" has been restored and the reference to the pie is back. However, the rewriter, who gets no credit, has still condescended to children in the particular choices of simplification. Here is Peter, caught in the gooseberry net:

> Peter was trapped! He started to cry, but his sobs were heard by some sparrows who flew over to him.
> "Keep trying!" they chirped. "Don't give in!"
> So Peter stopped crying and tried to free himself. Then, as Mr McGregor came up with a sieve to pop over Peter's head, he wriggled out just in time! (n.p.)

There are several pictures to an opening, often rectangular with the frame broken by part of the picture; a number are unframed. On every third opening, the text is overlaid on a faint background drawing of woods.

The pictures come from the animations which come from the original paintings, so the degree of reference to the first pictures is not surprising. To a greater extent than I had expected, however, the pictures are not direct imitations. I would always give a child the original text rather than this cut-down version, but I disliked the current Ladybird book rather less than I had anticipated. With so much that is new about it, it has at least generated the dynamism of its own limits. Like all the retellings, it is forced to take on the shape of a shadow already cast, but this version is less oppressively imitative than many of the others.

THE 1992 WARNE PAPERBACK

Warne also issued a paperback "book of the animation" in 1992. It combines the stories of Peter Rabbit and Benjamin Bunny, just as in the half-hour animation, and the opening picture is a photograph of the actress who plays Beatrix Potter in the frame story of that animation. After that, the emphasis is on producing many, many stills from the cartoon, a total of 118 pictures on 30 pages. Perhaps out of deference to the very firm way in which this book is located in its televisual origins, all of these pictures are strictly rectangular; there is not a frame-break to be found. The main dynamism and rhythm is created by variation in size of picture. This is sometimes used to good effect, as in the page opening where Peter meets Mr. McGregor (pp. 8–9). On the previous opening, no fewer than 10 small pictures appear, but page 10 and page 11 contain one large picture and one short line of text apiece: "'Oh help!' gasped Peter. 'It's Mr. McGregor!'" The large closeups of Peter's expression of consternation and Mr. McGregor's ferocious scowl do create a considerable impact, although it is far removed from Potter's subtlety.

In general, however, this version amounts to little more than a souvenir of the animation. A Guardian article on the subject of adapting *Pride and Prejudice* for television quotes Jonathan Miller on the relationship between films and books:

> I think that what happens is that when people have seen the film and
> go back to the book, the author becomes nothing more than a

projectionist's assistant, who simply enables people to re-run the film in their head. (Bennett, 1995, p. 3)

This particular version of the story would seem to me to be making heavy use of illustration to encourage exactly such a process in young readers.

This version of the story also contains the most banal wording of any of the specimens I have looked at, probably even slightly worse than the 1987 Ladybird edition. Indirect speech and thoughts are transferred into dialogue which is usually inane.

> First he ate some lettuces and some French beans. And then he ate some radishes. "Ooh! My favorite," he said happily.
>
> Then, feeling rather sick, he went to look for some parsley. But whom do you think he should meet round the end of a cucumber frame?
>
> "Oh help!" gasped Peter.
>
> "It's Mr McGregor!" (pp. 6–9)

To be fair to the unnamed editors, the suspense of the page turn is maintained at this point. This is more than can be said for the arrival of the sparrows followed by Mr. McGregor with the sieve, which occurs on the next page. This version is completely infantilized.

> Peter might have got away if he had not got caught up in a gooseberry net.
>
> "Hurry, Peter, hurry," urged some friendly sparrows. "Mr McGregor's coming! Quick, you *must* keep trying."
>
> Peter wriggled out just in time. (pp. 11–12)

In Potter's version, the sparrows make no mention of Mr. McGregor and his appearance over the page turn is a shock. These writers have eliminated not only the page turn but also the gap in Potter's text which functions almost like a shield; in this 1992 case, the sparrows warn about Mr. McGregor and, sure enough, there he is.

THE BLOOMSBURY BOOK

The World of Peter Rabbit Treasury (1994), published by Bloomsbury in association with Frederick Warne, is an activity book which includes a section called "Peter Rabbit's Story." It too is illustrated with stills from the animation. In this case, however, we can see even more sets of conventions at work. To the original picture book conventions we must add the conventions which go to the making of an animated cartoon and also the conventions which attend activity books. These last are eclectic and difficult to summarize but easy to spot in the book. On the opening pages, there is a "welcome" and a call to "meet your new friends." (p. 8)

> This is Peter Rabbit. He's a very *naughty* rabbit. He's always getting into trouble. You can read about his adventures on page 12. (p. 8)

And later,

> This is old Mrs. Rabbit with her daughters Flopsy, Mopsy and Cotton-tail who are good little bunnies. Peter is nowhere to be seen, of course; he's away in Mr McGregor's garden. (p. 9)

The subsequent opening (pp. 10–11) is a double-page picture which shows Peter in the wheelbarrow looking towards the gate. An inserted panel of text makes the situation clear, and correspondingly undermines the suspense in the story which follows next. The overall effect is to render the story less linear, in a way which is not particularly pleasing but which is at least interesting.

Twenty-three rectangular pictures of differing sizes appear on the six pages which constitute the story proper. Of these, only six have the frame broken even slightly, and the variation in size is the main source of energy or interest. The impact of the shifting sizes is compounded by the two double-page pictures; one opens the story and a second concludes it.

I shall return to the kinds of activities which comprise much of the rest of this book at a later point. At this stage, I want simply to compare the 1992 Ladybird edition with the Warne paperback and the *Treasury*. All three are authorized by Warne and stand as official spin-offs from the animations. I had never expected to warm to the Ladybird book, but it stands up better to analysis than many of the other versions. Perhaps Ladybird was stung by the response to the 1987 attempt; in any case, the Warne paperback and the Bloomsbury *Treasury* stoop to far greater depths of inanity and cliché. I don't particularly like the Ladybird book, but it serves a useful purpose in demonstrating that the book of the television program need not be inherently appalling; at the least, there are degrees of intelligence and care which can be applied to the process. This observation, of course, is a truism but it is one which is often overlooked in a culture which sometimes sneers automatically at the film of the book and the book of the film of the book.

IMPLICATIONS OF THE RECAST VERSIONS

The examples I have discussed are all relatively contemporary, but this does not mean the issue of Peter Rabbit recreated is a new one. In 1963, two influential essays were published on what was not yet called the "dumbing-down" of *Peter Rabbit* and of children's books in general, one by Rumer Godden and one by Jacob Epstein.

Godden created an imaginary correspondence between Beatrix Potter and a publisher, one V. Andel, who wanted to recreate *Peter Rabbit* using simpler words and pictures. Her sarcastic rerendering of the text reads perilously close to most of the examples described above. Mr. V. Andel, for example has this suggestion for the famous sentence about the sparrows imploring Peter to exert himself:

> Not all children will be able to identify sparrows; suggest the more general "bird-ies"; last five words especially difficult; suggest "to try again" or "try harder." (1969, p. 67)

Epstein puts his *Peter Rabbit* comments in the context of a wider discussion. He takes special umbrage at a picture in a "new version" of the book (unfortunately uncited), in which "over Peter's bed is the sign 'Good Bunnies Always Obey'" (p. 79). Epstein argues,

> [M]ost juveniles that are sold as merchandise can hardly be considered books at all. This is especially true of those specimens meant for children who are not yet able to read and which represent

the bulk of merchandise juveniles. These products are really nursery
fixtures made of paper. (1969, p. 82)

Epstein suggests that the real peril of perpetually writing down to
children

> includes the danger that the children may not grow up at all but
> simply grow older. For the appreciation of literature resembles the
> process of growing up in that they both involve the discovery of
> distinctions between the self and the world: the aim of both is
> differentiation, concreteness, and the development of a character of
> one's own. That is why literature is exciting and why it is, finally,
> inseparable from life. (1969, p. 86)

Where the purveyors of simpler texts go wrong, he says,

> is in [their] assumption that there is no particular need to distinguish
> oneself from the surrounding environment, that to take part
> uncritically in the common culture is the proper goal of growing up.
> (1969, p. 86)

A large number of children and parents and teachers do actually
assume exactly that point. Indeed the very scale and range of texts and
products designed to create just such a response actually lends the idea
an air of social verification and respectability. The quantity of such
material on offer makes it hard to avoid and also helps to foster the
logical conclusion that lots of other people must be reading this stuff
too, so it must be worthwhile.

GAPS AND INFERENCES

There are further questions about what children learn *about* literature
and *about* reading from a diet of constantly simplified texts. Reading
the words is only part of the story when it comes to understanding a
work of literature; as Wolfgang Iser (1976) has so thoroughly
explained, it is also a question of learning to understand what is not
present in the text. He quotes Virginia Woolf talking about Jane Austen
to make his point. Woolf said,

Jane Austen is thus a mistress of much deeper emotion than appears upon the surface. She stimulates us to supply what is not there. What she offers is, apparently, a trifle, yet is composed of something that expands in the reader's mind and endows with the most enduring form of life scenes which are outwardly trivial (Iser, 1976, p. 168).

Iser takes up this point and expands it.

What is missing from the apparently trivial scenes, the gaps arising out of the dialogue—this is what stimulates the reader into filling the blanks with projections. He is drawn into the events and made to supply what is meant from what is not said. What *is* said only appears to take on significance as a reference to what is not said; it is the implications and not the statements that give shape and weight to the meaning. But as the unsaid comes to life in the reader's imagination, so the said "expands" to take on greater significance than might have been supposed: even trivial scenes can seem surprisingly profound. The "enduring form of life" which Virginia Woolf speaks of is not manifested on the printed page; it is a product arising out of the interaction between text and reader. Communication in literature, then, is a process set in motion and regulated not by a given code but by a mutually restrictive and magnifying interaction between the explicit and the implicit, between revelation and concealment. What is concealed spurs the reader into action, but this action is also controlled by what is revealed; the explicit in its turn is transformed when the implicit has been brought to light. (1976, pp. 168–169)

I once read a reference to Beatrix Potter as "the Jane Austen of the nursery;" unfortunately I have not been able to track down the citation. Certainly Woolf's remarks about Austen apply in large measure to the way Potter's texts work. The implicit is an active force in Potter's texts. The clarity and simplicity of her writing and the fact that the pictures work on similar principles of the implicit informing the explicit combine to provide assistance to early readers. Thus, Potter allows young children to begin to come to terms with the idea that dealing with the implicit is one of the things that literature *does*. Child "readers" of Potter's *The Tale of Peter Rabbit* are learning very subtle lessons indeed about how stories can expand in your mind.

By and large, *The Tale of Peter Rabbit* retold and/or reillustrated loses many of the reverberations of the implicit. The original story contained many moments where the smallest child could make interpretations about a character's feelings or motivations. But David Hately in the 1987 Ladybird version, to take one particularly bad example, appears to feel that his obligation to his young readers involves the removal of any implicit points in the plot. Here, for example, is his account of Peter in the garden:

> There were lots of vegetables in Mr McGregor's garden. Peter Rabbit loved vegetables. He began to eat them. First he tried the lettuces. Next he tried the beans. Then he ate some radishes.
>
> Peter ate too much, because he was greedy. He began to feel sick. "I must find some parsley to nibble," he said to himself. "That will make me feel better." (n.p.)

Potter felt no need to inform her readers that Peter loved vegetables, or that he was greedy, or that the parsley might make him feel better. As a consequence, readers of the original Potter learn something about making inferences.

Ladybird, advertising the 1987 publication, said they were "delighted to present for the first time easy-to-read editions of Beatrix Potter's famous tales . . . an ideal introduction to the world of Peter Rabbit and his friends" (*Bookseller*, 11 September 1987, front cover). Implicit in this presumptuous blurb is the idea that first you learn about reading from a text which fills in the gaps for you, then you progress to the more sophisticated text where there is room for you to make your own inferences. This assumption would appear to work on the same principle as an exclusively bottom-up phonics-based approach to early reading: first you acquire a repertoire of bits and pieces, then you learn about assembling them. This kind of approach degrades the importance of how readers make meaning.

At one level, this issue is pedagogical; but there is also a sociological angle to some of the built-in assumptions which appear to be at work here. Sally Floyer of Warne, defending the Ladybird decision, said it represented a way to reach people who never go into bookstores. Why such people need a text which devalues the implicit and overloads the explicit is not clear. Why a simple distribution decision could not make a paperback edition of the original text available in supermarkets at an attractive price is also never discussed.

THE "ESSENTIAL" PETER RABBIT

A different kind of question also arises from the edited texts, a question rather more esthetic than social and pedagogical. At what point does Peter Rabbit cease to be the "real" Peter Rabbit and become an imitation or a travesty? The imitations (often trivial little books, apparently marketed to cash in on the popularity of an established cultural icon) do actually raise important and interesting questions about fictional truth and about authenticity and integrity in an invented universe.

What is striking in almost all the examples of *Peter Rabbit* that I have investigated is that the limits of his plot appear to be part of what makes him who he is. Potter herself told more about his life in *The Tale of Benjamin Bunny* and *The Tale of the Flopsy Bunnies*, but there does not appear to be much branching off from this firmly specified and located material. The company of Frederick Warne has guarded Peter carefully within the limits of its remit, but even in the free-for-all of the American market, I have found only a few examples along the lines of "The Further Adventures of Peter Rabbit." Peter's fictional existence is not confined to one text or one set of pictures, but it does appear to be confined largely to one plot: the garden, the vegetables, the threat of Mr. McGregor (with or without the pie).

The industry created around Peter Rabbit is all the more remarkable when this fact is taken into account. One of Peter's biggest rivals in the nursery marketplace, Thomas the Tank Engine, has the advantage of numerous plots and a relatively large number of supplementary characters. The television-based supercharacters, such as the Mighty Morphin' Power Rangers and Barney the Dinosaur, have been created with a view to merchandising from the outset. Peter, confined for the most part to the limits of his adventures in the garden, still manages to take them on in the marketplace.

For the most part, Peter Rabbit's existence in the world seems to be inextricably tied to his plot, but there are other questions. To what degree does he exist only as specific words and pictures in interrelationship? What adheres to him when he is removed from the dynamics of his original setting? Do traces of sophistication cling to

him in his coarsest manifestation or is it merely a reflected glow of a
particular cultural label, that of "literature?" And how much does it
matter?

I can think of numerous descriptions for many (though not all) of
the reworkings of *The Tale of Peter Rabbit*: "degraded" and
"exploitative" would probably be the kindest. I can also make
arguments for my preference of the original Potter text. What I cannot
do is legislate my own good taste for other people. There are
undoubtedly children who have met *The Tale of Peter Rabbit* in non-
Potter guises whose strong preference is for the version they know best.
There are certainly people for whom the Potter story comes with its
own baggage of associations with snobbery and with a particular kind
of middle-class Englishness that does not appeal to them at all. I feel
secure in the basis of my own literary judgement on this particular
book; I have thought about it very carefully and compared it to many
other stories. Yet I am aware that what I am calling virtues—delicacy,
reticence, profundity—can be attacked from many angles. And I am not
enthusiastic about a lingering aura of rank-ordering which seems to
hover around my strictures about the inferior versions.

Retreating from all judgement, however dressed in the virtues of
relativism, carries a tinge of cowardice. I did *not* find a variant version
of *The Tale of Peter Rabbit* which came close to Potter's original in
terms of insight, subtlety, or respect for children. After all my work on
these texts, my opinion is largely unchanged. We are fortunate to have
her version to give to our children, and insofar as the others interfere
with their encounter with Potter's book, we should be wary of them. At
the same time, we should not assume that we know how such
"interference" will work for each and every child; it is perfectly
possible that people who meet Peter Rabbit in an alternative version
may well come to appreciate the original for all the reasons I do or for
even better reasons of their own. A child's relationship with an
alternative version may be important and rewarding in its own right.
And a child may reject any or all versions.

CHAPTER 5

The Videos

Currently, the most ubiquitous *Peter Rabbit* video is the animation produced for Frederick Warne, first shown on the British Broadcasting Corporation at the end of 1992 and on the Family Channel in the United States in March, 1993. As part of a series entitled *The World of Peter Rabbit and Friends (TM)*, it is also readily available as a home video.

I want to discuss this animation along with three other screen versions of the story. Two are partial animations: the Coffee Table Videos production of 1986, which tells six Potter stories including *The Tale of Peter Rabbit*, and the 1988 video from Rabbit Ears Productions, which includes two stories, *The Tale of Mr. Jeremy Fisher* and *The Tale of Peter Rabbit*, using Potter's words and David Jorgensen's illustrations. The third video first appeared on the large screen, and involves a completely different approach to the challenge of bringing Potter "to life;" this is the filmed ballet, *Tales of Beatrix Potter*. Peter Rabbit's role in this film is small, but the approach to Potter's work is so fascinating and so instructive a comparison to the other productions that I want to include it here.

VIDEO AND TEXT

How does watching a story on video differ from reading it from a text? My pool includes two narrated, partially animated videos, one completely animated but only partially narrated video, and a filmed ballet. In some ways they are very different. In other ways they are all much more like each other than they are like the text on which they are all based. It may be useful to look at some of the differences between print and video.

In a video narrative, the pace of the storytelling is determined for you, with only the pause button allowing any kind of brake. The impetus of the background music is also forward-thrusting. The camera directs your eye to first one part of the picture, then another; it is impossible to resist and choose another order of regard. The relationship of the camera work to the narration is also highly directive; no matter how many times you watch the video, the same image always appears as a particular word is spoken, allowing for one kind of emphasis but not another. In short, it appears that latitude for interpretation, as we understand it in book terms, is considerably reduced.

Certain aspects of Potter's work may be difficult to convey on the screen; for example, the standard television picture always "bleeds" off the edges of the screen. It might be possible to find a way to recreate on the screen the effect of the white space on the page, but this was not attempted in any of the versions I saw. Peter, therefore, is seen against a continuous background in all the shots. The anonymous reviewer of the full animation in *Publishers Weekly* (1993) suggests, "It's only fitting that the books Potter originally designed for small hands be adapted for the small screen" (Review, p. 31). In fact, the small screen is really only small relative to the large screen; on television, Peter and his friends are magnified to a size much greater than even the largest text version. Television offers its own kind of intimacy but it is certainly very different from the experience of sitting with one of the little books.

It is very easy to get mixed up between questions of necessary change in form and content as a text is translated from one medium to another, and issues of personal taste where there is much more room for argument. In the hope of clarifying some of these issues, I want to deal with the four videos individually.

Tales of Beatrix Potter (Coffee Table Videos)

The video which comes closest to the original work in form and style is the 1986 *Tales of Beatrix Potter*, which includes narrations of six of Potter's books along with eight nursery rhymes. The pictures are based closely on Potter's own, the narration is of Potter's text, and the main change in form is the introduction of partial movement to the characters in the story. This partially animated narration of Potter stories manages to tell six stories and eight poems, with a reprise of the poems with text attached at the end, in a total of 43 minutes. The result is briskly paced with little in the way of delays. There is music, but it is always in the background of the narration. Sydney Walker tells the stories at what might best be described as a standard storytelling pace, not lingering but not hustling either. His approach conserves much of the austerity of Potter's own approach.

The animation is lumbering to my eye, and occasionally distracting. For my taste, there is rather too much of the rabbit "leaping" across the screen without moving a muscle. The effect is rather closer to a flick-book than to anything we would readily call animated these days. Once you acknowledge the limits of the technique it is possible to see that the producers have largely made the best of it; it is difficult, however, to avoid the strong suspicion that the techniques themselves were chosen for financial rather than esthetic motives.

The Tale of Mr. Jeremy Fisher and *The Tale of Peter Rabbit* (Rabbit Ears)

This version is also partially animated, but the effect is very different. First, and perhaps most obviously, the pictures are drawn by someone else, David Jorgensen. They are pastel drawings; the rabbits are much coarser and more angular than Potter's and the background is pale and grainy.

There are pros and cons to the idea of new illustrations. On the one hand, it is easy to raise the question: Why bother? On the other hand, the producers are not tied to making the best of pictures that were always intended to be viewed as stills. This argument would be more persuasive if I could see many signs that the producers had taken advantage of this freedom, but the technical approach to the pictures is remarkably similar to that of *Tales of Beatrix Potter*: zooms, pans, circular camera movement to denote confusion, etc.

The reillustration represents a clear-cut, public decision. Other aspects of Potter's work are altered in more subtle, even insidious ways. To my mind, the single most disastrous decision was to try to fill a 30-minute video with only two stories. There is a long filler at the beginning advertising other video stories (to which I shall return below), but even so the material is too short for the vehicle.

The stories are narrated from Potter's own text, and the producers' solution to the time problem is to stretch the text with long sessions of background music. This might work better if the music were better; Lyle Mays' music, however, has a number of drawbacks. It is anachronistic, being a mix of keyboard, bass and saxophone (a less Potteresque combination would be difficult to imagine). It is also unmelodic and highly repetitive, not up to the strain of expanding moments of text into longer moments of film. My impatience with the slowness of the story was compounded by my irritation at the boring, repetitious music.

In this kind of video, the role of the narrator is crucial. Meryl Streep has been given a very difficult task. The matter-of-factness of Potter's tone is partly conveyed in the way it never lingers, never wallows in a particular moment of stress or poignancy. That very specific advantage is lost when the story is stretched beyond its natural time limits. My analysis of the problems caused by this decision is partly an issue of judgement, but it is based on facts which can be commonly agreed upon; the proportion of narration time to the length of the video as a whole, for example, could easily be ascertained. When it comes to judging Streep's performance in esthetic terms, however, it is much more a question of taste and value. I find much of Streep's approach to be overdramatic and, indeed, rather soupy. I do not care for the way she lays substantial stress on particular words. There are probably others, however, who would argue in favor of the very points I dislike.

One aspect of this video is open to more definite discussion: the introductory advertisement for the "Video Playground," the collection of story videos available through the agency of Rabbit Ears Productions. This opening segment provides a very clear example of confusion about the audience to whom this material is addressed. A child's voice says,

> Okay, everyone, it's time for Video Playground. I bet you thought those characters just lived in books—well, not any more. Video Playground is a collection of classic kids' stories on video—with narration by some of Hollywood's *biggest* stars. They're all done with beautiful animation and original music.

So far, assuming small children can be interested in the importance of the Hollywood stars, this is unexceptional if uninviting. The child goes on to discuss various videos, laying heavy emphasis on the intertextuality provided by the stars with lines such as, "Listen to this next voice—it's Jack Nicholson, the Joker from Batman." References to films which children are likely to know are straightforward enough. I struggle to picture the viewer with the range of interests implied by the introduction to Meg Ryan:

> In *When Harry Met Sally*, Meg Ryan had her hands full with Billy Crystal. Let's see how she handles the voices of Little Red Riding Hood and Goldilocks, two of the most favorite kids' stories ever.

We all know that small children watch movies on television which can have little to say to them, but it surprises me that a company which brags about its awards, honors and value to children and parents would consider this kind of introduction to be meaningful to anyone likely to want to watch a partial animation of *The Three Bears*. *When Harry Met Sally* offers little to preschoolers; does Goldilocks really need this kind of come-on? Maybe I live in a peculiarly sheltered world, but I am not sure that I am the one with the problem. (A possible time-passer for a traffic jam would be to imagine Beatrix Potter's response to Meg Ryan's famous orgasm scene in *When Harry Met Sally*.)

The Tale of Peter Rabbit and Benjamin Bunny (Grand Slamm Partnership)

This fully animated video is Warne's great centennial gesture, celebrating 100 years since the writing of the original letter in which Peter Rabbit made his first appearance. *The Tale of Peter Rabbit and Benjamin Bunny* was the first in a series, now available in home video format.

The preliminary publicity about this animation stressed the technological miracles which are now possible. *The TV Guide* of March 1993 provides the most detailed account:

> Coates marshaled 300 artists, many of the book illustrators, to make sure everything, from the flap of Jemima's wings to the ripple of lake water, was perfect.

> Potter's wispy watercolors have been brought to life through a technique called "rendered artwork," pioneered by Coates. To achieve Potter-perfect reproductions, artists combined traditional

techniques with an additional overlay of wax. The effect infuses the
flatness of Potter's illustrations with shadow and depth. (Mitchard,
1993, p. 27)

The TV Guide may perhaps be excused for promoting its product rather
uncritically. But remarkably similar comments appeared in the
television review of *The New York Times*.

> But the cautious Warne company, now a division of Penguin Books,
> has finally found what it was looking for in an animation technique
> pioneered by John Coates, a British producer whose credits include
> "The Snowman," once nominated for an Oscar, "The Lion, the Witch
> and the Wardrobe," winner of an Emmy and "The Yellow
> Submarine." The technique in question is called rendered artwork, a
> process that allows the original Potter watercolors to be translated
> with stunning faithfulness into film and video. Some 300 animators,
> tracers and artists worked on these six episodes. (O'Connor, 1993,
> p. B10)

I had considerable trouble tracking down even a few reviews of
this video, but those I found were all highly enthusiastic. Writing in *The
Sunday Times* of London in December 1992, Craig Brown said,

> It is, quite simply, the most exquisite piece of animation I have ever
> seen. Not only are the pictures true to Beatrix Potter's beautiful
> originals, but the animators have obviously spent a lot of time
> observing the movements of animals, so that the birds flutter and the
> rabbits twitch just as they do in real life. Since last Sunday, my own
> children have watched it again and again, enchanted and enthralled. It
> was the television highlight of Christmas and will, I suspect, continue
> to be so for many years to come. (1992, p. 5)

John J. O'Connor was equally uplifted in *The New York Times* in
March 1993:

> The primal elements of a good children's story are all here: the
> forbidden territory, the fretting parents, the irrepressible child, the
> terrifying encounters and breathless chases, the safety of the family
> and the lesson learned.

The best thing that can be said about these painstaking
animations is that they are as utterly charming and beguiling as the
original books. Peter, Flopsy, Mopsy, Cottontail, Jemima Puddle-
Duck, Mrs. Tiggy Winkle and the rest of the Potter brood have
conquered a whole new world, one that should keep them around for
at least another century. (p. B10)

The *Publishers Weekly* review of the home video was also
complimentary:

Mr. McGregor's Scottish lilt and mama Josephine's worried tears are
just some of the finely conceived details that add warmth and heart to
the production. The episode strikes a nice balance between lively
action sequences—the famous chase scene—and quieter settings.
(1993, p. 31)

A finely honed sense of justice has obliged me to begin this
discussion with these rave reviews because I actually disagree with all
of them. It seems to me that the reviewers have been blinded by the
subtlety of the animation process, which is indeed fine. As cartoon
action goes, all the movements are relatively natural and convincing,
and Potter, who was famous for insisting on accuracy in her portrayals
of animals, might have approved at least of that aspect of the
animations.

Artistically, however, I have serious doubts about *The Tale of
Peter Rabbit and Benjamin Bunny*. It seems to me that the creators of
this film have recognized and triumphed over the technical challenges
of animating a set of small watercolors; but they have succumbed too
readily to the conventions and stereotypes which attend many animated
cartoons, especially those which feature animals. One convention is that
animals talk in cartoons. Only Mrs. Rabbit was given the power of
direct speech in the book, but in the animation, Peter, his sisters, the
sparrows, the mouse (incomprehensibly) and an observing robin are all
given plenty to say. Even more dismayingly, Peter and his cousin
Benjamin (who appears in the second story) speak with American
accents.

Some problems in this production seem to me to stem from the fact
that, like the Rabbit Ears producers, Grand Slamm Partnership wanted
to stretch two stories over half an hour. The opening sequences, which

are very leisurely, feature a live actress playing Beatrix Potter as she paints a picture, gets caught in a shower, goes home and writes the famous letter to little Noel. At the end of the two stories, we see her again, addressing the envelope and going out to post the letter.

This introduction gave the producers the option of using a "Potter" voice-over as a narration. They did not make use of this possibility. Although there are one or two narrative sentences, for the most part the plot is conveyed in dialogue. In theory, this is a reasonable choice for the medium. In practice, most of the conversations are limited and repetitive, augmented by much panting on Peter's part, grunting and groaning from Mr. McGregor, and a lot of giggling from Flopsy, Mopsy and Cotton-tail. There are also stretches where the music takes over, a far cry from the business-like pace of the faster video, *Tales of Beatrix Potter.*

The dialogue caused the *Publishers Weekly* reviewer to feel a few qualms:

> One small quibble: the young actors who read the voices of Peter and Benjamin are decidedly un-British and sound a bit forced when uttering some of the mannered phrases of the original texts, such as "Oh bother!" and "Whatever is the matter?" (Review, 1993, p. 31)

In fact, this reviewer should have felt more serious reservations; neither of the quoted lines of dialogue is actually uttered by anyone in *The Tale of Peter Rabbit* or *The Tale of Benjamin Bunny* as written by Beatrix Potter. In any case, there are phrases in the film which it would be very difficult to ascribe to Potter, "Oh golly! Mama will be furious!" being one prime candidate. Potter did not waste space on such empty interjections; most of her conversation is conveyed in indirect speech and it is usually to the point. No such scruples seem to have hindered the scriptwriters for the animation. Points are labored over and over again. Peter, lost in the garden, frets to himself: "Goodness—where am I now? I must get out—must get out. Is this the way? No. Oh, I don't know. Perhaps it's this way, or is it this way? No, this way."

The issue of the pie is dealt with in a very interesting way. The initial warning is defused. Mrs. Rabbit says, "Don't go into Mr. McGregor's garden. Your father had an accident there." Peter, mockingly anticipating, chants, "He was put in a pie by Mrs. McGregor," and Mrs. Rabbit repeats the line right on cue. Having thus enfeebled the threat, the producers then raise the issue again on a number of occasions throughout the film, something which Potter apparently felt no need to do. First spotted by Mr. McGregor, Peter hollers, "Mama! Oh no! I'll end up like Papa!" Caught in the gooseberry net, he shouts, "Mrs. McGregor will put me in a pie!" The overall effect of this repetition is, paradoxically, a coarsening rather than an intensifying of the sense of menace.

An article on Potter's 100th anniversary in *The Bookseller* talked about the animations in glowing terms and added an interesting point:

> Warne's determination to protect the quality of Potter (and to defend itself against charges of rank commercialism) has led it to produce an animation of the highest possible quality. It has been created precisely from Potter's own illustrations, thus making "live" pictures which are already familiar while also filling in gaps. As the Japanese publisher of Potter described it, "The video shows the secret Beatrix Potter, the bits which you have had to imagine in the past." ("Peter Rabbit Comes to Life," 1993, p. 32)

This Japanese publisher is not being very fair to the subtleties available to film, even to an apparently simplistic form of film such as animation. Even 30 minutes of story cannot show you everything you always had to imagine before; film calls for its own forms of inference-making, and the young viewers of *The Tale of Peter Rabbit and Benjamin Bunny* are as likely to be learning about the demands of this form through this text as they are in any other kind of encounter with a fiction. They must learn the vocabulary of cuts and camera angles, to take a single example. Nevertheless, the Japanese publisher is right about some things. The element of continuous movement in film does reduce the need for some kinds of assumption-making. It also plays its part in reducing the ability of the creator to be vague about some things: for example, the action of going "lippity lippity" is specific on the screen in a way which is not true on the page.

Video offers the possibility of a moving perspective, and this fact has led to some alterations. Peter, for example, is seen in the watering can exclusively from an internal point of view; at no time do his ears protrude. The producers have used their option of filling in the blanks to update the relentless and tiresome virtue of Flopsy, Mopsy and Cotton-tail; given voices and power of motion, the sisters whine and push at each other, spill blackberries on their napkins, and make merciless fun of Peter.

These changes can be defended; I find other alterations to be more irritating. My particular peeve is the talking robin, a Disney cliché imported to a text where he manifestly does not belong. His avuncular chuckles, his annoying habit of speaking to Peter in the first person plural ("Faster than Mr. McGregor, are we?") and his commitment to belaboring the obvious, all serve to reduce the subtlety of the story. It is the effect of the robin, above all else in this animation, which returned me to Jacob Epstein's idea that too many people think "that to take part uncritically in the common culture is the proper goal of growing up" (1969, p. 86). Look, the producers seem to be saying, we can make *Peter Rabbit* familiar to children who know only Disney; we can reduce the threat of the distinctive by introducing stereotypes where they were never needed before.

Similarly, some reviewers liked Mr. McGregor's Scottish accent; again, I found him to be a caricature with his repetitive, "Wee beastie!" and "Wee varmint!" Beatrix Potter had the advantage of print and picture in keeping him unspecific; but specifying certain aspects of his existence need not necessarily lead to cliché, and it is too bad that the producers succumbed to this temptation.

Many of these issues are questions of personal taste. There is no denying, however, that a child who meets Peter Rabbit in this animated format will be acquainted with an entirely different kind of story, in form necessarily but also, to a great degree, in content.

Tales of Beatrix Potter (EMI)

The version of Beatrix Potter's texts which, on the face of it, might seem the most implausible, is in many ways the richest and most successful. In 1971, after years of work, EMI produced a filmed ballet which merged several Potter stories and featured dancers from the Royal Ballet of Covent Garden, London, choreographed by Sir Frederick Ashton. Peter Rabbit appears in this film largely as a continuity figure, though he does get to do a "tarantella with lettuces" (Godden, 1971, p. 9). What this unlikely-sounding performance has to contribute to a consideration of the esthetics of adaptation is quite important.

The video is still in public circulation; I found it both in the public library and in the video rental shop. Furthermore, there is an invaluable book about the making of the film, written by Rumer Godden, who was approached by Warne to observe and record the whole complex venture of making the movie. Godden's background made her an ideal witness. She describes some of her qualifications in the Introduction:

> The Tales is a ballet picture: long ago I had trained, not as a dancer—
> a back injury prevented that—but as a teacher of dancing and, in a
> modest way, had choreographed ballets for my child pupils so the
> techniques of ballet and choreography were not a mystery to me . . .
> Similarly, with films: utterly disappointed with the first two made
> from my novels, I had had a "span" with Jean Renoir, perhaps
> greatest of all directors, working with him from beginning to end on
> *The River*, the beautiful picture he made from my book. And Beatrix
> Potter? True, I was not brought up on her—my Bengali childhood
> was too remote for that—but my children were, and her books had
> become a constant theme in the talks I give, articles I write—
> especially in America—in the cause of children's literature. (1971,
> p. 7)

In addition, as Godden does not mention, she has a long history as a writer for children herself. If anyone could be expected to understand the competing forces of different sets of conventions at work, she might be that person.

Not surprisingly, her comments are full of interest. She describes the many laborious processes which went into the making of the film: the complex, rarefied and meticulous operation of making all the masks and bodies which transformed the dancers into Potter animals; the elaborate research which informed the composition of the music (based on Victorian and Edwardian theater and dance music, which was tracked down in the British Museum and in secondhand shops); the choreography, rehearsal, film-making, editing.

Godden is interesting on more general issues, as well as on the many fascinating details:

> It is always a strange, almost startling sensation for the author of any
> work to see what was put down on paper take on flesh and blood, but
> one guesses that when Richard [Goodwin] and Christine [Edzard]

saw her sketches translated into Ashton choreography, it exceeded
even their vision. There is always "translation": Christine had not
"copied" Beatrix Potter's dresses and backgrounds, but translated
them into costumes and sets; nor did John Lanchbery "copy"
Victorian and Edwardian tunes: he translated them into music for The
Tales; and now, to Potter/Goodwin/Edzard/Lanchbery was added
Ashton.

All the Ashton light-heartedness is in this ballet, the wit and,
charm and something deeper; there are moments, only implicit in the
books, that become most moving in the ballet; the parting of Pigling
Bland and his brother Alexander from the farmyard and their
innocent excitement at being "sent to market"—their mother, Aunt
Pettitoes, knew very well what awaited them there; and that pas-de-
deux between Pigling Bland and Pig-wig, the black Berkshire sow. A
classical pas-de-deux is almost always a courtship and this is
deliciously tender, though "tender" is a dangerous word when
speaking of a pig. "Dear God, why did You make me so tender?" is
the Prayer of the Pig, and the pas-de-deux ends with a lift in which
Pig-wig's head touches the rack of sausages and flitches of bacon, the
hams and black puddings, hung up in the farmhouse kitchen.

"You *can't* put that in a film for small children!" some of the
Unit were to exclaim. Perhaps they had been schooled in the belief,
so prevalent nowadays, that books for small children must be
comical, facile, innocuous as to drama. The Beatrix Potter books are
none of these things; they are extremely dramatic, not blinking the
facts of life and birth and death. Under the prettiness of kittens and
rabbits, of ducks and mice, is this reality that does not mince matters.
"Nasty," said one of the men. Then is nature "nasty"? Beatrix Potter
knew that humans prey on animals, animals prey on one another, and
through all the books runs the toughness of real life. It is this that
gives them their drama: Peter Rabbit's tenseness and uneasiness in
Mrs. McGregor's garden is well founded—Peter knows about rabbit
pie." (1971, p. 37)

Ballet is a highly conventional art, and the choreographer of *Tales
of Beatrix Potter*, Sir Frederick Ashton, has adhered carefully to the
"rules" in this production. The mice perform a waltz, the two pigs do a
classic pas-de-deux, and so forth. At the same time, as Godden
suggests, the film addresses the real issues of the books, explores what

has been implicitly conveyed in the stories and allows intelligently for what will become implicit in the dancing. Unlike many other recastings of Potter, the ballet does not attempt to reduce ambiguity; instead it brings its own strengths and conventions to the exploration and celebration of exactly that ambiguity. One question which enriches the whole ballet is the classic question of all of Potter's work: are these animals animals or are they really humans in animal disguise? The animal dancers in the films exploit the potential of that question to the fullest. Both male and female pigs dance *en pointe*; the effect is one of very skillful dancers at work, but it also evokes the idea of tiny pigs' trotters with great success. Little hands and feet become twice as "twinkly" when contrasted to the bulk of the bodies. Similarly, Jeremy Fisher is simultaneously an exciting human dancer and a persuasive frog.

The film offers insights into the virtues of a robust approach to particular issues. In the opening scenes, the mice assemble to dance in front of the fender. They are filmed from above, at a sufficient distance to make them appear quite small, an effect greatly assisted by the scale of their setting: monster fender, large floor tiles, huge stairs. Having established the considerable charms of the miniature with great success and paid appropriate homage to one of the striking aspects of the books, the film does not then labor to recreate this effect in every scene; indeed in the final dance at the mouse picnic, all sorts of animals dance together. Cat, fox, squirrel, mouse, duck, pig are all roughly of a size (not surprisingly since all are created on the scale of the human form) but the effect is one of liveliness and harmony; details of relative size are simply not the most important aspect of this particular dance.

This production, in my view, successfully meets and makes creative use of the challenges which face any form of adaptation. The highly conventionalized demands of ballet meet and work with the specific demands created by the fact that it is Beatrix Potter's work and not somebody else's which is being turned into a dance. Each element creates its own restrictions; the success of the producers of this film is to use such limits as sources of energy. Perhaps this effect is only possible when the artists involved respect the original work in its entirety (in terms of what is absent and why, as well as what is explicitly present) and "translate" what they find important about that into the terms of the new medium.

GENERAL IMPLICATIONS

What is present in a text frames what is left out. The threat of Mrs. McGregor's pie, once made, informs Peter's actions throughout the story; he hurries to the garden, perhaps in defiance, perhaps in a state of misplaced confidence in his own immortality. Once discovered, he must reckon with the full force of the real danger he is in; Potter has no need to keep reminding us. Those retellings which eliminate the pie do away with a controlling element in the force of the story, but those who keep repeating the threat also do not appear to grasp that a plot element need not be constantly reintroduced in order to be present in the story. Potter never needs to mention the moment, implicit in the arrangement of events, when Peter suddenly realizes, *It could really happen to me too*. The implications of that discovery shadow many of Peter's subsequent movements in the garden; indeed, Potter was sure enough of the power of the tacit to include, without any further explanation, Peter's new awareness of his own mortality in the sequel to *The Tale of Peter Rabbit, The Tale of Benjamin Bunny*: "Peter did not seem to be enjoying himself [in the garden]; he kept hearing noises" (*Benjamin Bunny*, p. 30). The picture of Peter looking haunted reinforces the impact of this description, but Potter is never explicit about why Peter might be feeling this way. Later she picks up the theme, again without explanation: "Peter did not eat anything; he said he should like to go home. Presently he dropped half the onions" (*Benjamin Bunny*, p. 34).

A retelling of *The Tale of Peter Rabbit* which undertakes to set this story within a new set of conventions has to find a way to recreate that implied understanding as part of the overall effect of the new text. In my view, the approach of the Warne animation is the wrong one. Much of the sinister power of the threat of rabbit pie comes from the fact that it is never mentioned again after the first warning. This subtlety is lost when Peter keeps reminding himself of his mortal peril; that very sense of danger is devalued rather than heightened. This cannot be an absolute judgement, however. Clearly those reviewers who responded so enthusiastically to the video did not experience the same sensation of delicacy lost which I feel so strongly.

Obviously, in a moving picture of whatever sort, the way "gaps" work must be different from the workings of a text containing words and still pictures. One of the reasons why "translation" is needed is to find ways of expressing the explicit and the implicit. These are conditions of adaptation and in their expression we find the judgement of the adaptors on display.

There is also a question about the response of readers/viewers who meet, for example, the character of Peter Rabbit both in text and in video form. Gaps left unspecified in one format are made definitive in another; for example, we know from the text something of Peter's sense of consternation in the garden; we are told about this rather than having to infer it and that internal perspective can be transferred to the awareness we bring to the video version. On the other hand, Peter's voice, left open to be informed by the voice of the reader in performance in the text format, is specified (to my ear, unpleasantly so) in the video. A child familiar with both versions may therefore have a concept of Peter Rabbit which involves rather less filling in of gaps, a kind of palimpsest effect where specifications from different formats are overlaid to create a more explicit composite version of character or story. The final effect may be coherent or incoherent, and we know little about how children come to terms with contradictions in such circumstances.

There are many questions both about the making and the reception of adapted texts. Video offers access to what most people probably think of as the most common and striking form of adaptation. The video versions of The Tale of Peter Rabbit highlight some of the issues we need to explore further. The territory becomes even more complex as we look at other formats.

CHAPTER 6
Other Media

Although it is easy to think of print and film as the two main media of narrative text, the list of potential vehicles is much longer and still growing. In this section, I want to look at three formats: audio recording, filmstrip and computer program. I also want to look at the kinds of "educational" discourse which frame and accompany most of the versions of these formats which I have seen so far. I will return later to the newest medium for this story: CD-ROM.

AUDIOCASSETTES

I listened to six audio versions of *The Tale of Peter Rabbit*. Three were British: Warne's 1987 tape read by Rosemary Leach, Caedmon's 1974 reading by Claire Bloom, and the dramatized version derived from the Warne-authorized animation. Three were American: Meryl Streep reading for the Rabbit Ears 1992 production, linked to the video animation, and two nameless readers working for Listening Library, one in 1977 and one in 1983.

Perhaps the simplest transformation of a text from one medium to another is that from print to audio recording. A reader reads the story, with or without the embellishment of added music, sound effects, or dramatic voices. There are certain sacrifices: in the case of a picture book, there is the substantial loss of the pictures, and there is also the loss of control over pace. On the other hand, there are gains: the words are given a voice and a tune, and, for young listeners in particular, that can be very helpful. Many cassettes come with a matching text, in which case the advantages are strengthened and the drawbacks reduced.

Of course, nothing is ever quite so clear cut. Even in the case of a text as short as *Peter Rabbit*, there are issues of abridgement and alteration. The Listening Library tape, for example, inexplicably leaves out a single sentence: "It was a blue jacket with brass buttons, quite new." It also transfers the sentence about Mr. McGregor and the scarecrow to the end of the story, which irrevocably alters both the final cadences of the text and the ultimate balance of the opposing forces in the story.

Any oral reading raises questions about the accent of the reader; of the tapes I heard, half were read with an British accent and half were American. The effect on the pace and balance of the words was significant, although an American accent need not invariably cause problems in an English story. Decisions about the length of tape had a more profound effect on pace; the Meryl Streep reading, based on the video version, takes 14 minutes versus 10.30 for the longest of the other tapes (excluding the dramatization). The effect on the telling is striking.

Background music can remain in the background or take over the microphone on its own, with a different impact in each case, and a storytelling without music at all is different again. Sound effects also may alter the final shaping of the text. A dramatization works differently yet again. *The World of Peter Rabbit and Friends* dramatized audiotape of *The Tale of Peter Rabbit*, based on the Warne animation, achieves a balance between the text and the video. The narrative voice-over of Niamh Cusack, the actress who plays Beatrix Potter in the video, replaces many visual effects with Potter's original words, but wherever possible, the explication of the story is handed over to the dramatized voice of Peter. Peter thus gets to comment that there is no room for a fat little rabbit to squeeze under the door in the garden wall, for example. The action is augmented by background music and many of the video alterations, such as the more obstreperous behavior of Flopsy, Mopsy and Cotton-tail, are preserved in audio form.

Some audiotapes are more tied to an accompanying text than others; in tapes for young children in particular, it is common to find a little beep indicating either that the page should be turned or that the filmstrip should be moved ahead. The Listening Library tape features the same story on two sides of the tape, but on one side the beep is clearly audible; on the second side they fondly assert that it is inaudible but it can be discerned among the other background noises, a low-pitched tone to mark the adjustment of the accompanying filmstrip.

Roger Cox, speaking to the 1995 *Children's Literature in Education* conference in Devon, addressed some of the issues involved in the making of audio tapes out of children's stories.

All fiction involves complex processes of representation which the producers of fiction have to create and which children have to learn. In some areas which are particularly significant for children, for example with picture books and with animated films, the "layers" of representation become even more complex. Audio versions of stories are the newest example of this multi-layered process of representation, in which a layer of significance is added by the way the voice encodes meanings.

In both picture books and animations there is a clear tendency to use stereotype and caricature as effective ways to encode meaning— look for example at the animated film *The Animals of Farthing Wood*, or at the picture books of Babette Cole. These allow children to take short-cuts to semiotic competence, from the merest outline of a signifier to find the signified, its connotations, denotations, mythical aspects etc. . . .

There is a tendency to find these processes sinister and precisely because picture books, animations and audio-versions are more heavily and explicitly coded than the written word, to regard them as inferior forms of representation. (1995, p. 2)

Cox argues, however, that for learning readers the argument against stereotype and caricature is not clear-cut.

Whilst there are dangers in stereotype and caricature, they do extend the range of the child's experience and can add important information. As well as adding characterisation, they can often offer clues about the relationship between the narrator and the characters in the story and about the relationship between narrator and narratee, thus offering insights into aspects of focalisation and register that would often pass by an unsophisticated reader. (1995, p. 2)

The *Peter Rabbit* audiotapes offer a range of relationships between narrator and characters, and narrator and narratee. Rosemary Leach, in her aristocratic British accent, provides a very adult approach, stressing the detachment of the narrator from the pecadilloes of the main character. Niamh Cusack, narrating the BBC dramatized version in her persona of Beatrix Potter, supplies an even more impeccably chiselled tone, but the dramatized voices of the different characters are interwoven with her account and give the tape a much less austere tone. Meryl Streep, with her dramatic rendition of the story, creates a more immediately suspenseful and less thoughtful approach, calling for a more emotional kind of engagement. The gloss provided on the story by each version is substantially different.

THE FILMSTRIP

I found one filmstrip, produced by Listening Library in 1977, packaged with a tape and a teacher's guide. The filmstrip displays its own conventions in an interesting kind of way. For one thing, the backgrounds are no longer Potter's white page; text (printed in white) and picture are overlaid on backgrounds of various deep colors, presumably to add some variety to a relatively static format. In every case the picture is on the left-hand side of the screen, and all the pictures have been set in a uniform rounded rectangle shape. Where the text segment is shorter than on Potter's page, the picture may be repeated, sometimes with a slightly different focal point. The producers have also added pictures to supplement the text; of 41 pictures, 30 are by Potter, 11 by Margareta Larson, sometimes based on Potter pictures from earlier editions. With the pages freed from the confinements of the book spine, as it were, the producers also feel able to juggle the plot, and Mr. McGregor and the scarecrow once again appear at the end of the story.

Of all the versions I encountered, the filmstrip is in some ways the most linear. You thread the strip into the machine and then you move forwards or backwards through each picture; it is impossible to skip one, though the pace can be altered.

Unlike most of the other formats discussed here, the filmstrip still requires relatively cumbersome machinery. I tried to view it by holding it up against a window but it was too tiny to decipher. I had to book a projector and screen in order to make any sense of it at all. Compared to almost every other version, its rigidity in terms of both content and technology is now very apparent; it is startling to realize how very recently we took it for granted that alternative formats of a story would be cumbersome and irritating to use.

THE COMPUTER PROGRAM

Knowledge Adventures in the United States have produced a computer program of *The Tale of Peter Rabbit* (1993). This program uses Potter's text but replaces her pictures with Lonnie Sue Johnson's illustrations. These may have been tolerable to start with, though I have my doubts, but expanded to fill the computer screen they are simply dismal.

As with many CD-ROM versions of print books, the computer program provides word labels for bits of the picture as you point with the mouse. The word is pronounced and, often, a sound effect is added. It is in the provision of these sound effects that the banal becomes the ridiculous. *The Tale of Peter Rabbit* is full of items that, by their nature, do not make a lot of noise: trees, bushes, cucumber frames and so forth. Knowledge Adventure, presumably eager to make their program as lively as possible, have pressed all possible clichés into service, even when the overall effect is completely contradictory to the meaning of the story. Hence, the sound effect for the cucumber frame is of breaking glass; the sound for the bushes is a roaring wind which resembles a juggernaut rather than anything pastoral. The most remarkable effect is that of the fir-tree; its sound effect is of a tree crashing to the ground and a shout of "Timber!" (This is really true; I couldn't possibly make it up!) Poor Peter Rabbit, flopped in exhaustion on the sand bank; little does he know that his home is secure only until the child in charge asks for the name of the fir-tree.

The computer program is a relatively new format, but it proves that nothing establishes itself faster than a stereotype. The equipment will make sound effects? Sound effects we must have, and any cost to overall meaning will be disregarded. As with the Disneyesque talking robin in the Warne animation, the coarsening effect of cliché downgrades the individuality and subtlety of the original.

THE FRAMING DISCOURSE

The discerning reader may gather that I am not as excited about these versions as I might be. I had, in fact, expected much better. Furthermore, I must admit to being jaundiced by the accompanying rubrics in almost every single case.

The Listening Library filmstrip and audiocassette package (1977) is admittedly old, but it was readily available in the curriculum library at my university and, to that extent, is still part of the contemporary scene. To do the package justice, it does suggest that children's first viewing and listening experience should be for "enjoyment of the story and appreciation of its creative elements." However, the emphasis soon turns to "*listening* to phrases and sentences that make up the text narration." There are numerous questions, some to be used in preparation for viewing and some to explore comprehension. The most unlikely combination of exercises is the list labelled "To Do." This is the complete set.

> 1. Review these new words and phrases: sand-bank, root, fir-tree, fields, lane, accident, mischief, loaf, currant buns, gather, squeezed, radishes, parsley, cucumber frame, cabbages, waving, rake, altogether, unfortunately, gooseberry net, sobs, sparrows, implored, exert, sieve, wriggled, upsetting, trembling, damp, wander, puzzled, twitched, hoe, wheel-barrow, flopped, fortnight, camomile tea, dose, scare-crow.
>
> 2. Plant your own garden and make a scare-crow to keep the birds away.
>
> 3. Read the other books written and illustrated by Beatrix Potter. (n.p.)

The absence of coherent thought behind these questions is quite alarming. A child who needs this much "support" to read one book by Beatrix Potter is hardly going to sit down and romp through the remaining 22. And the idea that "reviewing" 39 words and phrases is something to *do*, let alone that it is an equivalent to planting a garden complete with scarecrow, is simply mind-boggling.

The discussion guide provided with the audiotape and books of *The Tale of Peter Rabbit* and *The Tale of Benjamin Bunny* (also produced by Listening Library in 1983) is longer and, as a simple consequence, worse. The authors do not flinch at leading questions, such as, "Why was Peter afraid to go near the cat? How does this show us that he did have good sense sometimes?" They do not hesitate to apply a large hammer to a potential moral: "Why did Peter almost give up when he was caught in the gooseberry net? What did the sparrows do? What does this teach us?"

For each of the two stories, a page of multiple-choice word definitions is provided:

"'It was a blue jacket with *brass* buttons, quite new.' *Brass* is a shiny, yellow-colored _____ a. metal b. cookie c. kind of cloth" Each story also gets a page of multiple-choice comprehension questions. To provide for the utterly unbelievable scenario that the teacher might not be able to work out the answers, a key is provided at the bottom of each page. There are two pages of vocabulary work, one working on definitions and the other on "spelling demons." An insipid list of suggested student activities ("Beatrix Potter says she cannot draw a picture of Peter and Benjamin underneath the basket. Can you? Use your imagination and remember the onions!") rounds off the booklet.

Every time I find myself thinking, "Well, that really is the limit!" another surprise comes along. I could have borrowed the 1974 Caedmon tape of Claire Bloom reading Potter stories from my public library and it would have come with no strings attached. As it happens, I went to the curriculum library at the university and my set came in a little package with a program booklet. Rather than providing instructional "support," this booklet supplies moral uplift in a disconcerting way. It cites Potter's meticulous detail in her descriptions of Mrs. Tiggy-Winkle, rabbit-tobacco, and Jeremy Fisher's return to the surface of the water. Such contemplation moves the anonymous writer to rapturous heights:

> Breathes there a child with soul so dead who could ever thereafter do harm to rabbit, frog or hedgehog? It is not of Beatrix Potter followers that the despoilers of nature are composed. Perhaps, in fact, it is more Peter Rabbit that the world needs now; more kinship with the green world at our feet, more sensitivity to the unthinking havoc of which mice and men are capable. (n.p.)

The computer program would appear to be aimed substantially at the domestic market but the instructional patter is nearly as unrelenting. Compared to some of the other packages, however, it provides a relatively enlightened guide to home use. The suggestions for parents include the idea that parents should let the child take the lead. "Aim to be a student of your child more than of the software. What can you find out about your child's learning style, interests, attention span, and thought processes?" (p. 8). Ask appropriate questions, they suggest, and have fun together.

Compared to some of the other rubrics, this text amounts to a monument of enlightenment. Nevertheless, it would be refreshing to come across some sense that children might learn about engagement, about subtlety, about irony, about the pleasures of meeting a challenging piece of *literature*. Literary understanding does not feature in any of these guides to teachers and parents. One is left with the question of why anyone would bother to introduce children to a sophisticated work of literature only to eviscerate it of all its interesting qualities.

CHAPTER 7

The Activity Books

The single most startling fact about the activity books associated with Peter Rabbit and other Potter characters is the sheer quantity. Considerable ingenuity has been expended on ways to repeat and recycle the same material over and over again in slightly different formats. Here, for example, are the entries in the name of Peter Rabbit alone from Warne's Canadian catalogue for the autumn of 1995, under the heading of "Beatrix Potter Activity Books:"

Big Peter Rabbit Coloring Book
Peter Rabbit and Benjamin Bunny Coloring Book
Peter Rabbit and Friends Cookbook
Peter Rabbit Craft Book
Peter Rabbit Make a Mobile Activity
Peter Rabbit Make and Play Book
Peter Rabbit Stencil Book
Peter Rabbit Sticker Book New Edition
Peter Rabbit Theatre: A Cut Out Theatre Starring Peter Rabbit,
     Mrs. Rabbit, Flopsy, Mopsy, Cotton-tail
Peter Rabbit's Christmas Book
Peter Rabbit's Cookery Book
Peter Rabbit's Puzzle Book
Scenes from The Tale of Peter Rabbit
Where's Peter Rabbit? A Flap Book
World of Peter Rabbit Sticker Book

Peter   remained   very   quiet,   but

just   then   he   sneezed.   "Ker Choo!

The Tale of Peter Rabbit Coloring Book as told in Signed English

Add to this the Ladybird contribution of a *Peter Rabbit Shaped Coloring Book*, a *Peter Rabbit Sticker Book* and a *Peter Rabbit Color In Storybook* and the scale of the marketing initiative begins to come clear. There are, of course, numerous variations on these themes featuring Jemima Puddle-duck, Tom Kitten and so forth. Other titles appear under different headings in the catalogue; there are also a number of pop-up books, hide and seek books, bath books, cloth books, board books, pictures, friezes and a *Peter Rabbit and Friends Poster Activity Book*. On top of that comes the collection of baby books, birthday books, address books, diaries and postcard books. There is also a monthly magazine for children, published by the Redan Company in the *Fun to Learn (TM)* series and entitled *Peter Rabbit and Friends (TM)*.

This enormous quantity of material represents the legitimate end of the market; there are also coloring books and other materials produced by American publishers without any acknowledgement to Warne. Of those that I have seen, the most extreme adaptation is a coloring book told in signed English, produced by Kendall Green Publications, an imprint of Gallaudet University Press. This project, no doubt worthy by some definitions, is "narrated" by an avuncular man whose outline is available for coloring over and over again as he appears with every word producing the appropriate sign. This edition does make a breakthrough in one particular convention by showing Cotton-tail in a pair of dungarees, a piece of rethinking which is novel by the standards of other retellings.

This piece of piracy is at least cheap; what is noticeable about the Warne publications in particular is that they are very expensive for material which is by its nature ephemeral. Perhaps to compensate, the coloring book comes loaded with credentials on the front cover; there is a triangular flash in the corner trumpeting, "Now a Major TV Series," the top of the book bears the logo, "The World of Peter Rabbit and Friends (TM)," and at the bottom another box says, "From the authorized animated series based on the original tales by Beatrix Potter." The coloring books from both Warne and Ladybird contain color pictures to accompany the outline drawings to "help you choose the colors to use." The practice of offering such assistance, which may seem oddly pedantic to contemporary tastes, in fact dates back to Potter's own coloring book which she produced in 1911 (Taylor, 1986, pp. 123–124).

The emphasis on relating this material to the television series suggests that the publishers hope to create the kind of "supersystem" which Marsha Kinder (1991) talks about in *Playing with Power*, a bandwagon effect in which hype and the sheer quantity of reproduction work together to persuade consumers to keep on buying (a subject to which we shall return later). To be fair to Warne, none of the material I looked at was completely meretricious, and *The Peter Rabbit and Friends (TM) Poster Activity Book* actually undertakes some ambitious projects in the cause of educating children about how film works and how animations are made.

The coloring books are relatively neutral, though they could be explored as yet further versions of the story. By and large, however, what happens to Peter Rabbit in the set of activity texts is that he undergoes a transformation into a domestic educational project. The effect of exploring a number of these books at once is a sense of overwhelming earnestness. "Where is Peter?" asks *The World of Peter Rabbit Treasury*.

> He's eating radishes in Mr McGregor's garden, of course! Paint or color this picture from *The Tale of Peter Rabbit*. Be careful—remember radishes are not the same color as carrots! (1994, p. 23)

Later, the same book offers the "Big Bad Crossword."

> How well do you know the Beatrix Potter stories?
> Try this crossword, and if you get stuck you'll find the answers on page 60. Once you've tried this crossword, you might also like to read the stories again.
> There's a complete list of the famous Peter Rabbit Books on page 61. (1994, p. 40)

The "Fun to Learn" magazine is even more didactic in tone. I looked at the June 1995 issue. Even the table of contents is relentless: "This month . . . lots to learn," chirps its heading (ellipsis in original). The rubric which attends the various exercises is thorough, to put it mildly. On the "Spot the Difference" page, for example, the instructions at the top say, "Draw circles round **4** differences between the two pictures." On the bottom of the page it says, "Did you spot **4** differences?" and includes boxes to tick yes or no. This incessant need for children to "do" something with all the material on offer perhaps reaches its apogee on the picture poster page. There is a dotted line for cutting out the full-page picture of a dormouse, but the average child's wish to do so might be severely undermined by the large panel superimposed on the picture, saying, "Picture poster page: Point to the dormouse's tiny, pink nose!" And the determination to draw a good moral is well represented on the "Look and Say" page, where the story of Peter Rabbit is retold in large letters. Here it is in its entirety, accompanying four pictures:

Naughty Peter Rabbit went to . . .
. . . Mr McGregor's garden.
He had to run all the way home.
Did he learn his lesson?

It will be no surprise to learn that the final caption accompanies a picture of Peter receiving the camomile tea.

The actual activities are harmless enough, possibly even worthwhile. It is the preachiness of tone which sets my teeth on edge with this particular publication. With some of the others, I am rather more perturbed by an inconsistency of address. *The World of Peter Rabbit Treasury* is apparently aimed at relatively literate children; *The Peter Rabbit and Friends Poster Activity Book* appears to be speaking to children of at least nine or ten. The introduction to "The Zoetrope" in the latter assumes quite sophisticated reading skills:

In the late 1700s Peter Roget wrote the first scientific paper on animation, and "persistence of vision." He saw that the human eye merges still pictures together when they are spun rapidly. Invented in the early 1800s, the zoetrope works on this principle. Pictures are drawn in sequence and spun inside a cylinder. As the viewer watches through slits cut in the side, the pictures blur together in a primitive form of animation. (n.p.)

I find it hard to imagine the reader who could make sense of that paragraph, yet who would need this help at the bottom of the same page:

* All areas where you apply glue are colored grey.

* Try not to let any glue get onto other parts of the zoetrope, to keep
it neat. When you stick two pieces together, make sure the glue has
dried properly before you carry on or it may fall apart. (n.p.)

SOME IMPLICATIONS OF THE ACTIVITY BOOKS

We do not normally perform any kind of close reading of the kind of
transient text represented by my examples above. Apart from anything
else, the ability to do so relies on a fairly elastic budget. For obvious
reasons, libraries do not stock copies of books for coloring or joining
the dots, and the Warne books are not cheap. The idea of any kind of
reviewing system for much of this material is, of course, out of the
question.

I inspected only a fraction of the entire list. Nevertheless, on the
basis of even the small sample I looked at, if I were a small child I
would feel I was being "got at" by these texts. The continuous
emphasis on instructiveness is wearing, to put it mildly. When we think
about the reception of different versions of *The Tale of Peter Rabbit*,
we should not overlook the impact of such didacticism on the way in
which children may respond to the story and the characters.

Of course, it is not the children who buy such material, and, in
many cases, it is not the children who pester their parents for it, either.
Much of the sanctimoniousness and relentless teaching tone is clearly
aimed at parents and grandparents, who may not have moved as far
from the preachy world of Victorianism as we like to think.

In any case, many of the children who read or watch *The Tale of
Peter Rabbit* will be bombarded with this form of follow-up activity.
Do such children, or some of them, feel they have reached the point of
exhausting the virtues of the text differently or more rapidly than
children who know only one or two versions? Does it matter? As more
and more books for children undergo commodification and strategic
marketing, such questions are not trivial. In some cases, such as that of
Thomas the Tank Engine, I would argue that the literary loss is not
terribly great if children either reach saturation point or are led further
and further away from the original texts. This is not such a clear-cut
argument in the case of Peter Rabbit.

EXAMPLES OF FRAGMENTATION AND COHESION

One particularly interesting text is *The Peter Rabbit Theatre*. My copy says it is "Starring Peter Rabbit and Benjamin Bunny" and I am not sure if this is exactly the same book as the one listed in the Warne catalogue as "Starring Peter Rabbit, Mrs. Rabbit, Flopsy, Mopsy, Cotton-tail." In any case, this book contains many fascinating contradictions. It largely consists of cardboard figures to be pressed out and used in a stage play; a cardboard stage with scenery is also provided.

The press-out figures consist of many versions of Peter, Benjamin, and the rest of the cast of the two books. They are simply Potter's paintings, removed from any background, and placed on a tab which serves two functions: when folded back, it acts as a base to enable the character to stand upright; each tab is also numbered and the numbers serve as an organizer for the production of the play.

The effect of seeing so many Peters and Benjamins in poses entirely familiar from the story but deprived of the normal background (which is, in some cases, recreated as "scenery" for the cardboard stage) is oddly disruptive. The fragmentation of the storyline is as complete as the most hypertext-conscious postmodernist could wish for. However, Colin Twinn, who is credited with creating and illustrating the Theater, is not interested in any way in the cognitive or artistic potential of fragmentation and fracturing. His instructions aim at a highly controlled activity; the numbers on the base take priority over any form of free imaginative play with the characters.

The instructions for "playing" with the Theater make interesting reading:

> Read *The Tale of Peter Rabbit* and *The Tale of Benjamin Bunny*, which you will find in this book [full texts are included], several times so that you know both stories and the pictures well. The next thing to do is to write the script. Decide whether you want to write two separate plays or one play combining both stories perhaps in two acts with an interval in between. You will see that some of the things that happen in the original tales have had to be left out of the play. Here are some guidelines to help you.

Act One
Scene One

Mrs. Rabbit warns her children Flopsy, Mopsy, Cotton-tail and Peter,
not to go into Mr. McGregor's garden, but Peter takes no notice.
While Mrs. Rabbit goes to the baker's and Flopsy, Mopsy and
Cotton-tail pick blackberries, naughty Peter squeezes under the gate
of Mr. McGregor's garden. (The figures you will need for this scene
are Nos. 1–7.) (*The Peter Rabbit Theatre*, 1983, p. 12)

There are equivalent instructions for a total of five scenes in *Peter
Rabbit* and three in *Benjamin Bunny*. The book continues with
suggestions for the script and the moving of scenery. Again, the
instructions allow little latitude for imaginative exercise.

If you are working the theater on your own, learn the play by heart so
that you don't have to hold up the action while you read the script. If
there are two or more of you, one person can move the figures while
the others read the parts. In the first act which tells the story of Peter
Rabbit, only Mrs. Rabbit and Mr. McGregor actually say anything.
You can write the script as though it is being told by a storyteller,
with only their parts being spoken. Or why not make up words for
Peter and his sisters too—and even the sparrows and the robin, if you
like . . .
The figures are numbered in the order in which they will appear in the
play, but because the numbers are on the flaps underneath, they are
not easy to see. It would be a good idea to write the numbers on the
backs of the figures themselves. (*The Peter Rabbit Theatre*, 1983,
p. 14)

I suspect, however, that no quantity of instruction can keep this
particular genie leashed to its bottle. Once the little press-out characters
are liberated from the page, they take on a life of their own, and their
only real limitations are those of pose, placed on them by Potter herself.
    The larger imaginative effects of an assortment of cardboard Peter
Rabbits are more difficult to envisage. The effect of the white space
surrounding Potter's pictures is suddenly expanded, as the characters
are detached even from their most vestigial backgrounds. A kind of
practical deconstruction is the outcome; instead of being an intellectual

abstraction, deconstruction becomes a manual activity. It is not difficult to imagine young children holding dialogues between one Peter and another. (I like to picture a crowd of Peters clustered around the Peter in the gooseberry bush, all imploring him to exert himself!) What would be surreal when confined to text alone becomes a simple action when the props are provided, as they are here.

A similar, though more restricted, effect is also possible with the sticker books. Both Warne and Ladybird have produced examples of these, both using illustrations from the animation. The Warne book offers rather more freedom to the user, with removable stickers which can be placed on the plasticized background and then repositioned at the user's pleasure. The Ladybird *Peter Rabbit Sticker Book* is more directive; although it offers "two blank play pages" with backgrounds where the stickers may be adjusted at will, the majority of the book offers prescriptive homes for the stickers. There are rectangular scenes from the animated version of the story; these are to be inserted next to the appropriate section of text. There are quiz pages where a sticker provides the correct answer to a sum or a shape puzzle; again, there is only one right place to put your sticker. The effect of a scene from the book with a shaped hole in the middle waiting for its appropriate sticker is one of reconstruction, rather than deconstruction; there is no sense whatever of any kind of open-endedness about the activities. Warne's *Beatrix Potter Sticker Book* offers other forms of activity such as recipes and the tried-and-trusted maze; the Ladybird book confines itself to sticker activity involving both pictures and single words. Whether this is a case of class distinction or a simple matter of pricing policy is not clear. In any case, the question remains whether such reiterative potential in the many recyclings of a single text holds important intellectual consequences for the way young children learn to think about a story.

The Peter Rabbit Spectacular

For those with luxurious tastes, substantial budgets and delicate fingers, the culmination of the activity books is probably the giant pop-up book which offers a three-dimensional rendition of a Lake District cottage complete with pop-up fir-tree, vegetable garden and lily-pond. Again there are press-out cardboard characters (though only one of each character this time), and a small book of two play scripts telling the story of Peter Rabbit and the story of Samuel Whiskers.

The book covers open flat and the pop-up scenery stands upright and is sumptuous in its level of detail. Both the back of the house and the roof open up, creating an effect of a rather delicate doll's house. A small and very careful hand could probably move the cardboard figures around inside but the effect of such details as the working staircase is generally more decorative than useful. It is really an interior to be peered into and admired, rather than a genuine setting for play.

The illustrations are all original Potter but the dialogue supplied in the play scripts comes straight from the animation; the authors are presumably counting on children either not to notice any discrepancy or to come equipped with a suitably flexible mindset. Once again, as with the play theater, the presumption of the creators (designer Kathryn Siegler and paper engineer Bruce Reifel) would appear to be that children will want to use this scenic playground only for the orthodox reproduction of Potter's story in dramatic form. The introduction is quite firm:

> These simple plays have been adapted from Beatrix Potter's tales and are great fun to act out.
>
> The cast and prop lists at the beginning of each play tell you which press-outs you'll need for that particular story, and to help you identify who's who, the press-outs have been numbered (you'll find a complete list in the back of this book).
>
> Read the plays a couple of times before you perform them so that you're familiar with the story and are sure of where to put the props. And, if you have Beatrix Potter's original tales, it might be a good idea to read them too. (n.p.)

Nothing in this prescriptive approach actually prevents a child from playing in more imaginative ways with this delicately constructed landscape, but the constant emphasis on simple reproduction and reiteration of a single plot does become overwhelming after a time. There are certainly many crasser forms of dictating how children "ought" to play with particular toys; many television advertisements come across in very authoritarian ways, for example. *Peter Rabbit* is clearly being used as a back story to this artifact, along the lines of many television-based toys which come complete with a predetermined plot. Perhaps I am simply jaundiced by looking at too many versions of the same small story; one can only presume that even the richest child Peter Rabbit fan would be exposed to considerably less material than I have explored and might therefore feel less bossed about. Nevertheless, I find something very tedious in this constant level of instruction and interference with ways of playing.

Having said that, there is no question that *The Peter Rabbit Spectacular* (1994) is a beautiful piece of work. Printed and bound in China, it stands as a testimonial to the care and attention to detail of its producers. Many children and perhaps even more adults would be enchanted by this "Pop-Up-and-Play Book." At the same time, it stands as a particularly vivid example of a Potter world eviscerated of all the nastiness that Rumer Godden describes as having been preserved in the ballet. Although Mr. McGregor is one of the cardboard characters in the collection, the overall effect of this world is overwhelmingly cosy, even dainty. Roses and lilies abound; even the cabbages are picturesque. Perhaps the insistence on adhering to the play script represents one last attempt to include some elements of the harshness of the real Potter universe, but in the face of the sensational prettiness of the landscape it seems doomed to failure.

THE OVERALL IMPACT

Presumably the market for these numerous and largely repetitive activity books sustains the apparently substantial investment in turning Peter Rabbit into various forms of instructional tool. It would be fascinating to have some idea of how many related activity books featuring a favorite fictional character are likely to be owned by the average child. Is there a point where even the most obsessed enthusiast says, "Enough"? Alternatively, especially with a character like Peter Rabbit, is it simply the case that the world is so full of grandmas and aunties and godmothers that the appeal to the child consumer is not the main priority? The pricing policies would suggest that many of these books are marketed with an eye to their potential as presents. Without more information, it is difficult to gauge the impact of so many reproductions of Peter in different instructive guises on those children who meet him over and over again. Does he eventually become more or less invisible, simply an adjunct to the mazes and crossword puzzles that occupy a child for a morning? Certainly it would not take many encounters before a child deduced that the potential for any new or exciting plot development is very slight, no matter how many times Peter reappears. That fact probably has its own impact; how many activity books would you have to work through before you decided that Peter Rabbit is actually pretty boring? At what point does the goose cease to produce golden eggs and does it really matter if a new batch of babies and toddlers, complete with loving relations, is always on the horizon?

CHAPTER 8

The CD-ROMs

In 1994, Discis produced a CD-ROM of *The Tale of Peter Rabbit*. Late in 1995, at least two Mindscape CD-ROMs became available, potentially the start of a long series of Potter products in this medium.

One of the things which makes CD-ROMs so interesting is their capacity to combine many of the formats already described and to develop forms of text which actively invite new kinds of reading behaviors and strategies. The three *Peter Rabbit* CD-ROMs I explored demonstrate some of the potentials, limitations and complexities of this new format. All three texts are hybrids of earlier forms, but each draws on a different combination of form and convention. By far the most intriguing of the three is the Mindscape production, *The Adventures of Peter Rabbit and Benjamin Bunny*; its mixture of other traditions of text and format does actually offer different reading and fictional experiences, the implications of which may be far-reaching for young learners.

The contrast between the three CD-ROMs offers a useful angle on some of the conundrums which attend the reworking of fictional texts within the parameters of a new technology.

THE TALE OF PETER RABBIT: DISCIS

Discis has produced a CD-ROM with Warne's approval, based on the original text and pictures. The most surprising aspect of this ultracontemporary version is how little it offers beyond the tried and tested combination of filmstrip and audiotape. "Pages" of text appear on the screen, framed as in a book. It is possible to activate a voice-over; the story is read aloud as the corresponding phrases of print are highlighted.

Certainly it is easy for children to be in charge of their own progress; as the "pages" of the book turn on the screen, they can pause to highlight certain words and phrases with the mouse, hear them being read aloud as often as they wish. They can also point to items in the picture and have the word appear in print on the screen with an appropriate pronunciation and the occasional perfunctory sound effect. As with an audiocassette, they can hear the story itself over and over again, the pages turning automatically and the words highlighted as they are spoken.

What I find remarkable about this version of the text is its extreme conservatism. Every obeisance is paid to the text; the potential of the new medium is exploited in a very minimalist way. The pages of the book appear on the screen as pages; sometimes the same picture appears on two adjoining openings when one of Potter's lengthier pages of text is split in two. There is some potential for moving around inside the text, but the overall impact is linear to an astonishing degree. In some ways, the lift-the-flap book, *Where's Peter Rabbit?*, is more imaginatively interactive.

Anyone who has seen one of the Broderbund CD-ROMs of children's stories (*Arthur's Teacher Trouble, Just Grandma and Me*, etc.) knows that there is great potential for reimagining the text (or at least the pictures) in new forms. Discis Books, however, would appear to place a higher priority on respectfulness than on wit or ingenuity. In its way, I found this approach as much of a disappointment as too much license. Simply reproducing the book on the screen (for a price of $30 instead of $3 for a paperback) seemed rather pointless.

Issues of quality control rear their head in the case of the CD-ROM. Reviews of such materials are scarce and there is no easy access to such reviews as exist. Internet reviews are interesting, but their authority is never entirely clear. Print reviewing tends to be patchy. A friend passed on a listing from *MacUser* from December 1994; presumably the fact that the Discis *Peter Rabbit* was listed at all had some significance, but there was little information to be gained from the annotation. *MacUser* suggests an age of 7+ years for this CD-ROM and says,

> This interactive read-along version of Beatrix Potter's story and illustrations is a fine introduction to this classic for young readers. (Shatz-Akin, 1994, p. 102)

None of that information is exactly untrue but neither is it very helpful—nor is it likely to be indexed in any useful place. As manufacturers rush to make and sell new multimedia products, the need to sort out selection criteria and a reliable reviewing apparatus is very obvious, and very important. The library journals are beginning to take clearer account of this need, and the number of computer magazines oriented towards family use will probably make a difference as well.

The rubric on the packaging of this Discis production is relentlessly didactic, with a reductive, utilitarian approach which is all too familiar. A Discis Book is "a gift of learning that will last a lifetime" (package back). There are various features for different kinds of emphasis and storage, all fairly pedestrian in my opinion, but the package description is enthusiastic.

> Children can learn from pictures too! They see an object's spelling and hear how to say it properly. And with hidden sound effects it's lots of fun!

> Your child may want to hear a word spoken slowly and clearly to help perfect his or her pronunciation. Readers can click for an in-context explanation of every word in the book to help them understand and learn from the story.

> The words your child found difficult and clicked on for more information are saved in a recall list which you can review with them.

Any hint that imaginative engagement might be a part of the learning process is lamentably absent from this reductive framework. The little booklet which accompanies the CD-ROM is not much better. The overarching objective of the program is well described in this summary sentence: "Children who read Discis Books have an increased opportunity to ensure their reading success by increasing their vocabulary, learning what words mean and learning how to read new words" (p. 11). The suggestions for home activities arising from the story are variable but also heavy-handed. "Good citizenship," begins one suggestion. "Rules and laws about trespassing, theft, and listening to parents exist to ensure that our community runs smoothly. Talk to your child about some of the rules and laws of the community, and some of the rules you have at home" (p. 13).

PETER RABBIT'S MATH GARDEN: MINDSCAPE

In the case of this CD-ROM, I viewed only a specimen snippet, part of a sample disk attached to the December 1995 issue of *CD-ROM Today*. As far as I could judge from a short example, the conventions merged in this particular product are those of an animated cartoon and those of an activity book. Various rabbits accompany the user to a collection of mathematical games: sorting, matching, adding, subtracting, and so forth. The games I viewed did not supply anything new and startling which a child could not encounter in a simple round of Memory or Kim's Game. Nevertheless, the computer is a profoundly patient partner, ready to play for an indefinite period of time. What is gained in the child's ability to persevere with the memory challenges is, of course, balanced by the loss of human contact. The complete disk may contain much more of a narrative element than I perceived in this sample, but that topic can be considered more carefully in the discussion of *The Adventures of Peter Rabbit and Benjamin Bunny*.

Elizabeth Weal, in an interesting review of this CD-ROM, suggests that Potter and computer graphics may not seem like the ideal combination.

> Anyone who has commiserated with Peter Rabbit's misfortunes knows the magic of Beatrix Potter's characters. What's hard to imagine is portraying these characters in computer graphics' hard-edged milieu. Mindscape, however, was not daunted by the challenge. The CD's lead artist traveled to Beatrix Potter's homeland, England's Lake District, to experience the countryside that inspired Potter's tales. The resulting CD is an artistic tour de force that drills children on basic math concepts within the context of Potter's world. Rather than the razzle-dazzle characteristic of most educational Cds, *Peter Rabbit's Math Garden*'s soft, highly detailed, airy screens create an environment that's warm, soothing and hard for children to leave behind. . . .
>
> At the completion of each activity, children are treated to Radish Time, unquestionably the most civilized zapping activity in multimedia history. During this ever-popular event, players collect radishes by clicking on the tasty veggies as they glide across the screen. As children complete activities and add to their radish stash,

they trade them for the seeds Peter uses to plan his interactive garden. (Weal, 1996, n.p.)

As is common with so many CD-ROMs, the question of drill is never far away. It is clear, however, that Mindscape is banking strongly on the idea that children will take to a kinder gentler CD-ROM universe. It remains to be seen how successful they will be with this gentle approach, and to what degree the normal computer conventions of flash, bang and murder have become entrenched in children's consciousnesses already.

THE ADVENTURES OF PETER RABBIT AND BENJAMIN BUNNY: MINDSCAPE

This CD-ROM struck me as the most interesting of the three, so I will take it as the main vehicle for exploring some of the ramifications which attend the development of this medium. *The Adventures of Peter Rabbit and Benjamin Bunny* offers many fascinating points of departure in such a discussion. It is a much more complex text than the Discis product, which is basically a screen reproduction of the book. This CD-ROM provides the complete text of the story, with the usual provision for having it read aloud with phrases highlighted as they are spoken. The story is illustrated by moving pictures, however; the movements of animated rabbits accompany the text, and instead of the page turning, the image on the screen slides smoothly around the landscape. The stability of the wording is maintained, but instead of relating to a still picture the words are attached to moving images (though the actions of the characters associated with any one set of words are restricted and repetitive).

The text is linear and conveys the normal narrative thrust we have come to take for granted. However, in the case of this CD-ROM, it is possible to interrupt the text not just once but many times. The reader/player can click on objects in the landscape for the usual oral and print label, or can follow the red arrows on the screen to explore further in Mr. McGregor's garden and shed, or can opt out to one of many games on offer at any point in the landscape where the scenery twinkles when the mouse is passed over it. Some of these extra attractions can be printed off (at least in theory, although I could not get my computer and printer to cooperate); thus when the child has assembled a jigsaw puzzle it is possible to make a hard copy. Vocabulary lists can also be printed. (Interesting copyright questions emerge at this point.)

It is also possible to interrupt the text with other texts; there are places in the pictures where a click of the mouse will bring up some of the small poems Potter illustrated later in her life.

Conventional and Esthetic Issues

Users of this CD-ROM will encounter some areas of similarity with the original book and some interesting points of departure from the kinds of convention we have long taken for granted. One very interesting aspect of the CD-ROM is that, unlike any other screen version I have seen, it respects Potter's use of white space and the pictures do not bleed off the screen. The 360-degree landscape, labelled as "Mindscape's unique Virtual ExploraScape (TM)" (package back), does offer a route into the fictional world which I have not encountered elsewhere; the closest comparison is the three-dimensional landscape of *The Peter Rabbit Spectacular: A Giant Pop-Up-and-Play Book*. At any point in the reading of the CD-ROM, the reader can move into the picture, activating red arrows on the screen to follow the path to another part of the wood or the garden or Mr. McGregor's shed. Even if the reader stays with the text, the action moves seamlessly around this landscape. There is no equivalent of a page turn; when Mrs. Rabbit leaves home, the viewpoint of the reader is simply moved over to the path on which she departs. Instead of being confined to separate pages or their screen equivalents, as in the Discis version, the actions of the characters lead the reader through the landscape. The words have their separate location at the bottom of the screen.

In many ways the landscape is the real "hero" of this text. The paths through the woods and garden are very beguiling, at least for the first few sessions before it becomes clear that their apparently limitless appeal is finite in reality. There is no attempt at humor or any real silliness. Clicked with the mouse, flowers add extra blossoms, squirrels run down trees, woodpeckers tap. The little games are clearly aimed at very young children and their impact errs on the earnest and educational side (though in some cases it is rather difficult to see what "skills" are being promulgated beyond an elementary control of the mouse).

The talking robin, who was a feature of the animated version of this story, takes an even more central role in the CD-ROM. He is the reader's helper, supplying the introductory commentary and providing guidance throughout. As you move the mouse over the landscape, what tells you that there is a clickable scene "beneath" the picture on the screen is the fact that the arrow changes to a dotted outline of the robin. The robin's tone is even more relentlessly avuncular in this CD-ROM than it is in the video.

The relationship of the stable text to the fluid pictures calls for a new form of attention to the balance between words and illustrations. The potential for almost infinite delay, both in progressing with the text at all and in pacing that progress, alters the point of control of narrative movement, away from the author, narrator and/or producer and towards the reader. Of the forms which I investigated for this study, only the book itself gave more control over pace to the reader—but the book offers fewer and less alluring distractions and diversions.

The Impact on Readers and Reading

This kind of text does in many ways call for a different kind of reading. At a very basic level, strategies for coping with unfamiliar words will probably develop differently when it is possible to click for an instant definition. Just as the spell-check has an effect on how children write and edit, just as the calculator has altered children's approach to arithmetic, so this instant glossary (with or without the corresponding print facility) will necessarily create an impact on how children learn to look at text.

An anecdote describing an adult reaction to the CD-ROM will perhaps clarify some of my points. A friend of mine, after just half an hour perusing the many charms of *The Adventures of Peter Rabbit and Benjamin Bunny*, came downstairs in our house. The old Elvis movie, *Jailhouse Rock*, was playing on the television set and we had some discussion about whether a character partially in view was really Natalie Wood. "I want to click!" said my friend, in some frustration. "I want to get her to turn around or at least get a label to say who she is." This friend is firmly book-based in her reading strategies; yet a short contact with the CD-ROM had her wishing to lean on the kinds of supports which permeate and supplement that text. No doubt the effect was temporary, but for a small child learning about reading, the consequence might well be more long-lasting.

Does a CD-ROM text, with definitions and pronunciations only a mouse-click away, encourage a more passive approach to print? I can remember myself at the age of six struggling strenuously with the word *Europe*. Nine times out of 10 I could not remember the pronunciation; I could only recall enough to know that *Ee-rope* was wrong. Clearly I would never have had such a problem with a CD-ROM text. Would the support of a pronunciation provision have reduced my frustration and encouraged me to keep reading? (I kept reading anyway.) Or did my frustration actually teach me something about the role of the place-holder in reading strategies as a consequence of not being able to produce the correct pronunciation every time? My work with older readers suggests that competent readers benefit from having access to a variety of strategies for dealing with unfamiliar material, and one of these strategies is simply to behave *as if* they understood in the hope that everything will become clearer later on. Does the instant explication of this kind of CD-ROM text reduce the reader's ability to function, at least temporarily, on inadequate information? If so, what is the consequence of such a change?

Julian Sefton-Green (1994) raises some similar questions about the kinds of CD-ROM which have so far been produced and the kinds of reading behaviors they invite. He comments on the various roles to which the format is suited, highlighting

> a discrete number of operations to be performed by the reader on the material on the disc. It is the potential of these which really define the special nature of the interactivity claimed for the digital book. In principle, the reader can manipulate the material in three ways. First the Search, Find and Link processes of Hypertext. Secondly the ability to play a range of multimedia recordings: sound, film and particularly animation. Thirdly the capacity to select and combine versions of the stored material. These three processes often combine in themselves, and frequently appear hidden beneath the surface of the material displayed on screen. It is important to remember that the process of reading digital books is both the activation of these programmes *and* the sense the reader makes of his or her experience. And because reading requires active physical participation beyond

turning pages, the *address* of digital books to readers may appear differently constructed. (p. 33)

Sefton-Green looks at the Broderbund CD-ROMs, *Arthur's Teacher Trouble* and *Just Grandma and Me.*

> The real genius of these publications is that the picture is also animated . . . Click in any part of the picture and the element will perform its programmed sequence. This can be unexpected, subversive, plain silly, or it can offer an opportunity for characters or environments to offer comments on the main narrative.
> The child (or spellbound adult) "reads" the book by playing with elements of the picture. The storyline thus becomes magnified to include all possible narrative implied by the world of the book. The original narrative of the written text is dethroned from its central position, and the reader can make the activity of reading be about what he or she wants—at least within the predefined constraints of the package. (p. 35)

Because the Broderbund CD-ROMs hit the market very early and because they are so engaging to adults as well as to children, it is easy to fall into the trap of using them as benchmarks for the judgement of other CD-ROM picture books. *The Adventures of Peter Rabbit and Benjamin Bunny* does not aspire to the level of wit and subversion which particularly marks *Arthur's Teacher Trouble*. Its elements are entirely unzany, utterly predictable. This does not necessarily make them better or worse. In fact, subversion of the text does occur but at a more generalized level: like many other reincarnations of *Peter Rabbit*, this one falls into a category that could qualify for the general heading of Misty Pastoral. Potter's words retain their austere ambiguity but the pictures are not equally reticent (despite the fact that Potter's picture of Mrs. McGregor with the pie has been reinstated). The 360-degree landscape of Mr. McGregor's garden and the surrounding woods retains its Potteresque prettiness but generally loses the underlying ferociousness which gives an essential edge to the story.

It is possible to supply a resistant reading to this kinder gentler Potter text (indeed I have just done so), but such an approach is not encouraged by the technology, by the kinds of content which have so far appeared in this format, or by the attitudes of many of the enthusiasts of hypertext literacy. Lynne Anderson-Inman and her colleagues provide a convenient example of what I am talking about in their account of work with older readers working with a short story on *ElectroText*, a hypertext authoring system.

> There are basically two types of enhancements available in *ElectroText* stories: Those designed to assist students' comprehension of the text (for example, definitions, fact questions, graphic organizers) and those designed to promote active reading skills and appreciation for the author's craft (for example, thought questions and notetaking options). Both types of enhancements reflect our view that the medium of hypertext is an ideal way to provide students with the support they may need in order to comprehend and appreciate good literature. (1994, p. 280)

The materials described by Anderson-Inman et al. do appear to foster a high degree of respect for and submission to the ideas of the author. They also appear to value a high degree of recall and a sophisticated understanding of such elements of the story as foreshadowing. This is one way of reading but it is not the only or even necessarily the most desirable approach. As Julian Sefton-Green points out, the emphasis in many such texts is on "the formal and traditional study of a text" (p. 34). This would be a grandiose description of the kind of material included in *The Adventures of Peter Rabbit and Benjamin Bunny*, but the emphasis on vocabulary is certainly one of the building blocks of this kind of approach to a text, and there appears to be no potential in the disc for creating any alternative readings of the story.

Sefton-Green, talking about the Broderbund discs, raises other considerations about even an accomplished transfer of a text from book to CD-ROM:

> There are a number of implications here which raise provocative questions about the shift in the reading processes heralded by the digital age. Firstly, the reader can only start and finish pre-programmed animations. Click in the hole in the tree on the first page of *Just Grandma and Me* and large eyes appear; they look from side to side, then a squirrel runs out of the hole, up the tree and back again. Click on the same spot and the same thing happens again. Part of the

pleasure in this is simply wonder and surprise, as with pop-up books, or reactions to early cinema. It is clever and fun. Often the animation bears no relation to other narratives; but first of all it has to be discovered and thus it stimulates children to play with the text. Secondly it continues the world of the book on its own terms. Reading thus becomes much more than just following the storyline. The kinds of meanings children get from pictures books and the ways they read pictures are extended. Most importantly the process by which we read pictures and make meanings from elements of the text is in itself made explicit through the deliberate act of clicking the mouse. It is thus a more precise and conscious process, and is obviously suited to joint activity between adult and child, or child and child, stimulating talk and discussion. (1994, p. 35)

Judith Graham, also discussing the CD-ROM of *Arthur's Teacher Trouble*, suggests that children may not spend so much time with a CD-ROM that it makes too much difference in any case. She speculates that once children work out all the jokes and activate all the animations, there will be little to entice them to return to the story. She describes her own reaction:

Once I was satisfied that I had exhausted the life hidden behind the screen, I really had no wish to play this program again. For all the inventiveness, in the end *I* was not being asked to be creative and for all the choice that I was offered, I couldn't actually change anything . . . These are not texts where one has a choice of how the story might proceed. For me that is not a major problem—I like feeling that I am in the hands of a storyteller who has shaped the story in only one way. What I felt, however, is that by exploiting every last ounce of potential in the illustrations, the makers of the program had made it unlikely that I would revisit the text . . .

All the evidence we have indicates that young children develop favorite texts which they request countless times. The "tune" then rings in the head as they turn the pages. They engage in "reader-like behavior" and grow more aware of how the print and the voice relate to each other. If other evidence is forthcoming, if their questions are answered, they make the intellectual leap that print has meaning.

> So if children do not revisit these books on CD-ROM because
> the work the reader has to do has all been done for them, the tune will
> not be in the head and the text will remain opaque. (1994, p. 16)

Graham rightly points out that we need much more research into children's behavior with CD-ROM stories. She points to the possibility that returning to such a text may actually become more a social than an individual project, with the child sharing favorite bits. She also suggests that in a program like *Arthur's Teacher Trouble*, where the added wit and humor is intensely visual, attention may actually be distracted away from the words. Clearly there is a great deal we need to know.

The Adventures of Peter Rabbit and Benjamin Bunny is an interesting piece of work. Great care has clearly been invested in its production and I can imagine that some children, especially gentle children with a predilection for the cosy, could well be delighted by it. After looking at the Discis CD-ROM and *Peter Rabbit's Math Garden*, I found its complexity intriguing. The kinds of reading it invites seem to me to be laying the groundwork for new kinds of approaches both to print and also to other visual and aural information.

It may be that the kinds of approaches to text fostered by current CD-ROM material simply reflect this current transitional stage where works created for the relatively stable world of print bound in pages are adapted for a new technology. Possibly the high level of respectfulness is even a nod to that disappearing stability. CD-ROMs are in their infancy and being marketed, at least to children, with a heavy emphasis on educational virtue. The day of a CD-ROM parody, however, cannot be far away—at least if the medium survives and prices continue to drop. Obviously the development of a recordable CD technology will also make a difference. The "Read-Only" factor is itself almost a kind of invitation to passivity.

Meanwhile, the potential for other, more flexible multimedia formats to take over the role of the CD-ROM is also developing at high speed. The kind of CD-ROM presently devoted to *Peter Rabbit* reminds me rather of the coloring books of this text: the expectation is that you will always stay within the lines and use the colors recommended.

CHAPTER 9

Consumables and Collectibles

If the variety of *Peter Rabbit* texts seems numerous and expensive, it fades to insignificance compared to the lucrative market in Potter-related objects which would appear to be largely aimed at adults. The scale of the money-making operation at work on the world created by Beatrix Potter almost defies belief. It certainly defies comprehensive description. I have been hanging around bookstores, department stores, china stores, gift shops and toy stores, simply listing the Potter variants which I found; my list now reaches many typed pages. And that is not counting the china specimens; two gift shops were kind enough to let me photocopy their catalogue entries for different kinds of china. The 1995 Wedgwood catalogue for tableware and giftware lists 27 separate Potter-related items; the total cost in Canadian dollars if I had bought a single copy of each item (mainly children's dishes and money boxes) would be $1,762.00. Even allowing for export mark-up and a bad exchange rate, that total is daunting. The Schmid catalogue of china figurines, waterballs, musical teapots and so forth is even more stunning, although my copy does not include prices. I counted a total of 151 separate items. An entire semiotic study could be devoted to the relationship between the china object depicted and the music-box tune chosen to accompany it. Some extracts from the catalogue will have to convey the spirit of the enterprise.

DESCRIPTION	TUNE
Peter Rabbit (R) On Books, 5 1/2"H (Peter Rabbit revolves)	"My Favorite Things"
Jemima Puddle-duck (R) Animated Waterball, 5 3/4"H	"Younger than Springtime"
Tabitha Twitchit (R) and Moppet (R) Animated Waterball, 5 3/4"H	"Happy Wanderer"
Jemima Puddle-duck (R) On Basket, 4 3/4"H	"April Love"
Little Old Woman In The Shoe (R), 4 1/4"H	"Love Will Keep Us Together"

Of the musical figurines I inspected in a jeweller's shop, my favorite was a china version of Mrs. Rabbit giving Peter the camomile tea; in complete contradiction to the implications of the story, the tune is "Just a spoonful of sugar to help the medicine go down" which, apart from its thematic incongruity, introduces a jangling tone of Disney. All this could have been mine for the expenditure of $42.95 Canadian; the larger items were retailing for $60.00.

In addition to the many china variations on the Potter characters, there is also a wide range of stuffed versions, including Mr. McGregor himself. These are produced by the Eden Gift company (which, for a while, was a branch of Pearson, though it has now been sold) and again prices are steep. Not surprisingly, I saw the largest selection in the largest toy shops I visited: F.A.O. Schwarz in San Francisco and Hamley's in London. The latter shop featured a stuffed Peter Rabbit, standing maybe two feet high and costing a mind-boggling £125. I saw many variants of plush rabbits, some with a radish, one with an umbrella, one lying down asleep. There was even the "Premier Peter Rabbit—Fully Jointed and Collectible." This is a stuffed Peter Rabbit wearing a badge which reads, "A Beatrix Potter Collectible." F.A.O. Schwarz featured a selection of porcelain bookends, properly sized for the little books and, at $90.00 U.S. the pair, a very expensive option for a child's bookshelf. It seems fairly clear that even in the toy shops much of the marketing impetus is being directed at adults.

There are toys and games clearly designed to be used by children: a set of plaster casting molds of different characters, for example, or a crib toy, or a baby mirror (with Peter Rabbit on the frame, "My First Beatrix Potter" on the label and a price tag of $54.99 Canadian).

However, much of this overwhelming variety of material appears to be directed towards adults. In some cases a child would be the end recipient, though it seems likely that the infant wearers of "Beatrix Potter Original" clothing or Peter Rabbit bibs and hooded towels might be fairly indifferent about Potter's role in their lives. In many other cases, the objects are designed and marketed specifically for adults. One seductive selling-pitch for the "collectibles," of course, is that they will appreciate in value. The Bradford Exchange, advertising a three-dimensional musical plate in a Canadian women's magazine, is clear about what it is offering. The advertisement pitches the esthetic line first but follows it quickly with the appeal to acquisitiveness.

> **An Affordable Art Treasure.** Now, their [Peter Rabbit and Benjamin Bunny] adventure comes to life on a richly sculptural and musical collector's plate. Each detail has been hand-cast and hand-painted to capture all the charm of Beatrix Potter's (TM) watercolor illustrations. What's more, a key-wind musical movement plays the tune "Oh, What a Beautiful Mornin'."
>
> **Exceptional Plates Increase in Value.** In addition to being a beautiful work of art, "A Pocket Full of Onions" has the potential to appreciate on the secondary market. Of course, like any marketplace subject to the laws of supply and demand, the plate market is constantly changing. Some exceptional plates appreciate in value; some go down and many remain at or near issue price. But right now, Bradford Exchange market analysts rate the "A Pocket Full of Onions" plate as one of the year's top prospects. (*Bradford Exchange*, April 1995, n.p.)

Apart from the seductive hint that this is a pleasurable way to get rich, there are questions about the source of Potter's widespread appeal. John Goldthwaite puts at least some of it down to a kind of twee charm in many of her books and makes explicit reference to the market in commodities to back up his claim:

> Of the more general claim that there is neither prettiness nor preciousness in her pages, there are, when you come to inquire, enough dear-littles and teeny-weenys to satisfy the most doting grandmother. Jeremy Fisher "had the dearest little red float." (What boy gone fishing ever thought of his gear in these terms?) . . .

> By the time of *Mrs. Tiggy-winkle* in 1905 Potter was a practiced
> hand at this whimsy . . .
> This quaintness, and not her ironic distance, seems to be the
> quality in her tales that many, perhaps most, readers respond to, given
> the strong market in Potterbilia; and they are responding to something
> that is in fact present in the work . . . Only in her few best books is
> falsification for effect negligible or absent. *Mr. Tod* is devoid of it;
> *Peter Rabbit* and *Jemima Puddle-duck* nearly so. (1987, pp. 119–121)

Goldthwaite continues in this vein for some time, and it is hard not
to agree at least to the suggestion that what fuels the purchase of many
Potter knickknacks is cuteness rather than austerity. Although the aura
attending a literary "classic" is doubtless behind some sales, the Potter
industry clearly runs on a stronger fuel than either literary taste or some
kind of associated literary snobbishness.

LICENSING AND MERCHANDISING

Most literate adults and many literate children are dimly aware that
there is a lot of Peter Rabbit about. As someone with an extensive
interest in children's literature, I thought I was rather more aware than
most and I was vaguely charmed to see a Peter Rabbit bib or
christening mug show up from time to time in a friend's house. When I
came to explore the extent of the commercial exploitation of the Potter
characters, however, the feeling of pleasure rapidly faded. The
industrial scale of the enterprise first dumbfounded and then appalled
me.

Perhaps this is simply literary puritanism on my part. After all,
turning out china knickknacks is an honest way to make a living and it
may just be a question of taste whether you want your revolving Peter
Rabbit to play a Disney tune. (It must not be forgotten that the literary
artifact also exists within a market; as I was in the process of working
on this project, a woman showed up at the BBC Antiques Roadshow
with a signed first edition of *The Tale of Peter Rabbit* which had been
lying in a tin trunk in her boiler room; the experts estimated the value
of her book at £20,000–25,000 ("£25,000 Peter Rabbit," p. 11)).

Warne spokespeople are quick to cite Potter's personal interest in
marketing, to justify their own activities, and there is no doubt that they
have a sustainable argument on this issue.

The marketing strategy behind Peter Rabbit's success was formulated by Potter herself. Deborah Hooper, marketing director for Frederick Warne in the U.K., says that Potter was involved in every aspect of publishing the books. Her development of related merchandise was simply an extension of that interest.

"She was extremely pioneering," says Hooper. "Peter Rabbit must be one of the oldest licensed characters and certainly is one of the few that was going at the beginning of the century that is still going now." Among the merchandise Potter developed were a Peter Rabbit doll, a board game, slippers and wallpaper. (Bodin, 1993, p. 19)

On the other hand, Potter had equally strong feelings about the need to have her merchandise made in Britain and to have the prices of her products kept at a level which children could afford (she even offered to reduce her own royalties if that would ensure a book being kept to the price of one and sixpence (*Linder*, 1971, p. 24)). Warne quotes these opinions less often. One striking aspect of the materials produced by Eden Gifts in particular is their international origins: Sri Lanka, Indonesia, China, the Netherlands. The activity books are not produced exclusively in the United Kingdom either; *The Peter Rabbit and Friends Poster Activity Book* and *The Peter Rabbit Theatre* are printed and bound in Hong Kong, the lift-the-flap book in Singapore, the carousel scenes in Colombia. As for current prices, they are often remarkable. A slipcase of the complete set of the 23 original small books can set you back as much as $160.00 Canadian; a set of six tapes of the 23 stories costs $40.00. The prices of many of the collectibles are equally daunting.

Apart from Potter's own efforts, the idea of marketing commodities has flourished throughout the 20th century, led, as so often, by Walt Disney who financed many of his early animated productions through money from tie-ins.

Here is a sampling of Disney products endorsed as of 1934, primarily through Mickey, "the biggest unpaid movie star" as he was described in *Fortune Magazine*: designs on the buckles of boys' belts, figures on the bottom of porridge bowls, ice cream, chewing gum, school tablets, dolls, books jewelry, swimwear, dresses, soaps, caps, neckwear, watches . . . these are just a few of the products that attest to the merchandising power of Mickey Mouse, and as such provide a major source of income to its creator, Walt Disney.

By the mid-fifties (this was *before* the Disneyland explosion) Disney endorsements had sold $750 million of products, some 3,000 different items (that is probably a low figure). (Klein, 1993, p. 53)

Warne's products are marketed through The Copyrights Company Ltd. The process is called licensing and, as an article in *The Bookseller* pointed out to its readers, it is an operation which is highly lucrative.

[L]icensing—the use of a known copyright character, brand or personality on a product as a means of increasing sales and profile in the marketplace—is now a firmly established business employing sophisticated marketing techniques and generating over $70 billion world-wide. (Lees, 1992, p. 1764)

Lees mentions Beatrix Potter but does not supply any marketing figures; some idea of the scale of sales possible for a children's text may be drawn from her claim that *Thomas the Tank Engine* "has generated retail sales of over £250m in the UK from some 500 products" (p. 1764).

Richard Paterson and Belinda Richards, also writing in *The Bookseller*, looked at the importance of brand valuation in assessing the worth of a company.

[A] brand name, or brand, contributes directly to the cash flow of a business through its unique selling power. As such, it often represents an unrecognised intangible asset. Brand valuation comprises valuing or putting a figure on these "hidden" assets. (1990, p. 1468)

It is surely not a coincidence that this article is entitled, "Is there a Peter Rabbit in the house?" The authors mention Peter Rabbit specifically by name as they explain how this concept applies to publishing.

Publishing companies could, arguably, be said to possess a wealth of brands. These range from imprints such as Mills & Boon, Ladybird, Virago and Penguin Classics at one end of the spectrum to strong and enduring titles such as *Who's Who* or *Peter Rabbit* at the other.

Advocates of brand valuation would maintain that publishers who failed to value their branded imprints or key titles were failing to reveal the full strength of their businesses. (1990, pp. 1468–1470)

The means by which a brand can be valued may provide distressing reading to those who like to think of texts in literary terms; somehow such terms seem more appropriate when applied to Mickey Mouse:

There are several different ways of valuing a brand. However, the most favored techniques generally boil down to versions of a single method: projecting the future cash flows attributable to a single brand and discounting them back over time (the discounted cash flow method). In order to project the cash flows, the market in which the brand operates has to be fully understood, as do likely future trends and competitor behavior. (Paterson and Richards, 1990, p. 1470)

A report on Pearson by C. Munro et al. for Hoare Govett Securities is explicit about Pearson's participation in brand marketing:

Pearson summarises its strategy as follows: continuing to select and invest in intellectual property and brand-driven markets; looking to invest further in Asia; developing the links between its operating companies; and moving increasingly into interactive multimedia. (1995, n.p.)

Commenting on Penguin's performance in 1993, Munro et al. return to this question of brand marketing:

The group sees itself as part of the entertainment and information industry, which adds value by obtaining and exploiting international property rights (IPR). Penguin's primary brands are its titles and authors; imprints and companies are of secondary importance. In the children's sector, brand exploitation includes special sales and mass merchandising of licensed characters such as Peter Rabbit and Winnie the Pooh. (1995, n.p.)

What this means in the shops is an ever-increasing range of literary-based commodities. The scale of the enterprise is almost beyond description. Bookshops, toy shops, gift shops and souvenir shops are perhaps obvious locations for toys, games and commodities based on texts, but Peter Rabbit is to be found in many other places as well. The British supermarket chain, Sainsbury's, sells an authorized Peter Rabbit cake; Liberty, the exclusive fabric merchant, offers four different bolts of cotton fabric adorned with Beatrix Potter characters. Kellogg's cereals in the United Kingdom feature a special offer for Beatrix Potter figurines. The gift catalogues of highly prestigious museums such as the Victoria and Albert supply Potter trinkets and knickknacks; and similar objects appear in charity Christmas catalogues. Flying out of Britain in September 1995, I was not even faintly surprised to observe that the last shop I passed in the passenger concourse on the way to my loading gate was a branch of Harrod's, with a large window display of exclusive china featuring who else but Peter Rabbit.

IMPLICATIONS

The complexity of the Peter Rabbit image in the world of commodities is intriguing. There would appear to be many consumers who are happy to acquire various artifacts related to Potter's world either for their children or for themselves, presumably with some view to preserving, recreating or perhaps even compensating for aspects of their own childhood.

I find my own approach to this world of commodities to be tinged with an unhelpful puritanism. On esthetic grounds I can discriminate between one kind of trinket and another, but my overall attitude is tainted by a kind of disdain not so much for individual objects as for the scale of the whole enterprise. Exploring a National Trust shop and a tourist souvenir shop in Cambridge, England, I came out satiated with the very idea of turning a nursery fiction into a large number of salable objects and turned into the premises of Liberty fabrics for some relief. My sensations on discovering in that shop no fewer than four different bolts of printed cotton featuring Potter characters can be imagined. The question of whether or when the British market in particular will be glutted with Peter Rabbit to the point of revulsion and consumer rebellion is one that would trouble me if I held any shares in Pearson. Is there an upper limit? Should there be? Is my reaction to what would seem to be the intrinsically harmless activity of making consumer goods out of a favorite story simply one of snobbery? Am I simply declaring myself as an inadequately postmodern citizen, unready to take my place in the 21st century? Or is there genuinely an element of exploitation and degradation at work in the constant recycling and reselling of this story?

In the appendix, I provide, not a complete catalogue of the items that I found, but simply a list of the *categories* of commodity related to Peter Rabbit which I saw in my explorations in three countries. There are more than 75 such categories, some representing large numbers of individual items. It would be fascinating to see a complete itemization of all the different ways you can purchase Peter Rabbit, but it is a list which would probably be impossible to acquire or create. Warne presumably holds an inventory of the authorized texts and commodities, but an enumeration of the unauthorized materials and objects would be just about impossible—and out of date the minute it was completed.

CHAPTER 10

Issues of Ownership

THE ROLE OF PEARSON

It is commonplace to read laments about how the large international conglomerates are affecting the old gentlemanly occupation of publishing. Looking at a single, specific example does help to ground the consequences of major financial moves in the publishing industry, particularly during the 1980s and 1990s.

Pearson plc (public limited company) is an international company which owns a sprawling range of companies—not as diverse as it once was in the days when it owned firms which made oil-rig drills and firms which made china, but still a wide-ranging conglomerate. It groups its holdings under three headings.

Information

Pearson owns the *Financial Times* of London and a number of local newspapers in Britain, as well as some European papers. It also owns FT Information, a company which supplies specialist financial and business information worldwide, both in print and electronic form. It is a part-owner of *The Economist*.

Education

Pearson owns the newly merged educational publishing firm of Addison Wesley Longman, whose imprints pretty much cover the English-speaking world. It now describes itself as the second largest book publisher in the world ("Financial—Pearson," 1997, n.p.).

Entertainment

Pearson is involved in television worldwide. The company owns Thames Television in Britain and has a minority interest in BSkyB, the British satellite broadcaster. It owns Grundy Worldwide and a quarter of the consortium which will be responsible for broadcasting the United Kingdom's new Channel 5.

In publishing, Pearson owns Penguin, which in turn owns such imprints as Frederick Warne and Ladybird Books. It also produces a number of special interest magazines.

It owns or is involved in a number of tourist attractions and theme parks in Britain and Europe, including Madame Tussaud's, the London Planetarium, Alton Towers (a British theme park) and others.

Mindscape is a computer software company which produces a variety of programs and games.

In addition, Pearson owns interests in Lazard Brothers and Lazard Freres, the major accounting firm.

THE PEARSON CONNECTION

Frederick Warne joined the trend towards conglomerate buyouts in 1983 when it was bought by Penguin, itself owned by Pearson. The Peter Rabbit merchandising operation was in full flow before this takeover, but the scale of the operation has increased massively since then, particularly in products related to the animations.

1993 was the first year in which the impact of the animations should have been felt, but it is difficult to be specific about the figures. Pearson's 1994 Company Report, like most of the other information emanating from Pearson, does not distinguish Warne's contribution to the overall Penguin figures. It does report positively on Penguin's overall record and its account of Penguin's plans makes interesting reading:

> PENGUIN. Sales £371.8m, up 2 percent. Operating profits £40m, up
> 16 percent. Penguin has a greater breadth to its publishing activities
> now than at any time in its history. It is one of the largest consumer
> publishers in the English-speaking world. It can also lay claim to a
> wider geographical spread of sales than any of its competitors.
> Penguin last year began the integration of the famous Ladybird
> imprint into a children's business now accounting for worldwide sales

of almost £100m. Characters from children's book [*sic*] have given rise to major merchandising programmes, and Penguin's book publishing has led on to a growing number of allied products. These range from book audiotapes, films and videos to initial forays into the world of multimedia publishing. (Extel Financial Limited, p. 6)

It is clear that the link between Penguin and Mindscape was intended to be a profitable one. Mindscape was purchased in 1993 and the Chairman's Statement in the 1994 Company Report speaks of Pearson's commitment to work with "steadily evolving technologies and shifting consumer needs" (1994, p.7). The chairman does give a nod to the idea of quality in his comments on print materials but goes on to talk about the importance of reformatting print works:

The traditional printed media accounted for well over half of our operating profits. Pearson's future still rests largely on long established strengths like the unassailable integrity of the Financial Times and the sheer quality and variety of our publishing lists and we see innovative products for the personal computer or television as a way of building on those strengths rather than eroding them. (1994, p.7)

M. Beilby et al., reporting to S.G. Warburg Securities on Pearson's prospects in January 1995, were more explicit.

It could be argued that, over the past 12 months, Pearson has been effectively re-rated. This is because it has been transformed from a multi-faceted conglomerate into a more focused developer and exploiter of copyright and content. The management's strategic intention is, in its own words, to become a "major international provider of media content, renowned for distinctive products, that deliver information, education and entertainment, in the ways that people want them." The business focus therefore, is the generation and exploitation of copyright and the operation of high growth delivery systems. Pearson is increasingly becoming a business that is driven by its back catalogue. Prima facie this should prove to be a high multiple business long term. The question now is how far the stock still has to run and what are the attendant risks. (n.p.)

"Exploitation of copyright" is at the heart of the commodification of literature. It is a process not confined to children's books (and not confined to "literature" either), as attested by this comment from my local newspaper, discussing the book and the film of *The Bridges of Madison County*.

> The *Bridges* phenomenon has spawned a healthy sideline featuring a journal/day book, a making of the film photobook, photobook of the actual covered bridges of Madison County, a three-hour unabridged-edition audiotape read by the author, a cookbook due out this fall, and tours to Madison County, Iowa. (Morash, 1995, p. E5)

Fiction now enters our lives by a number of routes and by processes of reiteration and recycling, happening today on a scale which makes it a qualitatively new phenomenon.

EXPLOITING THE BACKLIST

Pearson's capacity to "exploit" its backlist depends at least partly on its control of copyright. Beilby et al. are frank about this issue as well.

> Much of the growth in the book business has historically come from price inflation. This may become ever more difficult as far as the consumer book market is concerned. The prospects of the book division have, however, potentially been materially helped by the decision of the EC [European Community] to extend copyright protection to 70 years, as against the previous 50 years after an author or composer's death. This has considerable ramifications which, seemingly, have yet to be assimilated by the City. (1995, n.p.)

Later they say,

> UK Childrens' [*sic*] books have, in fact, shown consistent growth over the past decade. In the late 1980s, the childrens' [*sic*] market grew by a compound annual 7 percent in volume terms. The key is the demographic trend and consensus estimates suggest that the number of children will grow by between 9 percent and 10 percent between 1994 and 2000. This guarantees a consistent level of growth for printed books, even if children become ever more attuned to

screen-based entertainment. Pearson owns many important childrens' [*sic*] imprints and the extension of copyright to 70 years after the author's death will prove especially significant in this area of the business. (1995, n.p.)

Pearson is particularly interested in the potential of CD-ROM and, with a view to increasing its share of the CD-ROM market, acquired the company now called Mindscape which has considerable expertise in the production of software. Pearson's great advantage in working with a software firm should lie in its backlist, its storehouse of content and copyright. In the early days, the analysts were impressed with the potential:

> Mindscape has its own store of licenses and content, but Pearson is a vast repository of copyright extending from Penguin childrens' [*sic*] books through the Thames TV library to the extensive educational content owned by Longman and Addison-Wesley. Much of this content is ripe to be transformed into multimedia content, using proprietary Mindscape techniques and the company's proven expertise. (Beilby et al., 1995, n.p.)

In the face of such analysis, it seems sentimental to be talking about the drive to reimagine a work of art in order to produce something worthwhile in another format. Nevertheless, what has been done already with Peter Rabbit in the Discis CD-ROM and in the Knowledge Adventure computer program testifies to the hazard of ignoring this aspect, at least of fictional material. Fiction, by its very nature, involves a pragmatic contract with the user to imagine, to make believe. In order to be "ripe" for transformation into another medium, it needs further imaginative input. Corporate talk about quality does not allow much room for this kind of consideration, but at the level of production there needs to be a place for it. *Arthur's Teacher Trouble* demonstrates that there are ways of "exploiting" both the text and the technical potential of the new medium in ways which are clever and imaginative. The different CD-ROMs of *Peter Rabbit* show how the imaginative potential of the medium may evolve in various directions, and it is certain that new approaches are in store.

It may be that real art will never evolve on CD-ROM. It is certainly entirely possible that real art may never develop in terms of spin-offs from previously existing textual "content." In the meantime, we are left with considerations about what to do with multimedia transformations of printed fiction which move into the marketplace with a high price tag, but with variable degrees of added value.

In any case, it now seems clear that the early potential of Mindscape has not materialized, at least in the medium term. Its early connection with Pearson led to substantial losses—£45.5 million in 1996 by Pearson's own reckoning ("Financial—Pearson," 1997, n.p.). There now appears to be general agreement among the analysts that the gains of combining media were not as clear-cut as first seemed to be the case.

Kyle Pope, the *Wall Street Journal's* London correspondent writing in *The Globe and Mail*, specifically attacked the Peter Rabbit materials.

> Analysts say that Pearson, like many other media companies that jumped into the high-tech business earlier this decade, found that many of the synergies that had been promised weren't so apparent after all. The company has struggled in its efforts to convert its print holdings to CD-ROM. A multimedia version of *Peter Rabbit*, for instance, was panned by critics as being poorly adapted to the personal computer, while Pearson said it has been forced to take writeoffs for other products that were developed but never made it to market. (Pope, 1996, p. B10)

Emily Bell, writing for *The Observer* in London, was equally discouraging about the merging of print and software companies.

> The shimmering promise of synergies between paperbacks, television rights and CD-Rom—one piece of content across all formats—has so far flopped for Pearson and, indeed, other practitioners of the cross-media position. The truly successful media companies of the 1990s are proving to be those with a dogged focus and a determination to lead their market or maintain excellence in one area—even if it makes them as crushingly dull as Reuters or Reed ... If Pearson concentrated on one type of information or one sort of entertainment across a narrower range of formats, it might have more success. (Bell, 1997, p. 5)

As of March 1997, there were plenty of rumors about where Pearson would go next, but the interim statement which came out in that month did not give much hint about where the company saw its future, apart from a major investment in the *Financial Times*. The immediate response from the markets was unenthusiastic and commentators continued to point to the entertainment division as a major part of the problem:

> Much of Pearson's troubles were centered on its entertainment division, which includes Penguin books, software publisher Mindscape and Pearson Television. Operating profit dropped 50 per cent to £52.5-million from £110.9-million. Results exclude the Penguin accounting charge, but include a £45.5-million charge for restructuring costs, discontinued products and new accounting procedures at Mindscape. (Strassel, 1997, p. B8)

It is not possible to make general comments on the short-term success or failure of one attempt to rework backlists for profit, though it would appear that the straws in the wind do seem to be indicating that the process is not as straightforward as investors originally thought. The wider question of the general direction of Penguin Books may perhaps be answered, at least in part, by the appointment in August 1996 of a new Chief Executive, Michael Lynton, who came to Penguin from his previous job as president of Hollywood Pictures, one of Walt Disney's three motion picture production studios. Prior to that experience, he had started up and headed Disney Publishing, a group which included book publishing and the production of various magazines largely aimed at children and/or families. The comment of outgoing Chief Executive Peter Mayer on the arrival of his successor may be significant. Mayer said,

> Michael Lynton comes to Penguin with all my support and confidence . . . Knowing him well, I am certain he combines a publishing sensibility, management skills and background in media to succeed as CEO and to take Penguin further again. Pearson and Penguin are lucky to have found someone with such broad experience of books and brand management. ("Michael Lynton," 1997, n.p.)

It is sheer snobbishness to lament the fact that the historic firm of Penguin is now led by an alumnus of the Disney organization, but it is hard to ignore the implication that "brand management" is going to be an important feature of the new regime. Given Disney's success in saturating the market with every conceivable form and manifestation of its fictions, it is impossible to ignore the potential prospect that the Penguin backlist is just getting started. Peter Rabbit may serve as an exemplar for the marketing of many other fictional heroes and heroines.

THE ISSUE OF COPYRIGHT

Questions of copyright are clearly crucial, for the time being at least. Beatrix Potter's work came out of copyright in 1993, 50 years after her death. However, new legislation from the European Union may now alter this state of affairs. As of July 1995, copyright extends until 70 years after the author's death. Beilby et al. (1995), discussing Pearson's prospects, are enthusiastic about the utility of this legislation. Patrick Parrinder, writing in *The Times Higher Educational Supplement* at the time the legislation was passed is less impressed.

> Parliament has not debated it. The press has ignored it. The literary world has yet to wake up to it, and educationists were never consulted. The Government was unconvinced, yet voted in favor of it. If ever there was a textbook example of the European Union legislating behind closed doors, it is the directive on copyright that became law on October 29 [1993]. (1993, p. 19)

German law provided for a 70-year copyright term and the Germans put great pressure on the European Union to bring other countries into conformity. Parrinder's objections to the new copyright law, apart from his concern over the way it was legislated, lie in the area of scholarship:

> The real reasons for opposing the extension of posthumous copyright are not to do with royalties but control over texts and the right to quote from them which turns posthumous copyright into a restrictive practice inhibiting literary critics, scholars and biographers, and preventing the free circulation of ideas. One area which will be badly hit by the new law is that of textual editing. While it remained in

copyright, the work of many now classic authors was perpetuated in corrupt, haphazard and even bowdlerised editions. (1993, p. 19)

The end of copyright in such cases, he argues, allows for competing editions featuring new scholarship and editing techniques; it also makes critical comment easier.
Parrinder is not an impartial observer. His views are very clear.

Copyright was once a liberating force for writers and artists. By giving them legal ownership of their work, it confirmed their professional status and allowed them to deal with publishers on equal terms. But the more copyright is weighted against the public interest and in favor of the copyright owners, the more it will fall into disrepute. In future scholars as well as students may find that their needs are best served by a black market in American books.

The new copyright law leads to protectionism and the reinforcement of monopoly rights. (1993, p. 19)

THE PUBLIC STAKE IN COPYRIGHT

The Tale of Peter Rabbit provides a gloss on some issues of copyright. It is a special case for a number of reasons. The copyright is actually owned outright by Frederick Warne because of Potter's legacy. They claim to have spared no expense in protecting this inheritance. The level of argument over the 1987 Ladybird text would suggest that at least some members of the public think that there are also genuine public rights at issue in the question of a much-loved literary classic. But the history of *The Tale of Peter Rabbit* in the United States does not encourage a view that freedom from copyright is a helpful answer either.

The state of affairs at present raises many interesting questions. The authentic text is readily available at a variety of prices, ranging from a relatively cheap paperback edition to a top-of-the-market deluxe edition, with or without its own porcelain bookends. The legal questions, at least for the material authorized by Warne, seem fairly clear-cut. The esthetic and even moral questions are more complex. One question of considerable importance to the public (and I cannot think of a way to put it less tendentiously) is, to what extent do the many spin-offs actually affect or possibly even damage responses to the original text? Does market saturation have esthetic consequences? For everybody? Just for some? How much does it matter? Do the copyright holders have any kind of duty to the public beyond a perceived requirement to maximize profit?

A friend of mine, who works in a bookstore, told me she used to buy Potter "collectibles." "Not any more, there's just too much," she said, and her sigh spoke of a form of pleasure lost. Is there a kind of esthetics of scale, where one object is a way of extending an imaginative engagement with a text into some form of daily contact, but a hundred objects simply weary and disgust the potential user? Is the reverse true for some consumers? How does an explosion of commodities impinge on those who choose not to buy? Does it matter? What is the responsibility of the license holders to the public?

A different issue lies in the capacity of the copyright holder to restrict access to the words and images. Long years of convention have smoothed the way for me to quote short extracts from the various texts of *Peter Rabbit*. However, when it comes to images I am at the mercy of the copyright holders. I may not "quote" from *Peter Rabbit* by using the example of a single image. Most of the copyright holders have refused me permission to demonstrate with a single picture the points I am trying to make in this text. In a different context I have attempted to compile "quotes" of video and audio clips, but the project has failed because of copyright restrictions. The balance of ownership versus commentary is clearly very one-sided.

SUPERSYSTEMS

Marsha Kinder talks about commercial supersystems used to market toys and other "collectibles."

> A supersystem is a network of intertextuality constructed around a
> figure or group of figures from pop culture who are either fictional
> (like TMNT [Teenage Mutant Ninja Turtles], the characters from *Star
> Wars*, the Super Mario Brothers, the Simpsons, the Muppets, Batman,
> and Dick Tracy) or "real" (like PeeWee Herman, Elvis Presley,
> Marilyn Monroe, Madonna, Michael Jackson, the Beatles, and, most
> recently, the New Kids on the Block). In order to be a supersystem,
> the network must cut across several modes of image production; must
> appeal to diverse generations, classes, and ethnic subcultures, who in

turn are targeted with diverse strategies; must foster "collectability" through a proliferation of related products; and must undergo a sudden increase in commodification, the success of which reflexively becomes a "media event" that dramatically accelerates the growth curve of the system's commercial success. (1991, p. 122–123)

Peter Rabbit, in these terms, is not exactly a figure from pop culture in the way that Kinder defines it. Otherwise, the marketing of Peter Rabbit, especially in the years since the animations, bears many resemblances to the process described by Kinder. Peter Rabbit cuts across many forms of image production. He appeals to diverse generations with the targeting of various formats at babies, preschoolers, elementary school students and adults. The Ladybird books in particular represent a specific attempt to market to socioeconomic classes presumed not previously receptive to *Peter Rabbit*. Apart from the many translations, there has not been much ethnic work done with the story, but the issue of collectibility has entwined with the books right from the outset. Since the animations hit the screen, the rise in available texts, activity books, collectibles and toys has been astronomic. Because Peter Rabbit is a fixture of literary culture, this expansion has been less newsworthy than some of Kinder's other examples, but the attempt at saturation is clearly part of the process.

Marsha Kinder interviewed a number of children at a video arcade.

Even though . . . [they] were terribly naive about money and the capitalist system, they seemed keenly aware of the dynamics of consumerist desire. They knew from their own experience that the reported popularity of a commodity and its promotion through commercial tie-ins greatly intensify its desirability to consumers. (1991, p. 123)

What happens to literature when it hits that kind of escalator? If *Peter Rabbit* were a single exception, the question would probably not be worth asking. But anyone who frequents children's bookstores knows that *Peter Rabbit* is just one example, admittedly on the upper end of the scale of commodification. The number of stuffed toys, coloring books, audiocassettes, and other collectibles which connect with one particular book or another, seems to increase almost on every trip to the shop.

Stephen Kline, in a substantial study of children's culture and television marketing, comments on the importance which children place on the commercial elements in their lives.

> As we listen to children's conversations, we can't help but notice that the market touches their lives more directly than ever before . . . Given that merchants' attentions are increasingly focused on childhood, it is reasonable to expect that this nascent concern with children's consumerism will grow stronger. Yet the academic and journalistic commentaries on childhood seldom acknowledge the marketplace as part of the matrix of contemporary socialization or devote serious attention to how children learn those roles, attitudes and sentiments that reinforce the consumer culture. (1993, p. 13)

It is easy to become nostalgic about the way things used to be, but when I was a child, my books represented an escape from the pressures of the commercial world. To all intents and purposes, they came for free in the public library and their sober bindings were far removed from the come-ons of the toyshop or the sweetshop. There is little point in lamenting over irrevocable changes, but at the same time we need to pay attention to the consequences of those changes. Do children read differently when they perceive books as simply part of a larger market? Does a story function differently when it is inextricably linked with lots and lots of desirable objects which you covet, collect and brood over, or, alternatively, take for granted, treat carelessly and lose? When part of a story's role in your life is to help you to organize your plans as a consumer, does that alter the relationship between you, that story and your society?

There has not been much public debate about whether we, as a society, want our literature to be treated this way. Pearson is answerable only to its shareholders and the composition of the shareholding sections of society is changing. Lisa Buckingham and Roger Cowe raise some of the issues involved in this change:

> Shareholder power is, however, one of those shibboleths which closer examination reveals to be something of a myth. The problem is that the control loop has been broken. Major shareholders are no longer

the powerful individuals of the late 19th century, able to own a third of a company's equity and have equal influence over its mode of operation. Direct investment by individuals in the stock market has . . . shrunk dramatically in terms of value . . .

Instead, private investment has been increasingly channelled through collective savings in the form of insurance policies or company retirement schemes.

Shares once owned by retired bank managers, civil servants and the like are now under the control of giants such as Prudential, Standard Life and Schroders. These organisations collectively own more than half the equity in British companies but are ill-equipped to take a view on each and every issue at an annual meeting . . .

The mighty fund managers now stand as a wedge between individual investors and the companies. This makes it virtually impossible for private shareholders' concerns to find their way to the ears of company directors. (1995, p. 15)

Similarly, Karen Howlett and Susan Bourette, writing in *The Globe and Mail* (1995), comment that institutional investors (mainly pension funds and mutual funds) now account for 72 percent of the dollar value of trading on the Toronto Stock Exchange to the end of April, 1995. In the whole year of 1985, the total for institutional investors was 58.6 percent.

With patterns of investment such as these, the word "accountability" may have more of a meaning in its accounting sense than in the idea that businesses actually answer to someone. Frederick Warne owns Potter's copyright; Pearson owns Frederick Warne. Short of organizing a mass market boycott, it is difficult to see a viable route by which anyone might be able to raise objections to the way in which Peter Rabbit and his Potter stablemates are being forced into the marketplace.

On the other hand, it may be that technology will sidestep the entire issue. The whole idea of copyright and of intellectual property is altering as the Internet offers alternative forms of publication. On a very small scale, a friend of mine, hearing about my Beatrix Potter work, volunteered the information that he had used the text and some of the pictures of Potter's book, *The Roly-Poly Pudding* to practice with Hypercard. He gave me a disk containing his efforts, and perhaps, in a small-scale way, we were breaking the law. What should perhaps be concerning Pearson's shareholders is the potential for him to circulate this text anonymously on the Internet, perhaps as is, perhaps with insidious, even salacious changes. The photocopier simply opened the barn door; the Internet actively shoos the horses out of the stable. Copyright is not what it used to be and the struggles of legislators to gain some control of the situation are evident in many countries.

Esther Dyson, writing in *Wired* in the summer of 1995, suggests that the framework in which content and copyright rules have developed, is now changing.

> The Net dramatically changes the economics of content. Because it allows us to copy content essentially for free, the Net poses interesting challenges for owners, creators, seller, and users of intellectual property . . .
>
> What should content makers do in such an inverted world? The likely best course for content providers is to exploit that situation, to distribute intellectual property free in order to sell services and relationships. The provider's vital task is to figure out what to charge for and what to give away—all in the context of what other providers are doing and what customers (will grow to) expect. (p. 137)

For the present, the role of the Internet in the world of Peter Rabbit carries an all too familiar commercial flavor. When I used the search terms of Peter and Rabbit, I found numerous entries but every trawl drew mainly advertisements for shops, tourist trails and stuffed animals.

There are hints of change abroad, however. The behavior of some of Pearson's main competitors in the area of highly commodified literary characters suggests that the future for such enterprises is not entirely clear. Reed Elsevier, another enormous media conglomerate, in the summer of 1995 put some of Peter Rabbit's commercial competitors on the market; rights to Winnie the Pooh, Thomas the Tank Engine, and Babar the Elephant were put up for sale so that Reed could concentrate on scientific journals and business titles. *The Observer* of London viewed this move as part of a strategic turn to a computer-oriented marketing scheme:

> The areas Reed Elsevier wants to focus on are those easily distributed through new technologies—the potential for online distribution of

academic and professional publications is far higher than for
consumer titles. (Bell, 1995, n.p.)

It is interesting to note that as of May 1997 they have not found a
buyer.

Meanwhile, over the same time span, Walt Disney earned
headlines worldwide by purchasing the American television network,
ABC, thus opening up a whole new distribution route for its content
and commodities. Microsoft and another American network, NBC, are
similarly pairing up.

So the story is not over yet and it is not clear how Beatrix Potter or
any other author may fare in the 21st century. The real proliferation of
story and image may be just beginning.

CHAPTER 11

The Author as Commodity

In many ways, the author of *The Tale of Peter Rabbit* has been commodified in her own right. As with many other aspects of this case study, she represents an extreme of what can happen when an author becomes a public persona.

Beatrix Potter played a significant part in British public life in more than one way. She will always be remembered, of course, as the creator of the little books for children, but she played other roles over her lifetime. As a scientific artist, she presented (by proxy, since women were not permitted to address the Society) a paper on the spores of molds to the Linnaean Society of London (Lane, 1968, p. 43). As a farmer, she contributed in many ways to the study and preservation of particular species of sheep. As a woman of some means and influence, she made enormous contributions to the National Trust of Great Britain, in terms of money and land, and also in terms of direction.

In her own right, Beatrix Potter has also come to stand as one symbol of the escape from Victorian restrictions on women. Her biography tells a heroic story: the lonely child, isolated in a respectable nursery with only her clandestine pets for company, who turned that intense solitude to advantage; the young woman whose parents frowned on almost any form of normal social relationships with young men, but who nevertheless was engaged twice and married once over their objections; the dependent unmarried daughter who found a way to financial security through her own talents.

It is not surprising that, with such a rich vein of material, Frederick Warne, the National Trust and many others have found ways of telling the story of Beatrix Potter herself, and also ways of displaying and reproducing many of her own words and images beyond the texts of the little books. The proliferation of versions of this story seems almost obligatory, and there is no shortage of examples of reworking.

BIOGRAPHIES

There are many stories of Potter's life, some written for adults (Lane, 1968; Taylor, 1986) and some for children (Collins, 1989). At least one of these biographies, Judy Taylor's, has been made into a video production, narrated by Lynn Redgrave. The story is often retold for specific purposes; for example, I have a copy of a tourist magazine which provides an account of Potter's life, illustrated with paintings from Potter's books, photographs of Potter herself, and sumptuous pictures of Lake District landscape. The article concludes with notices of exhibitions (a topic to which I shall turn later) and some information about hotels in the district (Rose, 1993, p. 10). It is accompanied by advertisements for various other attractions in the North of England.

A friend of mine dimly recalls seeing a dramatized account of Beatrix Potter's life on *Masterpiece Theatre* but I have not been able to trace any details of this program. A one-woman play by Rohan McCullough played in festivals and on stages in various places in Britain, Australia, the United States and Japan. Potter's life story is also used as part of many different productions of her texts. Her solitary childhood and imaginative escape into the world of nature is the frame device of the ballet; her letter-writing activities to young friends, combined with a look at the beauties of the Lake District, form an integral and repeated part of the introduction and conclusion of all the Warne animations.

Indeed, Potter has even been reincarnated in a fictional role, featuring as a character in Robin Paige's (1995) Victorian mystery novel, *Death at Gallows Green*. It appears to be a contemporary trend to include Victorian and Edwardian authors in modern mystery novels and the blurring of boundaries between fact and fiction which ensues is interesting—although I would be more intrigued if the effects were less self-conscious and shallow.

THE HISTORICAL AND BIBLIOGRAPHICAL TEXTS

Even the definitive history of the Potter texts (Linder, 1971) is subject to recasting. Details are extracted and separately published in *The History of The Tale of Peter Rabbit* (1976), whose title page reads like something from the 18th century: "Taken mainly from Leslie Linder's *A History of the Writings of Beatrix Potter* together with the text and illustrations from the first privately printed edition." This text includes a facsimile of the original letter to Noel Moore, a facsimile of Potter's own privately printed version, and plates of some of the illustrations which were inserted and/or dropped in one edition or another. It also includes a great deal of Potter's correspondence with her publishers.

Potter's private journal has been decoded and published, as have facsimiles of many of her letters to children. A connection with Potter can actually be worth a great deal of money; a leather-bound photograph album containing about 200 pictures of Potter from childhood to old age, sold at Phillips in 1996 for $128,800 (Reuters news item, June 14, 1996).

Some of the biographical material has been recast in a form suitable for children. *Beatrix Potter and Peter Rabbit*, written by Nicole Savy and Diana Syrat (1993) and produced in the same size and format as the original *Tales*, provides a considerable amount of information about Potter's life and art, lavishly illustrated.

MUSEUMS AND EXHIBITIONS

I have not attempted to document the number of special displays and exhibitions which have been devoted to Potter over the years. Particularly in the centennial year of 1993, there was a flurry of activity on both sides of the Atlantic. Sue Rose's article for *In Britain*, a tourist magazine, provides a helpful snapshot of some possibilities for a visitor to the Lake District in 1993. She mentions five separate venues. The Old Laundry in Bowness-on-Windermere offered an exhibition entitled "The World of Beatrix Potter." The Windermere Steamboat Museum included Potter's own rowing boat among its exhibits of old steamboats and motorboats. The Beatrix Potter Gallery, housed in her husband's former law office, annually displays Potter originals; in 1993, it showed illustrations on special loan from the Victoria and Albert Museum. Packhorse Court in Keswick recreated a typical Lakeland farm, under the heading "Beatrix Potter's Lake District." The Armitt Library in Ambleside offered visitors a look at Potter's watercolors and drawings of fungi, mosses and fossils. The World Wide Web offers many sites which provide guides to tourists looking information about Potter and the Lake District.

According to an article in *The New York Times*, 80,000 tourists a year visit Potter's Lake District cottage, Hill Top. Nearly a third of these visitors are Japanese; and their tour buses are beginning to cause problems of congestion. Already tour buses must book in advance, and the administration of Hill Top is about to adopt a limit of 800 visitors a day (Darnton, 1995, p. A4).

The range of Potter's interests is clearly well represented in the Lake District sites. However, in 1993 in particular, there were Potter exhibitions in many different places. In the United States, for example,

> For bookstores, Warne is sponsoring a year-long Peter Rabbit window and in-store display contest. The publisher is offering a permanent spinner rack, a Peter Rabbit costume tour, a free 100th anniversary floor display, a free display kit and a Peter Rabbit birthday activity kit. (Bodin, 1993, p. 20)

In the summer of 1995, I saw remnants of a Peter Rabbit anniversary display still going strong in the window of a souvenir shop in Jasper, the town at the heart of the Canadian Rocky Mountains. At the center of this arrangement was a selection of Wedgwood china, and the implication that Peter Rabbit could successfully attract the world's tourists was very plain.

THE NATIONAL TRUST CONNECTION

A centenary is always good for business, and it is perhaps not surprising, given the very close links between Beatrix Potter, Frederick Warne and the National Trust, to find Potter being invoked in connection with the Trust's centenary. A friend sent me a card with a beautifully embroidered rendition of Peter's mother handing out baskets and warnings to her children. Inside she enclosed a bookmark, telling me "Beatrix Potter (TM) celebrates 100 years of the National Trust" and a little brochure announcing the National Trust Beatrix Potter Competition. The text of this leaflet is interesting:

> 1995 is the National Trust's Centenary year. Although Beatrix Potter is perhaps best-known for her world-famous Original Peter Rabbit Books (TM), she had a close association with the National Trust for much of her life. Her ideas about conservation and the preservation of

the heritage and landscape of the Lake District, live on through the work of the Trust. To celebrate the Trust's Centenary and the role which Beatrix Potter played in the development of the Trust, Frederick Warne & Co., publisher of Beatrix Potter's Original Peter Rabbit Books (TM), are offering you the opportunity to win a family holiday in a National Trust holiday cottage of your choice.

The leaflet goes on to describe the virtues of the National Trust holiday cottages. To enter this competition you answer three questions about Potter characters and send your entry to Frederick Warne.

The astuteness of the marketing symbiosis at work in this project is striking. There is also an interesting blurring effect at work in the prizes: first prize is a week in a National Trust cottage, second prize is "A selection of The World of Beatrix Potter (TM) books and merchandise worth £100" and there are 100 runner-up prizes of copies of *The Tale of Peter Rabbit*. The book, the associated merchandise and the experience of being in the beautiful British countryside are all tidily represented, and their virtues merged in this little list.

THE POTTER ACTIVITY BOOK

My personal favorite in all this associated material is an activity book produced by Frederick Warne with the National Trust: *Find Out About Beatrix Potter: Projects, Presents and Puzzles* (1987). The range of approaches to Potter and her work is interesting. There are several pages of biography, a section on keeping a journal, a guide to looking at trees, a join-the-dots picture, a picture letter from Johnny Town-Mouse to his country friend Timmy Willie, some instructions for making Christmas cards and place cards, a model of a Lakeland farmhouse to assemble, instructions for making traditional presents, a "Beatrix Potter country crossword," two pages on conservation in general and in the Lake District in particular, a picture of Tom Kitten and his sisters in which you have to find the missing buttons, a maze, a page on farm boundaries such as walls and hedges, a page on Herdwick sheep, and, finally, a blurb about joining the National Trust. Confusion of address marks this publication as it does other activity books; the assemblers appear to be trying to be all things to all children.

In this text, as in many of the others I have considered briefly in this chapter, the boundaries between fact, fiction and money-making are exceptionally tenuous. The back of the book assures us that profits go to the National Trust's Lake District Appeal, "to preserve the countryside and way of life which Beatrix Potter loved."

The commercial importance of Potter's name is apparent in the frequency with which it appears with the trademark logo attached. The cultural importance of the resonances which attach to her name, her art, her attachment to the British countryside and a way of life now effectively lost, would also seem to be meaningful to a large number of people.

THE GRAPHIC NOVEL

The associations of Potter's name with genteel aspects of the British countryside are moderately predictable, given the nature of her stories. What is perhaps more surprising is to find her biography and works an essential element in a graphic novel about child abuse. *The Tale of One Bad Rat* by Bryan Talbot, published by Dark Horse Books in 1995, draws on Potter's life and values in many explicit ways, both verbally and pictorially. The heroine of this book, Helen Potter, is a teenage runaway in contemporary urban Britain, driven from home by her father's sexual abuse. Helen is obsessed by the stories and the life of Beatrix Potter, and in the course of the book visits more than one site where Potter lived. Peaceful Potteresque images of the timeless Lake District act as a counterpoint to the dirt and danger of modern cities throughout the novel. On a visit to Hill Top, Helen actually finds a manuscript of an unknown Potter story, "The Tale of One Bad Rat," and the little book is reproduced as part of the novel. Ingredients of Potter's lonely childhood act as a major key to the development of Helen's story, which tackles major questions of child abuse.

Visual contrasts between the terrifying home and the frightening streets on the one hand, and the tranquil world of Beatrix Potter on the other hand are woven into the fabric of the story. Potter's work stands as an emblem of security in this story, but it is also used to represent an individual triumph over family problems and restrictions. The graphic elements of this novel are sophisticated; the text is complex but also didactic. Talbot provides an explicit afterword on the way the book was created as part of the battle against child abuse, and there are helpline numbers for three countries on the last page. Yet the book is more than a morality comic; the world and the values of Beatrix Potter are made an inextricable part of its fabric in a challenging, interesting, and highly contemporary way.

CHAPTER 12

New Adventures

As I neared completion of this project, I began to encounter texts which place copyright and ownership questions in a new context. My daughter arrived home with the news that she had seen a read-along tape and storybook of "The New Adventures of Peter Rabbit." I bought it at once and began to struggle with the implications of its content and presentation. The very next day, in my local paper, the syndicated cartoon *Peanuts* showed Snoopy the dog in the role of a world famous attorney going to court for a very important case. "Yes, your honor," says Snoopy, a dim-looking rabbit by his side, "we shall prove that my client never intended to go into the garden of Mr. McGregor" (Schultz, 1995, p. C6). A few days later, I encountered a "literary" picture book entitled *Dear Peter Rabbit.*

These three texts seem to me to suggest three different ways in which Peter Rabbit is escaping from the copyright garden of his plot. One is as a public icon, an identity who needs no labelling apart from a mention of Mr. McGregor's garden. The second, more disturbing, is an example of the kind of exploitation of children's books which is becoming commonplace with titles out of copyright. *Dear Peter Rabbit* involves a more respectable route out of the confines of the original text into a wider intertextual network.

There are other forms of text which dislocate Peter Rabbit from the constraints of his linear plot in various ways. These range from the simple, such as a mobile of characters from the book; to the more elaborate such as the variety of board games; to the tangential, such as Peter's appearance in that ultimate intertextual children's book, *The Jolly Pocket Postman.* Potter herself created an intertextual set of letters, now published in a book also called *Dear Peter Rabbit.*

As a last twist to the Peter Rabbit saga, I want to consider what may be the most amazing transformation of all, the appearance of our hero in a pair of Christian home videos where, as a giant puppet comparable to Barney the Dinosaur, he promotes a particular fundamentalist view of the universe to a group of sycophantic children.

And finally, of course, no study of texts in various media could close without a consideration of the Internet. Peter Rabbit is as much at home there as in all the other media we have discussed so far.

THE NEW ADVENTURES OF PETER RABBIT

Sony Wonder has produced this package of picture book and audiotape as an adaptation from the Golden Films Production of "The New Adventures of Peter Rabbit." I later found the film, but to begin with, I want to concentrate on the tape and book which I saw first. They raise a number of fascinating questions.

The cover of the book says that it is "Adapted from *The Tale of Peter Rabbit* By Beatrix Potter." The packaging slip is even more aggressive in its assertion of ownership. The first sentence and the last sentence of the blurb suggest that in reading and listening to this story, you are somehow participating in Potter's famous classic; the sentences in-between give some idea of the actual gap.

> Beatrix Potter's classic children's story comes to life in this whimsical, warmhearted, read-and-listen-along version of *The New Adventures of Peter Rabbit*!
>
> After telling one tall tale too many, Peter Rabbit fools himself into thinking his sisters have been shipped off to faraway Zanzibar. Determined to rescue them, Peter is joined by a comical cast of zany forest creatures on a hilariously heroic journey to bring his wayward siblings home safely. Join the fun, as you read the beautifully illustrated storybook and listen along to the audiotape version of this all-time favorite tale.

So just who is this Peter Rabbit who hangs about with a cast of comical, zany sidekicks and participates in hilariously heroic adventures? How can we make any connections between this world and the imaginative creation of Beatrix Potter? Does it take more than a brazen assertion or two to associate two wildly divergent universes?

This Peter Rabbit has acquired a fourth sister, Hopsy. This Peter Rabbit is warned about Mr. McGregor's garden because "his cat will have you for dinner!" (p. 1). This Peter Rabbit has a plump cousin Benny. This Peter Rabbit has an ear which flops forward when he tells an untruth. This Peter Rabbit lives in a world of American vocabulary:

> Just then, Mr. McGregor's sneaky cat dove from behind the bushes to snatch his prey. "Benny!" Peter shouted as he yanked him from the cat's path. Then the two scrambled underneath a large metal bucket. (p. 4)

Vocabulary aside, the intertextual links to both *The Tale of Peter Rabbit* and *The Tale of Benjamin Bunny* are probably at their most acute at the early stage of the story, as in the lines quoted above. Not only are we reminded of the escapade in the latter book in which the two rabbits hide underneath a basket to escape from the cat; even more unnervingly, the picture shows the two rabbits in the bucket with not one but two sets of ears protruding over the top. Later in this scene, however, we see the departure from the garden and an ever-increasing distance from Potter's world.

It is very difficult to convey just how bad a story this book is. The action is cluttered with helpers and villains who materialize out of the blue, sometimes to fade away after a small plot development, sometimes to hang around for longer. The escapes from various dangerous scenarios are both implausible and complex, a very bad combination (although, to be fair, it works much better in the animation, which is far better suited to the kind of ongoing slapstick mishaps which feature large in this story).

The overall plot is both stupid and complicated. At the risk of tedium, I want to recount it in some detail. Peter, set to mind his sisters, stows them in a box which he claims is labelled "Zanzibar." He and Benny go to Mr. McGregor's garden. The cat frightens them into a bucket from which they observe the mailman picking up the box. Peter fools the cat into thinking that he can smell salmon, so the cat goes away and Peter and Benny pursue the mailman. A mouse offers to show them a short cut across a creek. A turtle chases them through the creek but they escape and meet another rabbit, a cute one called Fluff. She suggests they find the mail train, but Benny wants to eat some berries. A "slimy" (p. 8) hedgehog complains that Benny is damaging his bush, but Peter comes to the rescue by telling the hedgehog that there is a stampede of cattle heading in their direction and the hedgehog runs for cover. They cross a wall by using a contraption made from ivy vines, a large rock and a basket. Benny, "being the pudgy sort" (p. 10), does not land square but rolls into a foxhole and falls into the fox's pot of boiling water. He leaps out and Peter distracts the fox by informing him that Benny is over the weight limit and it is illegal to eat him.

The four friends catch sight of the mail train, but it pulls away. Peter is forced to admit that he made up the name of Zanzibar. In disgust his friends desert him. The hedgehog, the fox and Mr. McGregor's cat accost Peter and it turns out they have already captured the friends and are carrying them in a sack. With a celerity that the Hardy Boys would envy, however, Peter and his friends dispatch the baddies:

> Suddenly, Peter leapt high into the air as the villains tried to catch him. He leapt again and again, in all directions, until they were so confused and dizzy that they fell over each other in a big heap. "Ouch!" cried the hedgehog. "Meooow!" screeched the cat. "Yikes!" bellowed the fox as he dropped the sack. Benny, Trevor, Fluff and the squirrel wriggled out to help Peter take on the evil rogues. With their combined efforts, they rounded up the scoundrels, and sent them hurtling down the hillside. (p. 15)

Peter is still gloomy, as he has to tell his mother his sisters are all missing. However, when they return home, the sisters are mysteriously all there. No explanation is given; we are left to assume that they must have escaped from the box in good time. Peter promises never to fib again (thus devaluing his own Trickster role as the resourceful liar who compensates for powerlessness with cunning) and Mother Rabbit serves a big dinner.

The story is bad; the writing is even worse. The vocabulary is demanding without being precise. The sentence structure is complex without being lively. Such suspense as there is becomes entirely overwhelmed by the flatness of the writing. In the film version the actions are active; in this text, all sense of activity is submerged in the complete passivity of the writing.

Trevor led Peter and Benny to a creek. "We must cross it," said Trevor. "Climb on my shoulders," Peter told him, "and I'll help you." But as they waded across, a giant snapping turtle rose up and chomped after them. The turtle chased them through the water with its jaws snapping, but the three managed to swim to safety. (p. 7)

The illustrations of this book are irritatingly derivative, not of Potter but of generic animated cartoons. The rabbits all sport buck teeth that would give Bugs Bunny second thoughts. Fluff, the cute girl rabbit, is dressed in a pink minidress with a pink bow on her ears. Benny, the plump one, wears a bow tie. The banality, the poverty of visual imagination, the heavy reliance on cartoon stereotypes, are all exceedingly depressing. The design is also unappealing with large amounts of text crowded on each page.

The audio recording of this story is as dull as the print version. The narrator struggles, understandably, with the turgid writing, and the music, while adequate, is not enough to compensate for the incoherence of the story as a whole. The size of the cast of unimportant and temporary characters is even more overwhelming in an audio version than on the page.

It is not entirely surprising to discover that some of these problems are less obtrusive in the film version. It is a fully animated cartoon. The characters all speak with American accents and the music is created out of well-known snatches and phrases from composers such as Bizet and Offenbach.

Some small mysteries of the print text are explained in the animation, which at 48 minutes is the longest video of any that I looked at, except for the ballet. It turns out that Peter's sisters are rescued from the mailbox by Mr. McGregor, who has already informed his cat that he has lost all taste for rabbit stew. The number of friends, allies and tag-alongs who join Peter and Benny on their pursuit is even larger than in the book (including a French cliché of a kitten called Perky), but because we are not struggling with names for all this crew it seems to matter less. The slapstick adventures, so boringly described in the print version, naturally seem more reasonable, if not plausible, in animated form. The cartoon is much more enticingly paced than the print version. And the absence of a narrative voice means that certain facts are less intrusively conveyed. Peter's ear flops over his face in the same way, but no one actually informs us that this is in response to a lie; we are left to work it out for ourselves. In short, the cartoon, while a travesty of anything that could tolerably be labelled as Peter Rabbit, is less of an esthetic disaster in its own terms than the book and the audiotape.

Overall, however, this story is an artistic product with very few redeeming qualities indeed. Yet it carries the label of "Peter Rabbit," uses the name of Beatrix Potter to help with sales. What are the implications of this kind of development? What exactly is this quality of Peter-Rabbitness which can be applied to a completely alien imaginative world?

The answers are not entirely clear in this collection of texts. Peter has a mother and sisters, but the adaptors who have produced the *New Adventures* have felt themselves able to add a fourth sister named Hopsy. Her plot function is negligible; if she is designed to serve as some form of protection against possible Warne lawsuits, it seems remarkably careless of Sony Wonder to throw so many references to Beatrix Potter around the packaging of the different texts. Mr. McGregor is still in the story, but he is a reformed character and all the danger comes from his cat. Benjamin Bunny, now transmogrified as Benny, lives on, but as a fat and greedy city boy who has a lot to learn about surviving in the countryside. Peter Rabbit himself is utterly transformed; completely American in tone, accent and attitude, he has long abandoned the original Peter's fine line between bravado and complete recklessness, and now occupies an imaginative space most easily described as standard cartoon-land, where issues are obvious and solutions are slapstick. It would appear that his entitlement to the name of Peter Rabbit lies solely in the fact of assertion.

IMPLICATIONS

I find it hard to imagine much consumer enthusiasm for this particular product, but such an assumption begs to be confounded. In marketing terms, the leading edge of the package is likely to be the film, but the theoretical and intellectual consequences of this development are wide-ranging, no matter which medium is involved. They are also not confined to the free-for-all of the North American market; I found this video for sale in Tesco's in Britain as well as in Canada.

Fulminations along the lines of, "Is nothing sacred?" are clearly a waste of time. Peter Rabbit is now public property, available for the cheapest and nastiest kind of character assassination (not to mention plot and narrative assassination as well!). Even if Frederick Warne were successfully to prosecute Sony for this piece of legerdemain, the material is in the marketplace for the moment, being sold as Potter's story "come to life."

There is no advantage to any child reader in having the name of Peter Rabbit applied to this trivial story. Any association with any previous text of Peter Rabbit, even (I think) with the 1987 Ladybird edition, could only lead to a disappointment here. The role of Peter Rabbit's name is purely to sell the package.

It seems likely that even quite young readers of previous texts may detect the element of exploitation at work in this story. How they respond may depend on the kind of adult support which attends their disappointment. Some children will be told, "That's not the *real* Peter Rabbit, that's not the *real* Beatrix Potter," and will learn something about authority and authenticity. Others will not receive such instruction and may develop a distrust of the text which washes back into their next contact with the original Peter, and, at worst, into their response to books in general.

At the same time, especially if the new film is adroitly marketed, there will be many readers who first meet Peter Rabbit in this guise. Assuming the story is at all memorable to them, they will surely feel some sense of dissonance if they later encounter the Potter version. By almost every term imaginable, these two texts are direct opposites; the role of the proper nouns in mangling them together is stretched to the point where it is barely comprehensible.

Yet we know that such exploitation of texts out of copyright is widespread. An animated cartoon of *The Secret Garden*, which aired on ABC and is currently being sold as a home video, recruits talking animals to the story of the sad, spoiled children, and gives Mary an American accent. Disney's Winnie the Pooh, which is ubiquitous, imports a gopher to the English nursery/countryside. Esthetic coherence is a sad loser when it comes to defining the rules of the marketplace for children.

Children and their families are not entirely passive in their interaction with this marketplace, of course. On the day that I bought *The New Adventures of Peter Rabbit*, I overheard a mother with two young children in a bookstore. The children had been offered a book each and the younger one was agitating to buy a book based on Disney's *Pocahontas*. The mother did not even pause for thought; "I'm not buying film books," she said, and there was no further argument. The older child had strategies of her own. She was looking at a numbered series of titles and deciding whether to buy one. "I want them all," she said, "but I want to read them in the right order." In fact, she left the shop with a different title altogether, and whatever the long-term success of the marketing ploy of listing series books in numerical order, in the short term it cost the publishers a sale.

There are, of course, families who use such marketing tactics as film-related books or numbered series as positive strategies, who organize their book-buying behavior within the frameworks that the market provides. But this is not a necessary response.

In accounts of life in heavily centralized countries, there is often a mention of how people learn to read *against* the prevalent censorship. There are many descriptions of such kinds of reading, but Lesley Krueger's example has the virtue of being pithy:

> I lived in Mexico for a few years and the official newspaper Excelsior, like government-allied papers elsewhere, had to be read for its subtexts. If a headline appeared across Page 1 saying something like Oil Industry Jewel of Mexico, you knew there had probably been an accident somewhere. (1995, p. A20)

I suspect that in a patchy and semicoherent way, there is something of a tendency in our culture for people to learn to read *against* capitalism. Some parents certainly instruct their children directly: "They're only doing that/saying that/selling that because they want to make money." A certain amount of such conversation also occurs on school playgrounds, and the ubiquity of advertisements means that even very young children are never short of examples of salesmanship at work. Resistant reading may be random, ill-organized and inchoate, but it certainly exists.

At least some disillusioned Peter Rabbit fans (anywhere from $9.99 to $12.99 sadder and wiser in Canada, £8.99 to the bad if they buy the video in Britain) may decide that Sony Wonder are simply in it for the profits. Of course, they will not have access to sophisticated insights into Warne's efforts to preserve Peter Rabbit from such predatory reincarnations; they may indeed blame Warne or Potter herself for letting such a blatant piece of manipulation loose on an unsuspecting public.

As our society is presently organized in the West, there may be some recourse available to Frederick Warne in this particular case, but there seems to be little protection offered to the public. Where is the standard of truth in advertising which prevents Sony Wonder from asserting that by listening to their travesty of a story, you are actually listening to "the audiotape version of this all-time favorite tale!"? (North American package back). What protection is offered to those who are sufficiently naive or ill-informed that they simply take as true Sony Wonder's claim on the cover of the picture book that this story is "adapted from *The Tale of Peter Rabbit* by Beatrix Potter." What does a child, puzzling out the intertextual relationship between the two stories, learn about what we now mean by "adapted?" What does this child learn about the trustworthiness of imagined experience when your attachment to a particular character is used to sell you a fraud? And does it matter? Do children simply acquire a certain suspiciousness about the provenance of related texts which may actually serve them well in the long term? Do they learn something about discrimination by the yoking of two such blatantly dissimilar texts? Are they simply rendered cynical at an early age? Do they develop a postmodern sensibility which precludes any notion of authority? Or do they simply and unquestioningly include such peculiarities as part of their working understanding of what makes fiction?

Whatever the answers to these questions, it seems plausible to assume that many children are learning to approach the world of literature with a certain leeriness, which may be entirely appropriate to the marketing techniques involved in the sale of that commodity, but which may have a deleterious effect on their interest in engaging with that world.

Protecting our children from the kind of exploitation represented by *The New Tales of Peter Rabbit* would appear to be difficult on any level larger than that of the individual family. It may well be that protective procedures would cause more problems than they solve; certainly the debate over the V-chip, which might reduce children's access to violence on television, suggests that the issues are not clear-cut. Who decides what, and for whom? And how do we legislate for (or indeed against) the child who falls passionately in love with *The New Adventures of Peter Rabbit*, treasures it throughout childhood and remembers it fondly in later years? Anyone who has ever read to a child knows that literary quality is not necessarily the most compelling criterion when favorites are being established.

In short, we are back to what I am beginning to think of as the Standard Mackey Cop-out: it is all very complex and there are many questions to which we do not have answers.

DEAR PETER RABBIT

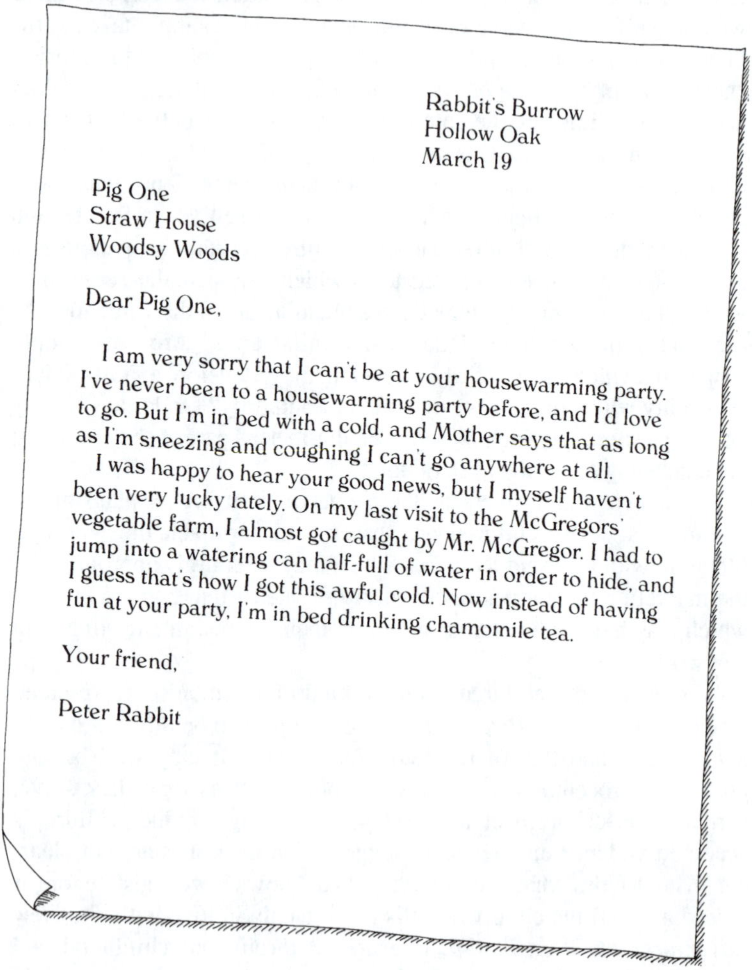

Rabbit's Burrow
Hollow Oak
March 19

Pig One
Straw House
Woodsy Woods

Dear Pig One,

I am very sorry that I can't be at your housewarming party. I've never been to a housewarming party before, and I'd love to go. But I'm in bed with a cold, and Mother says that as long as I'm sneezing and coughing I can't go anywhere at all.

I was happy to hear your good news, but I myself haven't been very lucky lately. On my last visit to the McGregors' vegetable farm, I almost got caught by Mr. McGregor. I had to jump into a watering can half-full of water in order to hide, and I guess that's how I got this awful cold. Now instead of having fun at your party, I'm in bed drinking chamomile tea.

Your friend,

Peter Rabbit

Dear Peter Rabbit by Alma Flor Ada.

Dear Peter Rabbit by Alma Flor Ada.

Further light is shed on this highly complicated topic by another text which I discovered in the late stages of this project. *Dear Peter Rabbit*, written by Alma Flor Ada and illustrated by Leslie Tryon (1994), is an epistolary picture book, involving letters to and from a variety of characters, all but Peter Rabbit himself taken from fairy tales and folk tales. The plot has to be assembled from the letters and the accompanying pictures. The first Little Pig invites Peter Rabbit to a housewarming; Peter has caught a cold from hiding in Mr. McGregor's watering can and is unable to attend. This turns out not to matter because the wolf blows down the house before the party can be held. A similar problem attends the housewarming party for the house of sticks, but Peter finally makes it to the party held in the house of bricks. Meanwhile, Goldilocks, who turns out to be Mr. McGregor's daughter, is corresponding with Baby Bear about a little blue jacket she found in her garden, and the wolf is commiserating with his cousin over the loss of his tail in the Little Pigs' cauldron. In the end, the wolves reform and the other characters have a great time together at Goldilocks' birthday party (Mr. McGregor does not seem to be too happy with his daughter's choice of guests).

Any fiction composed entirely of letters naturally involves lacunae. In this case, some of the gaps are filled by information provided in the pictures and the two sources of information complement each other quite cleverly. Peter Rabbit and his mother are drawn in Potteresque form, but the pictures add details to the plot and also to the reader's understanding of Peter's relationship with his mother. Other gaps, of course, are covered by previous knowledge of the original texts.

I found the overarching plot of this book to be rather bland, but there is no doubt the story is cleverly put together. I also have no doubt that this kind of use of a previously established fictional character is in a different literary league from the crude exploitation of *The New Adventures of Peter Rabbit*. Is this simply because literary people have their own labels for work they approve of? Why am I comfortable in describing this kind of reworking of Peter Rabbit as intertextual rather than cheaply derivative? What is the quality of reimagining which makes this text acceptable, even respectable, whereas *The New Adventures of Peter Rabbit*, especially in its book form, is simply horrifying?

It is not a simple question of quality. *Dear Peter Rabbit* is cleverly constructed but it is not a major work of art. It is intertextual both in its content (which refers to a number of well-known characters and uses their stories in the development of its own plot) and in its construction (which irresistibly brings to mind the Ahlbergs' *Jolly Postman* and its successors, although it is not as ingenious or as funny).

One factor which makes this account of Peter Rabbit considerably more legitimate than the cartoon is the care with which the author attends to the limits of the original work and locates them within the other, different limits of her own construction. The cartoon *New Adventures* locates Peter entirely within the limitations of its own genre, with only the slightest attention paid even to the plot of the earlier story. *Dear Peter Rabbit* takes account of the imaginative world of the first text, even as it dislocates Peter into its own world. This book, with some small lapses (such as placing Peter's home in Hollow Oak), actually attempts to make room for Peter's implicit as well as explicit experiences. The author is not always entirely successful; Peter's idiom errs on the American side of plausibility. Nevertheless, there seems to be a genuine effort to respect the subtleties of the original.

No doubt there is an element of social and literary prejudice in my preference for the subtle over the coarse and the clichéd. The only alternative is an entirely relativist acceptance of every variant as equal, and I find myself unable to take that step. Every variant is equally interesting in the illumination it casts on the whole intellectual issue of versions, but when it comes to the crunch they are not all of equal value in terms of what they can offer to young readers. It seems to me that a nonjudgemental approach runs the risk of validating many forms of exploitation of children.

A different question relates to the elevation of Peter Rabbit to the status of folk character. One of the American reillustrated books made the same connection, quoting Bettelheim on the importance of folk fairy tales to young children. The fact that such a connection can be asserted, whether correctly or not, is related to the assumptions made by Charles Schultz in his *Peanuts* strips, the idea that Peter Rabbit is a culturally complete figure in his own right and that any reference to a single part of the story will automatically invoke the whole.

OTHER NONLINEAR REPRESENTATIONS

A baby's mobile consisting of characters from The Tale of Peter Rabbit offers the very youngest consumer a route into the deconstruction of the story. This capacity to take apart and reassemble a text which began life in a highly linear format is reinforced by the variety of board games which use the characters and elements of the plot to create new patterns and relationships. One catalogue description of a set of these games may convey the rather precious approach emphasized by the marketers;

this is how the Letterbox mail order catalogue describes a set of the games:

THE BEATRIX POTTER COLLECTION £29.99

Excellent value with 3 enchanting Peter Rabbit games in one—Draughts, Ludo and Paths & Burrows—based on Beatrix Potter's stories and using her original illustrations. With 4 painted rabbits, 2 wicker baskets, terracotta flowerpot shaker and Mr McGregor's sack to store dice and cabbage counters. Age 4+. (p. 18)

I inspected "Paths and Burrows" and found it to be a fairly pedestrian version of Snakes and Ladders; no amount of excitement over shaking your die in a terracotta flower pot would seem to me to compensate for the fact that all the gains and losses are relatively small and painless. What is the point of playing Snakes and Ladders if you never swoop from 89 all the way back to 11? Be that as it may, the games do release Peter from the tightest confines of his plot and offer another way for children to meet the story on different terms.

A more complex and satisfying reincarnation of Peter Rabbit is his cameo appearance in that epic of children's intertextuality, *The Jolly Pocket Postman* by Janet and Allan Ahlberg (1995). In this book we get a brief glimpse of Peter, in Mr. McGregor's garden as usual—but that garden is located within a wide-ranging literary geography, so that it lies alongside Neverland, Treasure Island, the Land of Counterpane, and the Yellow Brick Road. The map literally sparkles, with glitter outlining the Yellow Brick Road and the Emerald City; the book sparkles on a more metaphorical level as well with its riot of literary juxtapositions, stories crowding up against each other, enriching each other just with the awareness that there are, indeed, so many stories to be told.

The Jolly Pocket Postman by Janet and Allan Ahlberg.

These examples show various artists, with highly diverse levels of skill and integrity, making new uses of elements of the Peter Rabbit story. It is fitting, but not really surprising, to discover that Potter herself was aware of the potential for disrupting and realigning her story. In 1995 Frederick Warne published *Dear Peter Rabbit*, a story assembled out of miniature letters, purportedly written by characters in her books, which Potter composed for young friends. These letters now appear as part of a book, tucked into their own miniature envelopes attached to the pages. Peter writes to Mr. McGregor and to Benjamin Bunny, his mother writes to Mrs. Tiggy-winkle; Squirrel Nutkin writes to Old Brown. The frame story is fairly clumsy (I believe an earlier edition omitted it altogether and simply laid out the letters without elaboration), and while Colin Twinn is given credit for the illustrations in this book there is no acknowledgement of any author; the title page has no author's name at all and the cover merely says, "A story featuring the letters written for children by Beatrix Potter."

No doubt, the ingenuity of the marketers and/or the devotion of Potter's admirers will lead to further reinventions of the story of Peter Rabbit, further reverberations and echoes. The question of where it will all end is unanswerable; the more immediate question is what it may mean for young readers. The Ahlberg book in particular demonstrates how even very small children can participate in the kinds of literary games which delight many of their elders; *The New Adventures of Peter Rabbit* shows that such games can be played in the interests of rapacity as well as of delight.

THE PARABLES OF PETER RABBIT

The creation which perhaps stands as the ultimate retelling is the Peter Rabbit created for the Christian videos which portray Peter as a man-sized puppet, a human inside an animal costume along the dimensions of Barney the Dinosaur. This Peter Rabbit briefly establishes his credentials by referring to how lonely he is now that Flopsy and Cotton-tail have moved to the meadow, but for the most part he confines his conversation to discussions of what God wants of and for us. His proselytizing is directed at four suitably multicultural boys and girls who accidentally tumble into his rabbit hole and who lap up his homilies with sugary enthusiasm.

This Peter and his creators waste little time or energy on subtlety. Peter introduces himself to his new friends with a song:

> My name is Peter Rabbit.
> I have a happy habit
> Of hopping everywhere I go
> And telling everyone I know
> That Jesus lives inside me
> To love me and to guide me.
> He fills my heart with a happy song
> That keeps me hopping all day long.

Far from being a predator on vegetables, this Peter keeps a window box of animated vegetables who sing and dance and cringe at any idea that you might ever cook a vegetable, let alone eat it.

I find it very difficult with texts as perversely bad as this one or *The New Adventures of Peter Rabbit* to distinguish between my instinctive recoil at the sheer lack of quality and my strong sense of being offended by the assumptions of the video-makers that they can do what they like with a fictional character in whom I have, over many years, made my own personal emotional and artistic investment. *How dare they?* is not necessarily a useful critical response, but it is one that is very hard to avoid. I can accommodate the idea that some Christian children might conceivably like stories which accentuate those qualities which are regularly impressed on them in their daily lives; in any case, numerous children's stories have had to carry didactic weight and there is nothing intrinsically offensive about such didacticism being of a fundamentalist Christian nature. I do query whether such stories need be told so poorly, with such inane lyrics and bad acting (not to mention the dancing!). And I object to the presumption of these video-makers that they have the right to take a fictional character already established in the public domain (with or without legal copyright protection) and hijack him for their own propaganda purposes.

The blatant way in which Peter Rabbit is turned into a mouthpiece for ideas so clearly foreign to his creator could possibly be described as a testimonial to the universality of her work, but I think that approach probably stretches charity beyond its reasonable limits. This particular version of the story would seem to be available to a limited and self-selecting audience (my resourceful daughter found these videos in a specialist Christian bookshop and I have not come across any reference to them in any broader context), but I cannot see that this fact in any way mitigates the scale of the offence.

Would I be so offended if, instead of pushing a specific ideology, the giant puppet of Peter Rabbit merely exhorted his young friends to be kind and loving to one another, along the lines of his saccharine inspirer, Barney? The videos would still be sappy and silly, but the specific missionary element would be slightly diffused. I think it is possible to distinguish between the qualities of esthetic scorn and of political indignation. On an esthetic level, there are arguments to be made over whether *The Parables of Peter Rabbit* or *The New Adventures of Peter Rabbit* is actually the worse production. The lyrics quoted above are pretty bad, but they are incisive and clever compared to the song which introduces *The New Adventures* in which a chorus of rabbits sings,

> Hop to the left and hop to the right,
> Hippity hoppity day and night.
> Hop right on till the day is through,
> That's what all of us bunnies do.

The Parables of Peter Rabbit: Friends. Illustration by Jerry Hopper.

The question of whether explicit Christianity is more insidious than implicit sexism and chauvinism (as manifested most completely in *The New Adventures* in the clichéd character of Perky, the French kitten) is a debatable one. It is difficult to assess the impact of either on very young viewers, and of course the questions of provenance, of moral rights to intellectual property, of esthetic integrity, are matters which mainly trouble adults. In both these cases, as in the other forms of text described in this chapter, Peter Rabbit has escaped from the confines of his originating plot more or less comprehensively; it will be interesting to see if such departures are harbingers of a future where the controls over the essential qualities of Peter Rabbit become ever more tenuous.

THE INTERNET SITES

A number of Internet sites relate to Peter Rabbit in one way or another. Given the hit-and-miss nature of the Internet, I do not feel confident that I have made any kind of a clean sweep of the possibilities; however, what I have been able to find is all depressingly similar.

Using the Webcrawler browser, I turned up 82 sites when I typed in the phrase "Peter Rabbit." I did not visit all 82 of these, but it seemed fairly clear that the general drift of these sites was commercial, very largely connected to the vast tourist industry in the Lake District with some sidelines devoted to merchandising; one site, for example, lists more than 30 varieties of Royal Doulton Beatrix Potter china you can order. Some sites offered reviews of various versions of the Peter Rabbit story, or opportunities to order, say, the CD-ROMs.

Pearson has established an official Peter Rabbit Home Page (http://www.peterrabbit.co.uk) and it does contain some material with child appeal, along with a considerable quantity of marketing of all kinds of attractions, from china to an ice show at Alton Towers featuring Peter Rabbit and his friends. I found a few sites where young children and/or their parents had created links to Peter Rabbit, and there were some sites offering reviews of various texts, most particularly the CD-ROMs. For the most part, however, the huge majority of the Internet material I found on the subject of Peter Rabbit involved a sales pitch of one kind or another.

The certainty that something idiosyncratic will turn up whatever you type in is one of the more beguiling aspects of cruising the Web, and my most preposterous finding (though one I am not sure little children would appreciate) was one I turned up using Lycos when I used Peter and Rabbit as subject entries. A site called "Amorous Poems" gave me a poem called "The Way of the Flesh" by David P. Shreiner, and I can only assume it made it through the filters because the hero is called Peter and late in the poem a rabbit dashes across the lawn. The opening lines will illustrate the level of incongruity:

> At the age of twelve, precocious Peter sees nothing
> but rounded hillocks, swaying hips, bouncing breasts.
> Trees with sturdy limbs erect, point
> to downy swells of clouds, maidenhair drenched
> in dewy sex of virgin cumulus . . .

My first reading of this can only be described as a postmodern moment, and my bemusement must be imagined.

A slightly more substantial connection led me to "Peter Rabbit Sex Poem" by Marilyn Bowering, which gave me three stanzas of coital perplexities, illuminated by a reference to Peter Rabbit in the vegetable patch with his passion for carrots undiminished. In keeping with the standards of Peter Rabbit sites on the Internet, this one offers a link to an order form for your own copy.

There is no real reason why adults should not introduce Peter Rabbit into their poems about sex and it is probably unlikely that many children small enough to be upset by this poetry would find their way to the sites. Nevertheless, there is something going on here which affects readers; the jarring incongruities between my motives in searching and my findings would be difficult to replicate in ordinary print-oriented life. It is hard to imagine the context in which I could set out to check print sources on a children's book and wind up in sex poems inadvertently. The fact that Peter Rabbit can be located so unpredictably in that set of random juxtapositions we call the Internet demonstrates yet another way that he is clearly in the public domain, whatever his technical copyright position may be.

Either way, being sold to or being startled by sex, I found little on the Internet to enrich children's encounters with Peter Rabbit, though as usual there is nothing intrinsic to the medium which makes this prospect impossible.

CHAPTER 13

Implications

Peter Rabbit does not exist. He is a fiction. His material existence amounts to a small quantity of ink, paint and paper.

And yet, Peter Rabbit is an industrial reality. His existence, virtual though it may be at one level, fills lines on balance sheets and employs workers in many countries. He affects the price of shares on the stock market; his image provides wages for attendants in museums and exhibitions. He supports a substantial tourist industry and provides a major boost to the National Trust of Britain.

Peter Rabbit also exists, in a different kind of way, in the minds of little children. Their image of Peter Rabbit, however, is not the same as mine when I was a child. Their image of Peter Rabbit is fractured, multiple, shifting, decentered, perhaps above all unclosed—and yet, almost always, recognizably, the same character.

Fiction is an important part of most children's lives. It gives them ways to explore and understand the world. Their sense of how stories work comes to their aid when they begin to learn to read. And, as a consequence of their experiences with versions, their sense of story may very well be working in different ways from those of the adults around them.

The most rapid technological change is taking place in the West, but the revolution does not stop at the boundaries of the richer countries; I met a five-year-old in Zimbabwe whose great passion was for *Thomas the Tank Engine*, which he knew by way of a weekly television program. Technological change may permeate developing countries in more selective ways than in the West, but the stability of text which was taken for granted in childhood by almost anyone over the age of 40 is a thing of the past, world-wide. What are the implications of that shift, esthetically, pedagogically and academically?

THE ESTHETIC IMPLICATIONS OF FICTIONAL PLURALITY

Do stories work on us differently when they are put through a prism, refracted in one version after another, meeting us on varying terms of engagement which differ between one medium and another? It seems as if the answer must be affirmative; we can never erase all traces of one encounter with a text in order to approach it anew in a different format. Not only that, it seems reasonable to posit that we now also read those singular texts which exist only as texts in a slightly different way; this specifically limited route to a fiction is now only one possibility, no longer the norm, no longer completely taken for granted. Habitual ways of thinking probably camouflage this change for adults, but children take acute note of what is happening around them and formulate their own ways of paying attention.

It is possible indeed that young children, exposed to the range of texts on offer in today's bookstore or library or video outlet, develop a kind of rough-and-ready definition of a new canon: there are stories which are important enough to exist in multiple manifestations, and then there are the others which they may perceive as also-rans. Particularly in the case of a novel being made into a film or a television series, there is a specific ritual of canonization as the text passes into the new category; much publicity, possibly some commercial tie-ins and gimmicks at McDonald's, a sudden rush of associated texts and toys. Children attend to such ceremonies and draw their own conclusions about the importance of what is being marked. They may also notice, within themselves, qualities of engagement which differ between those texts offered in multiple formats and those texts which exist only singularly in print.

As well as altering the rules of intertextuality, many of the new developments also alter the rules of interaction with fiction. Lifting the flap, watching the mobile, playing the board game, assembling the theater figures, playing in the CD-ROM garden, meeting Peter Rabbit as a character in other fictions, all such operations enable readers to engage differently with the fictional world. For adults, whose awareness of the rules and protocols of fictionality is well established, these developments may not mean very much; for children, who are coming to terms with the whole idea of the fictional contract, the implications may be more far-reaching. The questions about what happens to a text rendered nonlinear and/or interactive in some or many of its versions are very important.

This issue, like many others over the course of this project, is illuminated as much by news items from the daily papers as by more theoretical studies. We are now told that movie theaters are about to become megacomplexes "replete with virtual reality and motion-based simulator games tied to the film" (Bourette and Grange, 1995, p. B1). In such a megacomplex there will barely be time to digest the movie in its linear form before the various agents of deconstruction are set in motion. Again, it seems plausible to suggest that the implications for children will be greater than for adults.

Even though it is a simple text, *The Tale of Peter Rabbit* in its many incarnations provides a case study of startlingly expansive dimensions and raises many important questions about fiction in contemporary society, about the role of the marketplace, and about the impact on children learning about their world.

AN ESTHETICS OF VERSIONS

In exploring a large number of renderings of *The Tale of Peter Rabbit* and a smaller number of texts which use the story as a starting point (the filmed ballet *Tales of Beatrix Potter, The New Adventures of Peter Rabbit, The Parables of Peter Rabbit, Dear Peter Rabbit*), I found myself asking certain questions over and over again. I want to explore some of these questions here.

First, there is the question, for want of a better way of expressing it, of what makes the quality of Peter-Rabbitness. Does Peter Rabbit really exist only in his specific words and pictures, as created by his author? It seems as if this cannot be the case, because otherwise we would not recognize any of the retellings—yet it is relatively straightforward to establish that certain qualities are lost irrevocably when the original balance of print and illustration in the original format is altered. With a text which has so long been stable, it seems possible to assert that no recast version contains *all* the qualities of Peter-Rabbitness which attend the original. A pure definition of Peter Rabbit, as it were, would involve the idea of a rabbit getting into trouble in a garden *as told and pictured by* Beatrix Potter in her small book.

The classic statement of the impact of the original work of art is probably that of Walter Benjamin in his essay, "The Work of Art in the Age of Mechanical Reproduction," first published in 1936. He says,

> Even the most perfect reproduction of a work of art is lacking in one element: its presence in time and space, its unique existence at the place where it happens to be. This unique existence of the work of art determined the history to which it was subject throughout the time of its existence. This includes the changes which it may have suffered in physical condition over the years as well as the various changes in ownership . . .
>
> The presence of the original is the prerequisite to the concept of authenticity . . . [T]echnical reproduction can put the copy of the original into situations which would be out of reach for the original itself. Above all, it enables the original to meet the beholder halfway, be it in the form of a photograph or a phonograph record. The cathedral leaves its locale to be received in the studio or a lover of art; the choral production, performed in an auditorium or in the open air, resounds in the drawing room.
>
> The situations into which the product of mechanical reproduction can be brought may not touch the actual work of art, yet the quality of its presence is always depreciated . . . The authenticity of a thing is the essence of all that is transmissible from its beginning, ranging from its substantive duration to its testimony to the history which it has experienced. Since the historical testimony rests on the authenticity, the former, too, is jeopardized by reproduction when substantive duration ceases to matter. And what is really jeopardized when the historical testimony is affected is the authority of the object.
>
> One might subsume the eliminated element in the term "aura" and go on to say: that which withers in the age of mechanical reproduction is the aura of the work of art. This is a symptomatic process whose significance points beyond the realm of art. One might generalize by saying: the technique of reproduction detaches the reproduced object from the domain of tradition. By making many reproductions it substitutes a plurality of copies for a unique existence. And in permitting the reproduction to meet the beholder or listener in his own particular situation, it reactivates the object reproduced. These two processes lead to a tremendous shattering of tradition. (1969, pp. 220–221)

The issue of "aura" is relatively straightforward when applied to a unique creation which is later reproduced, and of course there is no question that there are elements of Potter's original watercolors which cannot be transferred to a print by even the most sophisticated printing techniques. Nevertheless, the question of reproduction becomes more complex when applied to a work of art which is actually created to be reproduced. Perhaps there are, as it were, "degrees of aura;" such a suggestion would certainly help to explain the response of the auctioneer on the BBC *Antiques Road Show* television who encountered a rare signed first edition of *The Tale of Peter Rabbit*.

> "As soon as I saw it, I started shaking and had to put the book down," said Clive Farahar, the programme's book expert. "Another signed first edition was recently sold for £45,000 in the United States, but that was in much better condition and was inscribed to a member of the owner's family.
>
> "Because Beatrix Potter is so popular at the moment, I am sure this book would achieve at least £20,000–£25,000 at auction now."
>
> For the past four years, the book has been locked in a tin trunk in a boiler-room at the home of the owner, who wishes to remain anonymous.
>
> It had been left to her by her great aunt Daisy—Margaret Wilson—who was a contemporary of Beatrix Potter and had studied at the Slade School of Art. (£25,000 Peter Rabbit, 1995, p. 11)

The implications of this little story are complex. The book thus discovered was one of the original 250 copies which Potter herself had privately printed. Its provenance, history and tradition are as carefully described in the article as those of any one-off "original" would be. It is, of course, possible that the book expert began to shake simply because of the high financial value he was able to place upon this find, but that does seem like a heartless explanation; it seems more psychologically likely that he was responding to some version of "aura."

How much of this aura passes on to the "authentic" (or to use Warne's terminology, "original" and "authorized") texts which are mass-produced but which work from Potter's own plates? To what degree is that concept of aura or authenticity tied up with the identity of the particular author, and does the importance ascribed to that association increase when the number of imitations also rises?

Michel Foucault (1984) has considered the role of the author as a label:

> The author's name serves to characterize a certain mode of being, of discourse: the fact that the discourse has an author's name, that one can say "this was written by so-and-so" or "so-and-so is its author," shows that this discourse is not ordinary everyday speech that merely comes and goes, not something that is immediately consumable. On the contrary, it is a speech that must be received in a certain mode and that, in a given culture, must receive a certain status.
>
> It would seem that the author's name, unlike other proper names, does not pass from the interior of a discourse to the real and exterior individual who produced it; instead, the name seems always to be present, marking off the edges of the text, revealing, or at least characterizing, its mode of being. The author's name manifests the appearance of a certain discursive set and indicates the status of this discourse within a society and a culture. It has no legal status, nor is it located in the fiction of the work; rather, it is located in the break that founds a certain discursive construct and its very particular mode of being. As a result, we could say that in a civilization like our own there are a certain number of discourses that are endowed with the "author function," while others are deprived of it. A private letter may well have a signer—it does not have an author; a contract may well have a guarantor—it does not have an author. An anonymous text posted on a wall probably has a writer—but not an author. The author function is therefore characteristic of the mode of existence, circulation, and functioning of certain discourses within a society. (pp. 107–108)

It seems relatively clear that Potter's name is an important part of what makes Peter Rabbit a viable cultural counter; the insistence with which her name is prominently displayed on many of the pirate editions suggests that they want to use that stamp of authority to enter their work into a particular exchange of discourse. Foucault, of course, is not dealing with the idea that such authority may in effect be a forgery. The number of texts of *Peter Rabbit* which stress the Potter connection does suggest, however, that such a stamp of authority does contribute to some sense of aura, however attenuated or falsely based it may be.

As so often in the Peter Rabbit story, however, there is an example to contradict any general conclusion. My indefatigable daughter found a copy of *The Tale of Peter Rabbit* in a store that specializes in taking "historical" photographs of tourists. Published by Gallery Graphics of Missouri in 1993 and printed in Hong Kong, this large-scale picture book uses Potter's words and the pictures of an unknown artist. Beatrix Potter's name appears nowhere, but the book cover is full of references to the antique and classic nature of the story. It claims to be a "version of the original antique book," but gives no publication information about this original text. The back cover lauds the virtues of the Gallery Gold (TM) Little Classics, saying, "All books are reproduced from the original Antique Lithograph. Collect the complete series of Little Classics." The sample titles include fairy tales, an ABC and *The Night Before Christmas*, and it is clear once again that Peter Rabbit is a creature of the public domain as well as a particular creation of Beatrix Potter. In this case, a kind of all-purpose antiquarianism would seem to be providing an aura of sorts.

The singularity and uniqueness of a particular work of art may still be an issue, even when the world is full of equivalently authentic reproductions. *The Tale of Peter Rabbit* in a version approved by its author (small book, page design, complete text, authorized page turns, etc.) is perceived differently from a text which contains some or many but not all of the original ingredients. William H. Gass provides a metaphor for the work of art which suggests something of the dimensions of the problem:

> On the other side of a novel lies the void. Think, for instance, of a striding statue; imagine the purposeful inclination of the torso, the alert and penetrating gaze of the head and its eyes, the outstretched arm and pointing finger; everything would appear to direct us toward some goal in front of it. Yet our eye travels only to the finger's end, and not beyond. Though pointing, the finger bids us stay instead, and we journey slowly back along the tension of the arm. In our hearts we know what actually surrounds the statue. The same surrounds every other work of art: empty space and silence. (1979, p. 49)

The Tale of Peter Rabbit, as created by Beatrix Potter, sits both literally and metaphorically in its own white space, created as a complete work of art on its own terms. Gass's is a highly romantic description and one which ignores the social, economic and cultural roots of any work of art, but it does help us to contemplate some of the issues which arise when such a work is translated into other terms, not once but many times. It is a tribute to the artistic power of the original that any sense of its free-standing powers survives the pressure of numerous reiterations.

But what of the derivative versions? Do they stand alone, perhaps in a slightly different surround of "empty space and silence" or are they dependent (even parasitic) on the first text? It seems to me that there are at least two ways that a secondary text may be successful within the terms of this discussion. It may succeed in a completely free-standing way, making its own terms of engagement with the world, so that the original text is rendered if not unnecessary, at least an optional extra. The televised version of *The Jewel in the Crown* provides an example of this kind of achievement. I did not find a complete example of this kind of success among the many texts of *Peter Rabbit*; the Warne animation, for all its weaknesses, probably comes closest to this model, and some of the pop-up books do succeed on their own modest terms. Alternatively, the secondary text can make positive and creative use of its dependency; the Potter ballet is the obvious example of this kind of work in the *Peter Rabbit* collection. In the terms of Gass's statue metaphor, the derivative work of art may include the primary text as part of its overall universe, so that the texts work in combination. But, to stretch Gass's parallel a little further, what many new versions do is simply "point" to the original, saying in effect, "Look, there's a better or more famous statue over there."

Any new version probably involves some form of trade-off. What is startling in this case, though it would not necessarily be the same with every text, is how few of these trade-offs seem to offer a balance of something new and worthwhile in exchange for the loss involved in moving away from the original text.

This view, of course, is only my opinion. The Ladybird publishers, the animators of the authorized cartoon, and the producers of "Family Classics from the Stars," to take just three examples, would undoubtedly argue that the trade-off involves greater access to the story for those unfamiliar with it; and this is not an argument to be taken lightly, although the statue metaphor highlights some of the problems with this justification. My condemnation of the animation, in particular, is a personal judgement not supported by such critical accounts as I have been able to discover. And there are undoubtedly people who would make a more generic argument that the destabilization of text involved in the creation of different versions is a contemporary inevitability and a liberation from the stifling restrictions of the past.

Whatever the outcome of such an argument, there is still a case to be made for holding the recasters accountable for what they have made of their reproductions. A useful ground-rule for assessing new versions of an old text might involve the way in which the new producers have considered the limits of their material. In the case of an adaptation, the first set of limits is that which attends the original story. Alterations to the original should have some point and purpose to them. Substitutions should work intelligently and subtly, grappling with the overall issues (described both as presences and as absences or gaps) involved in the original text. Simply saying what the book does not say (as is the case, for example, with Peter Rabbit's several reminders to himself about the pie, in the Warne animation) can be heavy-handed and uninteresting. The forces of ambiguity in the original text need to be respected and to be given their due importance in the new version.

Seymour Chatman, who has done a great deal of work on the conversion of print narrative to film, says, "Film adaptations often face a familiar charge: that they fill in too many gaps" (1990, p. 161). In the terms often used by critics, he says, this charge "seems a little unreasonable" (1990, p. 161). Films do not stimulate the visual imagination in the same way as print, because the visual element in the story is made determinate and specific on the screen in a way which is impossible on the page (though more possible in a picture book than in any other, of course). Other aspects of storytelling may be far more difficult to convey on the screen.

> Though the visual imagination may be less stimulated by a film than by a novel, the conceptual imagination may be very much stimulated by, say, a face filled with emotion that goes unexplained by dialogue or diegetic context. In a way, the challenge is greater, and our capacity to interpret faces is not innately up to our capacity to image from words. Film has just as much room for artistic gapping—though

it is an artistry of its own. In some cases, the film is better suited to a subject than the novel that inspired it.

Still, good film adaptations of good novels are not a plentiful commodity, for reasons that are of narratological interest. The central problem for film adapters is to transform narrative features that come easily to language but hard to a medium that operates in "real time" and whose natural focus is the surface appearance of things—hence film's traditional difficulties with temporal and spatial summaries, abstract narratorial commentary, representations of the thinking and feeling of characters, and so on. (1990, p. 162)

As Chatman's remarks demonstrate, our reflections on adaptations can call on a theoretical framework supported by detailed examples in the area of film studies, to take the most obvious example. The case of *Peter Rabbit*, however, also offers examples of reworkings in fields far too trivial, too ephemeral or too new to attract the attention of theorists and critics. Is it worth the time and energy which would be required to explore the theoretical implications of turning a text into an activity book? If we decide that the answer to that question is no, we must still pay heed to the practical and pedagogical implications of a social and cultural arrangement which bombards children with very many fragments of their favorite stories. Individually, each example may mean little; the cumulative effect is overwhelming and important. And every straw in the wind seems to be blowing in the same direction: this multiplication of text "bits" is going to increase rather than decline.

New media also deserve critical and theoretical attention. In my view, the CD-ROM produced by Discis with Warne's permission (the disk which basically just transfers the page of print onto the screen) does very little justice either to *The Tale of Peter Rabbit* or to the artistic and intellectual potential inherent in the CD-ROM format. How many such examples of timid practice must we accumulate in this field before we have a trend worthy of theoretical study? And how, in the meantime, do we adjust our practices to take account of the changes happening so quickly in the world where we join our children in trying to make sense of the new?

There is another way in which fiction for children is breaking ground new for everybody, not simply jumping on board an adult bandwagon. Unlike adult fiction, children's stories, with attendant forces of commodification and marketing, are making transitions in many directions. Consider the genesis of many popular children's narratives of the past ten years. The Teenage Mutant Ninja Turtles started life in a comic book. The Flintstones moved from animated cartoon to live action film. SuperMario began life as a Nintendo game but ended up in film as well. Garfield the cat began life as a strip comic, and has moved so far into the territory of domestic consumption that he now adorns a bag of cat litter presently sitting in my kitchen. The Mighty Morphin' Power Rangers and Barney the Dinosaur began as television programs. As a kind of apotheosis of this process, the movie *Toy Story* was developed from preexisting toys and then recommodified. Print may be involved in some or many of the spin-offs involving these stories, but it is not the primary source. The plurality at work in the marketing operations puts pressure on the singular version in a way which does not yet occur in the adult market.

Disney provides perhaps the largest range of examples of adaptations from the world of print, but there are many other examples of literary characters holding their own in this wide-ranging field of salesmanship which operates simultaneously in the world we describe as real and in the terms of a fictional universe. Print may not be the exclusive or even the major source of fictional "supersystems," but it has certainly established its right to participate in the domain of hype. The implications of this fact for children today and adults tomorrow may be very significant.

The Importance of Hand and Eye

Aidan Chambers has an interesting point to make about how children's approach to books differs qualitatively from that of adults:

> What is the mystery of the page? Young children, when they are learning to read, demonstrate one aspect of it that literary adults often forget. They chew books, and hug them and paw at the pages. One of the reasons the page is so important is that it is tactile. The book, an object made of pages, is designed for holding in the hand; the binding is designed so that the pages can be turned. The physicality of book reading, its appeal to our fingers, is hardly at all attended to by researchers into reading. In earlier times, when the book was dominant, this didn't matter. Now that there is a variety of electronic print that does not involve pages, the book's touchability does matter,

makes it special and different, and needs to be thought about. (1995,
p. 251)

Chambers' reminder about the importance of touch in relationship
to understanding is an important one, although I believe he
underestimates the different forms of touch involved in other media. As
with so many other topics in this area, there is a great deal which we do
not know. It is possible to relate to computer text or CD-ROM with a
mouse or a joystick; are there implications in the fact that such a
relationship normally involves only one hand (and maybe one side of
the brain)? Film allows for no tactile engagement, but television and
video now offer the option of manual connection via the remote
control. Is the importance of tactile engagement one reason for the
arguments which seem universally to attend family discussions about
who controls the remote? Toys and activity books necessarily involve
many "hands-on" operations; is this fact intellectually as well as
manually important? What is the difference between "pretend" play
which engages the whole body and play with toy proxies where only
the hands are involved? Does the plethora of miniature toys, especially
but not exclusively aimed at girls, have an impact on learning about
make-believe disproportionately through the hands rather than through
a bodily acting out?

Chambers perhaps romanticizes the importance of the page to the
touch. There are many circumstances in which the rule concerning
books is *noli me tangere*. Historically, the norm was for one text to be
read aloud to many people, whether in church, coffee house, or family
drawing room. Small children do chew and tear their books; for this
reason, they are often the book users least likely to be allowed to hold
the page in their hands. There are many impoverished communities
around the world today where literacy involves reading print in a book,
but where the amount of physical contact between reader and text is
necessarily slight; and often, use of a slate or writing paper or even a
stick in the dirt replaces most of the tactile relationship with an already
printed text.

Nevertheless, there remains a question about whether narrative is
differently received and processed when the hand as well as the eye or
the ear is involved. If this is even slightly the case, does it impinge on
the reception of different versions of a core story? Do all fictional
experiences, whether seen, heard, or fiddled with manually, eventually

contribute amorphously to the overall sense of story which most human beings develop? Or is there some form of mental differentiation of the route by which a narrative is experienced? Or both?

The Importance of Conventions

Seymour Chatman (1990) rightly argues that film has its own conventions and its own "gaps." The same can be said for other forms in which narrative fiction can be conveyed. The study of *Peter Rabbit* has revealed the rich potential for a transfer from text into a different medium to lead on to further extrapolations; the spin-offs from the official animation provide the largest range of materials, but it is actually quite difficult to find any version which stops at a single text. There are a number of packages involving video, audio and print (Warne's own authorized versions, of course, but also the Rabbit Ears package of "Family Classics from the Stars" with the David Jorgensen illustrations and *The New Adventures of Peter Rabbit*). There are activity books which trumpet their relationship to the original text and those which stress their linkage to the animation. The clothes, the china and the stuffed toys largely rely on the Potter originals and, for the most part, their prices would seem to reflect the snob value attached to the idea of a "classic."

Each version must find a way of dealing with the constraints of its own method of production. In some cases, as with an activity book based on the animation which reworks the original text, a number of sets of conventions are at work. In many cases of *Peter Rabbit* examples, what we find is that the demands of convention (sometimes combined with the demands of didacticism or the need to make the item sound like a persuasive investment) have triumphed over the need to make the story interesting within the terms of its new format.

Aidan Chambers quotes John Berger: "Authenticity comes from a single faithfulness: that to the ambiguity of experience" (Chambers, 1995, p. 250). Berger is writing about singular works of print literature, and it is an interesting question whether that faithfulness can remain single in the process of adaptation. It is important to acknowledge the ambiguity of experience, but in the case of an adaptation, it is an issue of ambiguity *as already expressed*. The case of *Peter Rabbit* provides a clear example of many transfers in which the ambiguity of Potter's original attitude to Peter's transgression has been hopelessly lost in the process of reworking. Presumably, in at least some cases, what has been expressed instead is the adaptor's own belief, which may be described for our purposes as an assumption that disobedience is always reprehensible even when understandable. It might even be possible (though there are few examples in the *Peter Rabbit* collection) to express this view with subtlety and suppleness; the question is whether such an expression violates the terms of the original text.

The challenge of adaptation, in Berger's terms, may be described as an issue of whether the creator is to be faithful to his or her own understanding of ambiguity or to the original creator's. The answer may not be clear-cut. There are few good examples of *Peter Rabbit* providing a starting impetus for a thoroughly reimagined work of art, but I do not find it impossible to imagine a case where Potter's own dry ambivalence about morality provided a starting point but not a finishing point for a different author.

In any case of adaptation, Berger's call for faithfulness to the ambiguity of experience should somehow be coupled with a respect for the original artist's take on the world. The new work must also allow for the strengths, weaknesses and conventions of its own format, using them to reexpress what is said and not said in the original work. There is no such thing as eliminating all the gaps in the old text by means of the new text; all that can happen is that the nature of the gaps will change. An intelligent appreciation of how to make use of absences in the new version is one of the features which contributes to a good adaptation.

Talking about the way any single adaptation is composed from an original text is an operation which still retains some vestiges of singularity. What of the reader/listener/viewer/player? What of the consumer of numerous versions of a single story? As the encounters with different versions of the same text mount up, it may well be that attending to different kinds of absence in different forms eventually adds up to a gap-reduced experience, as it were, a kind of palimpsest effect in which one version provides closure for an aspect of the text left open in another. Is this a plus or a minus for the experiencer?

There is undoubtedly not a single right answer to that question. I found my own experience with *Peter Rabbit* interesting in this regard. For the most part, I was annoyed by texts which crudely attempted to fill gaps best left unspecified in my opinion. When it came to an alternate text of real subtlety, the ballet *Tales of Beatrix Potter,* however, my attitude was very different. The character of Peter Rabbit is not developed in any way in this ballet, so I must talk about my reaction to other stories. It is easier to do so in metaphorical terms; I found, for example, that my response to *The Tale of Pigling Bland* involved a sensation that the gaps had been multiplied rather than closed in. Instead of the new version filling in the blanks of the old one, it took those blanks and added its own; for instance, the convention that ballet dancers never speak meant that gestures had to convey ideas of considerable subtlety. The overall effect was one of an elaborate fretwork of gaps which had to be closed by my own powers of inference—which meant that every time I looked anew, the effect of the fretwork was still there, lacy and delicate. The most crashing contrast in the entire collection of *Peter Rabbit* versions, I think (though there is considerable competition), comes in the *Fun to Learn* magazine, asking in as heavy-handed a way as possible, "Did Peter learn his lesson?"

There are many examples in the *Peter Rabbit* oeuvre where the conventions and stereotypes associated with a particular format would seem to have triumphed over the organic needs and demands of the text itself. The talking robin in the Warne animation, the "participatory" question ruining the poster in the *Fun to Learn* magazine, the manipulation of pictures in the pop-up book so that continuity and sequence are sacrificed to layout on the page, the misapplication of inappropriate tunes to the china wind-ups—these are just a few of the ways in which stereotypes of format have downgraded the integrity of the original account of Peter Rabbit. In both esthetic and pedagogical terms, it seems to me that this is a territory rife with peril for developing readers and appreciators of literature. One of Potter's strong points as an artist is the way in which she rejects the obvious development in favor of "the shock of the new." If your contact with Potter's text is mediated by an avuncular talking robin, a species of character already familiar to you from countless other animations, you lose out in many ways. You lose the specific pleasures of reticence and understatement which attend the original text. Your access to the idea that there are many different ways of mediating a story is also reduced if the same kinds of stereotype appear in every text you encounter (this, of course, is one of the main charges against Disney). It is not exactly fair to call it a question of lowest common denominator; there is nothing *inherently* wrong with the character of the robin. Nevertheless, the approach involves a tactic of levelling down to the commonplace and the familiar which is particularly unsettling in the case of an artist like Potter who did not patronize her readers with a commonplace approach.

QUESTIONS OF IDEOLOGY

Teasing out the ideological threads of a text as subtle and sophisticated as the original *Tale of Peter Rabbit* is a complex undertaking in itself. Is Potter on Peter's side or on the side of law and order and Mr. McGregor? Or is she offering a more detached observation on the nature of nature, as it were, on the need for rabbits to dig up vegetables regardless of the consequences? If the latter (which does seem a more plausible interpretation of the book), does this detachment carry its own ideological freight about the relationship between rabbit protagonists and human author? How much ideological weight attaches to the author's address to the readers? Is Potter presupposing a particular kind of readership or offering reading "lessons" in creating a particular kind of approach to a book?

These questions become at once more complicated and more straightforward when we begin to look at the range of alternative versions of the story. At one level, a text like *The Parables of Peter Rabbit* illuminates the subtlety of the original by the light of the crude ideological overlay, in this case of fundamentalist Christianity. A very different kind of text, the filmed ballet of *The Tales of Beatrix Potter*, offers a different form of commentary; as a friend of mine has rightly observed, whatever is gained or lost in this retelling, one element of the original production which is recreated very successfully is the appeal to a sophisticated audience. The degree to which the ballet, like the original book, actually develops the needed sophistication in its viewers/readers is a testimonial to the striking qualities in the overlapping nature of the address to the audience.

Peter Hollindale has explored some of the important issues concerning ideology in children's literature. He talks about three levels of ideology, and all three can usefully be investigated in the context of the many versions of *Peter Rabbit*.

Ideology, then, is present in a children's book in three main ways. The first and most tractable is made up of the explicit social, political

or moral beliefs of the individual writer, and his wish to recommend
them to children through the story . . .

It is at this level of intended surface ideology that fiction carries
new ideas, non-conformist or revolutionary attitudes, and efforts to
change imaginative awareness in line with contemporary social
criticism. (1988, pp. 10–11)

The importation of conscious and explicit ideology into the story of
Peter Rabbit is carried out in many of the texts produced by hands other
than Potter's, some authorized by Frederick Warne and some published
without that authority. The domestication of Peter Rabbit and his
enrollment in the cause of enforcing childish obedience is relatively
commonplace. His more egregious conscription as an agent of assertive
Christianity seems almost parodic in its aggressive extrapolation of a
few surface essentials from the original story; Peter is lonely because
Flopsy and Cotton-tail have moved to the meadow, so he is glad of his
new friends. For the most part, however, every detail which survives
the transfer to *The Parables of Peter Rabbit* is stood on its head: even
the vegetables are transformed into actors in their own right, with their
own singing and dancing routines. The whole video raises questions of
the degree to which readers need to reach a working assessment of the
author's intention; it would be extremely easy to view this film as a
caricature, but all the external and internal evidence suggests that its
creators were extremely serious in their project.

Hollindale distinguishes between overt and covert ideology and
suggests that,

> in literature as in life the undeserved advantage lies with *passive*
> ideology. The second category of ideological content which we must
> thus take into account is the individual writer's unexamined
> assumptions. As soon as these are admitted to be relevant, it becomes
> impossible to confine ideology to a writer's conscious intentions or
> articulated messages, and necessary to accept that all children's
> literature is inescapably didactic. (1988, p. 12)

Children's literature, Hollindale suggests, represents and even
embodies an important part of what adults hope to teach the next
generation. The values taken for granted in any given text may slide

into the assumptions of the child reader in an unquestioned and unquestioning way.

> This is merely to accept what is surely obvious: writers for children (like writers for adults) cannot hide what their values are. Even if beliefs are passive and unexamined and no part of any conscious proselytising, the texture of language and story will reveal them and communicate them. The working of ideology at this level is not incidental or unimportant . . . Unexamined, passive values are widely *shared* values, and we should not underestimate the powers of reinforcement vested in quiescent and unconscious ideology. (1988, pp. 12–13)

Thus in Potter's *Peter Rabbit*, we may, to take one obvious example, see the assumption that girls are more likely to be obedient slide through in an almost invisible form until readers begin to pay conscious attention to that particular detail.

When we get to commercial remakes of an original text, we may find it difficult to disentangle ideological and commercial considerations. The Warne animation redresses the balance between the sexes by giving Peter's sisters a small amount of gumption (though they still giggle and backbite in a way that could be described as stereotypically feminine). On the other hand, it allows its hero to speak with an American accent. Is this an invisible ideological assumption that American will do perfectly well in the circumstances, or a carefully calculated commercial decision that the largest quantity of home sales will be in the United States?

Hollindale's third element of ideology rests on the tenor of the age.

> The individual writer is likely, as we have seen, to make conscious choices about the explicit ideology of his work, while the uniqueness of imaginative achievements rests on the private, unrepeatable configurations which writers make at subconscious level from the common stock of their experience. Our habit is so much to cherish individualism, however, that we often overlook the huge commonalities of an age, and the captivity of mind we undergo by living in our own time and place and no other. A large part of any book is written not by its author but by the world its author lives in. To accept the point one has only to recognize the rarity of occasions

when a writer manages to recolor the meaning of a single word: almost all the time we are the acquiescent prisoners of other people's meanings. As a rule, writers for children are transmitters not of themselves uniquely, but of the worlds they share. (1988, p. 15)

Peter Rabbit, in his original incarnation, inhabits a world which is recognizably late Victorian/early Edwardian, a fact which is even truer of other Potter characters. Some of what we now value about the story, maybe even some of its "aura" develops from our response to the window it offers on another time.

The alternative versions of the story, especially those which aspire to do more than offer a limited form of copycat approach, equally offer windows on their own times in ways which are sometimes obvious and sometimes oblique. It has been noticeable to me, showing versions of different retellings to a wide variety of people, that those reworkings which date from times now recognizably past offer elements of their own nostalgia to individuals. Thus it is that at least some readers looking at the Grosset and Dunlop "animated" pull-the-tab book from the 1940s are taken with the now old-fashioned drawing, the cheap paper, the crude images—not for any esthetic virtues on offer, but for reasons of sheer nostalgia for the often inadequate books of their childhood. Similarly, I find myself approaching the Little Little Golden Book, which was originally produced in 1958, with a decidedly less stern attitude than that which marks my approach to some other retellings, because I actually enjoy the relentlessly 1950s-housewife apron, pearls and pose of Mrs. Rabbit, even as I reject most of what she implicitly stands for and do not long for the time when women put on their housedresses and high heels to look after their children.

The complexities of such built-in associations with a particular time are compounded not only when it comes to questions of reinterpreting an already given text, but also when it is clear that the inextricable associations with a particular time are part of what fuels an enormous marketing campaign. The intangible associations with a perceived golden age are clearly a major factor in the contemporary selling of Beatrix Potter; it is hard to stand back from that overwhelming factor and reach any disinterested conclusions. I may be revolted by the assumptions implicit in many Potter books that everyone in society has a rightful place and trespasses at his or her own peril; equally I may be revolted by the way these assumptions are now "sold" to us as something desirable even if lost. Disentangling those responses is a complex and perhaps impossible endeavor.

This complication leads me to question whether there is a further level of ideological encounter with any particular text. Can the conditions of presentation of the text be subtracted from any interpretation? Certainly, it is now difficult to consider the ideological baggage of *Peter Rabbit* outside of the conditions within which we make its acquaintance. *Peter Rabbit* is now part of an enormous sales pitch; how do we, or should we, eliminate this factor in weighing the implications of the text in any particular society?

Similarly, there is a question about whether or not it is possible to subtract the format of the presentation from the way we receive it. Robin Buss (1992) raises an interesting point about whether we may accept the ideology implicit in *The Tale of Peter Rabbit* in ways that are affected by whether the format is congruent with the time of its initial production or is more contemporary, appealing to current sensibilities.

> The films . . . takes [*sic*] the story out of the child's grasp and delivers it into the grown-up screen world.
>
> Here, it shifts in time, from late Victorian storybook to late 20th-century screen product; and, as such, invites questions we may not previously have thought to ask: is it politically correct, for example, for Peter to have the adventures and his sisters Flopsy, Mopsy and Cottontail to pick blackberries? Is the fact that one of the girls stains her apron, suggesting that they are not just goody-goodies, enough to salve the contemporary conscience? (p. 33)

ISSUES OF THE MARKETPLACE

Art, of course, rarely exists in a financial vacuum. Beatrix Potter herself was glad of a chance to establish an independent source of income which emancipated her, to some degree, from the stifling restrictions of the life of an unmarried Victorian gentlewoman. Her financial circumstances certainly affected her enthusiasm for marketing Peter Rabbit commodities. Many of the early decisions about pagination and pictures took financial implications into account; most of the alterations in Warne's early printings of *The Tale of Peter Rabbit* were organized to allow for monetary considerations of one kind or another.

Nevertheless, it is possible to argue that financial motives seem to play a more dominant role in publishing decisions nowadays, in children's literature as in other forms of publication. Undoubtedly a number of factors have worked together to affect the contemporary market for children's fiction and its attendant trappings.

Stephen Kline (1993) argues that the deregulation of children's television which occurred in the United States during the Reagan administration was a major element in changing fiction for children. With the advent of program-length commercials, the role of the story in selling the goods altered radically, and the number of goods to be sold rose in correlation. While such levels of commodification may have started with television programs, it is obvious that the publishers of print literature have not been slow to see the potential for expanding the range of commodities they offer.

Simultaneously, the great wave of publisher takeovers accelerated in the 1980s. There is an enormous amount of testimony to the ways in which new ownership affected publishing decisions; the bottom line became more important than ever before and gambles which once would have been possible were ruled out. It is easy to sneer at the gentlemanly role of the prewar publisher, but the individual decisions of an Allan Lane or a Frederick Warne do read rather more heroically than the ready references in current business analyses to the "exploitation of content and copyright."

At the same time, trends in public services have played their part, at least in Western societies. With a crunch in public spending, both public and school libraries have often found themselves with reduced budgets; school libraries in particular have also lost librarian time. Librarians play many roles with children and books; in particular, they often stand as mediators, making selections in advance of the children's choice, weeding out much of the kind of material I have explored in this project. It was noticeable, when I tried to obtain a copy of the 1987 Ladybird *Peter Rabbit* by interlibrary loan, that both my public library and my university library had to travel very far afield to acquire a copy for me; all the nearby libraries had never selected this version. It is possible to argue for and against the role of such a filtering process, but its decline does make a difference to the ways in which books and other materials are marketed.

With library budgets under attack, publishers, who for a long time had relied on such institutional support, found themselves in the position of having to appeal directly to the public. The ongoing paperback revolution was a factor here as well; it is much easier to appeal to a child's taste and pocketbook with a cheap paperback. And developments in other technologies have clearly played an important role in the kinds of changes we are witnessing today.

Not all the consequences of this concatenation of circumstances have been bad. New writers, new books, new approaches, to beginning readers and teenagers in particular, have all appeared in the past 20 years. Nevertheless, it is clearly fair to say that not all the changes in the publishing industry involve a disinterested analysis of what child readers need and want. And it is often the case that the multiple reworkings of particular texts reduce one of the most important elements in the whole book marketing world: space on the bookstore shelf. Once it was one of the objections to Enid Blyton that her numerous works filled up too much of the space available for selling other better books. Now fictional works that were once part of the solution are perceived as part of the problem. Nicholas Tucker describes the situation succinctly:

> Books once created characters; now increasingly it is newly licensed characters who are producing books. Pooh Bear, Barbie Doll, Peter Rabbit and various other childhood celebrities now stride through the bookshops like all-engulfing monsters, spawning multitudes of forgettable spin-off titles plus assorted merchandise in their wake. Those new authors and illustrators normally expected to create characters for the next generation of readers meanwhile find it increasingly hard to get published and then stay in print. (1997, p. 25)

IMPLICATIONS FOR CHILDREN

Fictionality

In learning to listen to stories and then to read, children must learn, among other things, to imagine with words. With many of their stories today, that kind of imaginative engagement is often supplemented by props: toys, games, artifacts resembling those used by the fictional characters, and so forth. It is important to remember that different children may respond differently to the same kinds of experience with such objects. The ability to play with officially endorsed spin-off toys or dolls may intensify children's engagement with a story, or it may simply diminish the importance of the verbal element, or it may be neutral, or any of a number of alternatives, which may vary from one child to another.

Learning about how a fictional world relates to the real world is an important project for children. Ellen Winner suggests that the most basic component of story-making which children must tackle from the outset "is the construction of a boundary between the fictional world of the story and the everyday world of reality" (1982, p. 318).

Children's developing awareness of the fictionality of fiction may be routed differently according to their experiences. How fictional is Thomas the Tank Engine when, in your hand, you hold a real and solid toy which is more or less identical to the image in the book or on the screen? A plastic toy and a line drawing from an animation can be close to identical, much more so than, for example, a plush toy and a watercolor picture; does the latter combination lead to the development of a more sophisticated concept of representation than the former? McDonald's is a real place, but also a site of some ceremonial importance in the lives of many children; does a plastic toy from McDonald's bring its own ritual trappings to the complex intertextual mix which builds up a child's understanding of fiction?

Children have always used their games to develop, focus and practice their sense of make-believe. A narrative fiction draws on that sense of make-believe in developing the pragmatic contract between text and reader. When commercial considerations are built into the game-playing, when consumption becomes part of the ritual of engaging with a fiction, how is that pragmatic contract affected? Are the commercial ingredients simply subsumed in an overwhelming need to engage in the fictional world? Do they become part of the pragmatics surrounding the primary fictional engagement? There are adult readers, for example, who are not willing to surrender to a fiction unless they know it comes from some commercially validated source such as a bestseller list; it is this sort of mentality which concerns Tom Engelhardt (1991), looking at how children read today. What does seem clear is that the changing nature and expanding scope of fictional offerings to children entail many complicated questions.

Engagement

Having learned some of the elementary rules of engagement with fiction, children often then engage with great intensity. Paula M. Salvio provides the account of an adult student recalling a book which strongly affected her as a child.

> I fell in love with a book in the third grade. I no longer can remember the title or the author's name, but I can remember the story in vivid detail . . . I don't remember reading another book the whole year. I became consumed with the story. When I wasn't reading the book, I was dreaming about being a character in the book. After each new reading, I would add a new embellishment to the story. Sometimes I was the little girl, sometimes I was the nice young nun. At other times, I made up a character: I would be a friend of the little girl at the orphanage. My character would try and help the girl find her family. Or the new character would secretly be the little girl's older sister. (1995, p. 11, ellipsis in original)

This same student, Kathy Rogers, draws a more general portrait of herself as a child reader:

> The common thread that tied all the books together was the way I read each of them. I didn't just decode lexicons: Oh no, I crawled inside the pages, elbowed my way through the words, and made a space for myself in-between the lines. I was able to connect and move with the words. I lived the life and emotions of the characters. I would engage characters in a conversation, change the story-line, or imagine them in different situations. (Salvio, 1995, p. 11)

This kind of reading could be either augmented or disturbed by props of toys and dolls related to the text. Does the fact that we cannot specify individual outcomes neutralize the impact of commodification in a more general sense? The answer will obviously be different for different children, but Salvio goes on to make a point about Kathy Rogers' reading practices which seems to me to be very relevant:

> Kathy not only slips between the complex lines of her books, she inhabits them. In this passage, which captures Kathy's habit of

dwelling in a text and coming to know the characters through imagined conversations and improvisations, she remembers using her body as a vehicle for interpretation. Yet while Kathy reads imaginatively and with feeling, she reads alone, amidst classmates who silently read beside her. Kathy's readings are set apart from public scrutiny; they are housed in a private location, cloistered, so to speak, for she learns early on to self-regulate her emotional responses to literature by keeping them to herself. (1995, p. 11)

Toys, games and artifacts may open more of a child's engagement with text to social reenactment. It is an area about which we know too little; children have obviously always played games based on their familiar stories. And there is nothing about a set of toys which would eliminate the kind of intense in-dwelling experience described by Kathy Rogers; indeed, the reverse may be true and it may be that a set of connected toys actually encourages such a form of commitment to a fiction.

Clearly, the issue is complex, but it seems important to render it at least visible. Shelby Anne Wolf and Shirley Brice Heath (1992) provide one example of a child's developing response to story over a number of years, but their guidance is only partially useful here because they describe a child who was deliberately kept away from television, let alone other forms of multimedia. Nevertheless, they make some interesting points about how children may engage with a text.

A text that is known to a child does not remain in its original state or even in a steady, stable form; instead, the child rewrites it. Texts become transformative stock to which young readers can return again and again as they figure out their own roles, words, actions, and critiques of their current situations. In addition, literary words amplify in memorable chunks the language abilities of children, who know the appropriate emotions to express but who may yet be unable to formulate complete grammatical utterances or call up precise, politely acceptable words. (pp. 109–111)

There are many things we do not know. If children come in contact with an incident, say, of *Thomas the Tank Engine*, recreated in many formats (text, simplified text, video, audio) with very little permissible change in terms of plot and character, does that foster or retard a capacity to rework privately for themselves? Does it matter if their model of reimagining is a limited and exploitative one? And to whom? Barry Diller (1995) makes a distinction between repackaging and redefining.

> Taking a movie like *Jurassic Park* and turning it into a videogame— that's repackaging. Taking a bestseller and putting it on tape—that's repackaging. Taking magazine articles and slapping them online, word for word—that's repackaging. And if you think this is the work of the "New World," you're kidding yourselves. It's more like strip mining. After you've extracted the riches from the surface, there's nothing left—and you're probably too tired to do any real development . . . Redefine, don't repackage. Redefining the mission of your ventures is slow, brain-bending work. (p. 83)

Many children are given a model of reworking texts which is all too close to the concept of strip mining. In some cases, their imaginations will triumph regardless, but in other cases they will not. Is this important? If it is, how should we attend to the implications?

The New Adventures of Peter Rabbit is a text which refines Diller's argument. In one way, this production can hardly be called a case of strip mining; the producers have indeed redefined the territory and the mission. The problem is that they have done it both badly and dishonestly. Like the 1987 Ladybird edition of *Peter Rabbit*, the *New Adventures* proves that reimagining is a necessary but not a sufficient condition of adaptation. The creators of the *New Adventures* have not reimagined the world of *The Tale of Peter Rabbit* in any coherent or careful way; they are not strip-mining in Diller's sense of simply exploiting the surface plot, but they are certainly running a bulldozer through the garden. What do children learn about reimagining from this clumsy assault on a good story? What are the implications for teaching a child who has already learned in front of the home video that it is okay to substitute slapstick for subtlety?

Closure

Engaging with a story is something which children must learn how to do. They also need to learn something about how to exit from a fictional world. Children's reading behaviors reflect their awareness of strategies available to them at the end of a story. They can read it all over again, at once or later; they can find books which are part of a series and have more of that universe available in another title; they can continue the story in their own imaginations or in their games. Nowadays, there are other options: they can turn to the same story, or a story involving the same characters, in a different medium.

As with very many other aspects of the early stages of reading, we know relatively little about the ways in which children saturate themselves in a particular fiction, and about the ways in which such behavior may affect their ability to come to terms with closure. We know even less about how an abundance of related texts and toys might affect children's development in this regard.

The question of closure is one of great importance to children, and not always in ways we can anticipate. Jerome Bruner (1990) suggests that some aspects of narrative are built into a child's very early understanding of the world.

> The young child, moreover, is early and profoundly sensitive to "goals" and their achievement—and to variants of such expressions as "all gone" for completion and "uh oh" for incompletion. People and their actions dominate the child's interest and attention. This is the first requirement of narrative. (p. 78)

Children learn to apply these concepts to whatever texts are available. I watched a two-year-old observing his sister play Nintendo. He had a vocabulary of very few words and he certainly did not have the dexterity to manipulate the controls, but he knew enough about the action that when Mario died, he chipped in with an acknowledgement of a break in the story: "Uh oh!"

Ann Trousdale (1989) tells the story of Christie, aged two and a half, being read the Disney version of "The Three Little Pigs," in which the wolf does not actually eat the pigs and is not actually eaten himself.

> We turned the page. The Big Bad Wolf did come down the chimney into a kettle of hot water placed there by the third little pig—but, to my surprise, rather than being cooked and eaten for dinner, he screamed "Yeeeooow!" and scurried back up the chimney and escaped back into the woods.

> Christie turned to me. "He's gonna come back," she announced.
> I tried to reassure her that the wolf was so scared he wouldn't ever
> come back, but she seemed unconvinced. "Let's read it again," she
> said, and we did. Again, the wolf escaped up the chimney and into the
> woods, and Christie turned to me and said, "He's gonna come right
> back." The next morning Christie wanted to read the story again. We
> did—twice more. Both times, Christie made the same prediction of
> the wolf's return. As we put the story away, Christie asked me, "Does
> the Big Bad Wolf come to *your* house?" I assured her that he did not,
> but she did not seem much comforted. (pp. 69–70)

Christie's mother, who had been using the Disney version of this
story to "shield" her daughter from the more gruesome versions,
described some of the ways in which Christie tried to come to terms
with the story.

> Christie had been asking for that story often, and . . . she also
> frequently initiated dramatic play involving the Big Bad Wolf at her
> pre-school. She had had several nightmares in which she saw the Big
> Bad Wolf, or the Big Bad Wolf had come to her house. (Trousdale,
> 1989, p. 30)

In the end, the cure for Christie's obsession turned out to be a copy
of the unbowdlerized version in which the wolf is more thoroughly
dispatched by being cooked and eaten. This extreme closure proved
sufficient.

Trousdale worked with children and their responses to texts in
various media, but her conclusions about the way the children
internalized the stories are remarkably similar to those drawn by Wolf
and Heath who were operating in a situation confined to verbal stories:

> [T]here were varying interactions between children and media, but
> . . . regardless of the medium of presentation, the children were
> actively constructing their own inner text for the tales. This inner text,
> as represented in their own tellings of the stories, was influenced by
> the version or versions they had had exposure to as well as by their
> own active, selective, imaginative and interpretive mental processes.
> It is the inner text that seemed to be the key to the children's
> responses to the dangerous or evil elements in the tales. (1992, p. 32)

There are many artistic, social and educational questions about how children learn to process stories to which we simply do not know the answers. There is no question that endings are important to children; anyone who has ever tried to omit "The End" when reading a story to children is aware of the significance of that phrase. But "The End" implies a linear construction which is no longer a reliable index of story. The CD-ROM of *The Adventures of Peter Rabbit and Benjamin Bunny*, for example, allows children the possibility of constant deferral. (The scenario of a CD-ROM at bedtime, with the parent looking for closure and the child looking for stalling potential offers us a perspective on new forms of frustration all round.)

There are stories for quite young children which draw on the esthetic option of nonclosure in ways which are relatively new to our culture. David Macaulay's prize-winning *Black and White* is a picture book which defies linearity in highly creative ways; Allan Ahlberg's *Ten in a Bed* provides a set of stories which, among many other things, are actually *about* resistance to closure. Ada's *Dear Peter Rabbit* offers one example of this kind of game-playing with previously closed texts. Children at an early age can grasp highly sophisticated forms of parody. Aesthetic forms are altering in reaction to social and technological changes. Yet we do not know whether small children have specific psychological needs for closure, for security, for a safe harnessing of ambiguity. Nor do we know whether the repetition of a story in numerous formats stretches or shrinks a child's sense of the potential for story, augments or distorts the developing understanding of closure.

Discussing her young readers, Ann Trousdale (1989) suggests, "Many other elements were seemingly negotiable, but a safe and secure happy ending was not" (p. 72). Is this an inviolable fact of childhood, or a culturally specific aspect of the relatively secure life of children in the West, or a romantic notion which will soon vanish as postmodernism makes it to the nursery? I am not sure we know the answer. What I do suggest is that we are meddling with big questions when we alter, defer or devalue closure in our children's stories.

Directionality

The linear nature of the narrative thrust is just one aspect of direction in story-making. There are many questions about directionality in children's exposure to story to which we do not have clear answers.

Does it matter which text a child encounters first? Is an attachment to clarity about the pedigree of a text (is it the book of the film or the film of the book?) simply a reflex response by people who grew up in a more print-based era? Is a generational shift occurring even among today's children?

Are some texts neutral? If a child first encounters Peter Rabbit in the form of a china cup or bowl, does that fact alter a later relationship with the book? What if the first encounter is with the official animation? Are we moving towards a world where any of these questions simply seem hopelessly old-fashioned? Erica Carter, in her Translator's Foreword to Frigga Haug's *Female Sexualization* suggests,

> In the broadest of terms, "postmodern culture" is seen to be characterized by a superabundance of mass-produced cultural artifacts which, though their origins are dissimultaneous, are endlessly reproduced in relations of simultaneity. (Carter, 1987, p. 15)

We operate, she says, "[w]ithin the framework of a cultural logic that anaesthetizes history, reducing it to a synchronic assemblage of esthetic objects" (p. 15).

Our cultural logic may work thus, and indeed it would be easy to illustrate such a thesis by the proliferation of Peter Rabbit materials which I have described. Nevertheless, history lingers in the domestic world of families, even when routed from public sites. Margaret Meek, describing parents reading Beatrix Potter to their children, makes an alternative point, that we cannot subtract our own experience with these texts when we read them to children.

> My suggestion so far has been that we cannot know how children read the little books, what they "make" of them, unless we understand something of what we, the older generation, are up to when we read to inexperienced readers these laden texts from a culture that is part of our history but no longer present. (1995, p. 5)

The Tale of Peter Rabbit bears the weight of these kinds of ambiguity in the many ways it relates to our culture. In what form(s) it survives the kind of saturation marketing which presently engulfs it is a question which remains to be answered.

IMPLICATIONS FOR SCHOLARSHIP

The scholarly study of children's literature is an expanding field, but all too often scholarly attention has been highly filtered in its approach to the field. David Lewis, who describes the picture book as "a form awaiting its history" (May 1995, p. 99), suggests that too much academic attention is paid to a highly selective aspect of the territory. Providing a list of the texts for children which he found in a single large bookshop, Lewis takes account of the junk as well as the quality. It is important not to overlook the rubbish, he says; "a survey that sifts out the better from the worse *before* analysis will not get us very far" (May 1995, p. 100).

> Furthermore, it seems to me that this diversity, this intrinsic heterogeneity, is a most important feature of the picture book. It is easily obscured, however, for those adults who stand between children and the books they read—parents, librarians, teachers, reviewers—tend to filter out whatever is thought to be shoddy: the TV spin-offs, the tackier pop-ups, the unimaginative and the derivative. I am sure a trawl through a good primary school library rather than a high street bookshop would have turned up a very different sample, one that foregrounded narrative, imaginative writing and high quality illustration. The diversity is real, nonetheless, and is a cardinal feature of the form. It is the one characteristic above all others that persuades me the picture book is not a genre but a much more flexible and open-ended type of text. (May 1995, pp. 100–101)

Lewis goes on to suggest that academic study of the picture book is deficient in the way it ignores the ephemeral and the exploitative.

> Surprisingly, there is little in the critical literature on children's books that takes this flexibility and diversity seriously. There is no agreed or established taxonomy of picture books, and rarely do critics consider the form as a whole . . . Put bluntly, the history of the picture book simply does not explain how the picture book came to take on the form it now has. (May 1995, p. 101)

It will be clear that I agree with Lewis, and that this study is one attempt to encompass the scale of the enterprise known as children's literature (or, perhaps more cynically, the enterprise known as selling to children). *The Tale of Peter Rabbit* is something of an exceptional case in the access it provides to extremes of diversity: a subtle work of literature, some complex examples of the challenges of reinterpretation, and many crude examples of exploitation, all parading under the same title. However, the issues raised by this one book are issues which are important for the whole field. To a large extent (and with the notable exception of that helpful and fascinating book *The Brilliant Career of Winnie-the-Pooh* by Ann Thwaite [1994]), they are issues which have been documented and discussed too little. Studies of popular culture take proliferation for granted, but literary studies tend to focus on the original and unique.

A bad worker blames her tools, but it is easy to list ways in which an academic study such as this one lies outside the remit of the formal guidelines. Bibliographic control of the kind of material I have investigated in this project has been a source of constant struggle. Even the brand new MLA Handbook, which was published during the course of my work, does not provide a complete guide to the kinds of problems represented in the bibliography. (At one point, I seriously considered renting out the bibliography as a full-term project for a university cataloguing course!) One particular test case is the issue of the little trademark logo, (TM). I have included it in all references because, for my purposes at least, it carries an important freight of meaning. Should it always be included when the title page includes it with reference to title or author? MLA is silent.

Quality control of the newer media is another issue. The reviewing apparatus for CD-ROMs is lumbering far behind the proliferation of titles, and access to such reviews as do exist is still very difficult. Even gaining access to reviews of television programs (particularly those aimed at children and even more particularly animations) was a laborious process.

On the other hand, some developments are helpful to the person trying to make sense of what is going on in the world of children's literature. I am no business specialist, but I found it extremely simple to gain access to up-to-date analysis of Pearson's strategies and prospects, online in the library and downloadable to my own computer. Pearson's own website could be printed off in my own home. The current social arrangements for the production, presentation and framing of literature, in which very many publishing decisions are made by large international conglomerates, mean that scholars and critics should take full advantage of this new ability to gain access to financial analysis of these companies. The creative artist working in a void, if such a creature ever existed, is not a relevant image today, and we should not be treating children's texts as if they were developed by such a figment of wishful thinking.

As we get used to a new way of thinking about publishing, some of these demands and problems will be resolved with further time and attention; but there are other issues which are more difficult to resolve. As will probably be obvious to all my readers by now, I found it very difficult to write about a seemingly endless set of reiterations of a single story without becoming highly repetitive. With the print versions, it is possible to help readers keep track of different retellings with the judicious use of quotes and illustrations; even this crutch is not available in the discussion of different video or audio versions, and many of the publishers and producers of *Peter Rabbit* material were unwilling to let me reproduce their still images. The sheer scale of the enterprise of recycling makes it hard to be comprehensive in documentation, let alone useful description. Until the day when we make active use of the multimedia potential of computer or CD-ROM to let us "quote" from many media in our critical discussions, we will continue to face problems of how to represent different forms of production within the confines of a print-based analysis. And until the copyright situation is clarified, it will continue to be easier to make references to print than to any other format.

In the meantime, it is important to acknowledge the real size and scope of contemporary publication and production of fiction for children. I have two file storage boxes overflowing with texts of *The Tale of Peter Rabbit*. With an unlimited budget, I could probably fill one or two more, simply with texts of one kind and another; a collection which included a single example of everything I have seen, toys, clothes, china and so forth, would undoubtedly fill a good-sized storeroom. And I am under no illusion that I have seen everything available or even come close.

To register and make sense of this scale of production without being overwhelmed is a challenge. To find useful ways of thinking and talking about what is happening to some forms of fiction for children is an even greater challenge. And yet we must, because what is happening is important and we do not know what the consequences are going to be, for our children, for those who deal with them, and for the works of art which undergo this kind of commodification.

The implications for what we call reading are also very important. The minimal degree of hypertext involved in the *Peter Rabbit* CD-ROMs is perhaps not all that important in itself, but in very real ways it is serving as an introduction to a different kind of reading process. We are already getting a glimpse of a kind of reading in which fragmentation and discontinuity are the strategic norm and in which gaps may actually be created by an individual reader's decisions. We know too little about where technological developments are taking us *as readers*.

Patrick Bazin, the director of the Bibliothèque de Lyon, describes some of the contemporary changes in reading very succinctly:

> Struggling free from the straitjacket of the book and directing its efforts toward a true polytextuality—in which diverse types of texts and images, sounds, films, data banks, mail services, interactive networks may mutually resist or interfere with one another—this process of reading generates progressively a new dimension (polymorphic, transversal, and dynamic). We might call it metareading. (1996, p. 154)

It may be possible to make the argument that the realities of commercial multiplication of children's texts are, whether deliberately or inadvertently, creating the conditions for the development of a kind of metareading skill which will suit today's children to the new demands of reading in the 21st century. Alternatively, it may be that children who are learning about reading in this context will grow up to demand and create their own new forms of reading and of fictional engagement and of nonfictional organization.

Such outcomes are possible, but it is difficult to see any form of cultural wisdom at work in the conditions which have created the current glut of *Peter Rabbits*. Most of the current revolution is led by scientific and financial determinants; the cultural implications trail behind. Artists have always made use of prevailing technology and market conditions but it is not clear how much genuinely new art for children is being produced in current technology; most material for young children today derives from works in earlier media. Will reading change as these conditions change? What will be the impact on future art—literature, music, illustration, animation—of the expectations being inculcated in today's children?

And what of the impact of this situation on one specific artist, Beatrix Potter? Humphrey Carpenter has described Potter's effects on some notable 20th-century writers for adults. He speaks of "the force of her imagination, the acknowledgement that she had the power of creating archetypes that remain with her readers for the rest of their lives" (1989, p. 277). Can we safely take for granted that an archetype is something so powerful that we need not worry about the effects of constant and repeated trivialization? Can we blithely assume that any rerendering of a work of art is culturally interesting in its own right and not an issue of concern in the long run?

I am, of course, weighting my questions unfairly. I do not know what Beatrix Potter's powers of survival really are. The little books have lasted pretty well up to now, but the effects of the new multipliers applied to them in the 1990s are far from being clear. In some very real and important ways, her books have moved into the territory of the folk tale and are seen as public property, fair game for reworking. In Marina Warner's useful phrase, they may now be seen as "porous" (1995, p. 255). Yet, as we have seen, such porousness, such plasticity, comes at the cost of the loss of much of what made the original work so striking and significant. Benjamin's "aura" is more than a token of artificial market value.

Meanwhile, children keep coming along, learning about the world, at least in part, through the texts made available to them. Children's literature is important for many reasons, but as David Lewis points out, it is not only the good stuff that matters. The questions about fragmentation, proliferation and salesmanship are ones which we need to acknowledge and to try to begin to answer.

References

BIBLIOGRAPHY

"£25,000 Peter Rabbit Unearthed." *Daily Telegraph*, June 27, 1995: 11.

Ada, Alma Flor. *Dear Peter Rabbit*. Illus. Leslie Tryon. New York: Atheneum, 1994.

Ahlberg, Allan and André Amstutz. *Ten in a Bed*. London: Puffin, 1990.

Ahlberg, Janet and Allan. *The Jolly Pocket Postman*. London: William Heinemann, 1995.

Alderson, Brian. "Peter Rabbit's Fate Worse than Death." *Times*, September 17, 1987: 16.

———. "Peter's New Colors." *Times Educational Supplement*, June 5, 1987: 63.

Anderson-Inman, Lynne, Mark A. Horney, Der-Thanq Chen and Larry Lewin. "Hypertext Literacy: Observations from the ElectroText Project." *Language Arts* 71, April 1994: 279–287.

Bazin, Patrick. "Toward Metareading." *The Future of the Book*, ed. Geoffrey Nunberg, with an afterword by Umberto Eco. Berkeley: University of California Press, 1996.

Beilby, M. et al. "Pearson—Company Report." S.G. Warburg Securities, January 19, 1995. *Investext*. Online. InfoTrac. May 26, 1995.

Bell, Emily. "Publish and Broadcasting Be Damned." *Observer*, January 12, 1997: 5.

Bell, Emily. "Reed Lays Future On-Line." *Observer*, July 23, 1995.

Benjamin, Walter. "The Work of Art in the Age of Mechanical Reproduction." *Illuminations*, ed. Hannah Arendt. Trans. Harry Zohn. New York: Schocken Books, 1969.

Bennett, Catherine. "Hype and Heritage." *Guardian*, September 22, 1995: 2–4.

Bodin, Madeline. "100 Candles for Peter Rabbit." *Publishers Weekly*, March 29, 1993: 19–20.

Bourette, Susan and Michael Grange. "Mega-complex coming to a theater near you." *Globe and Mail*, August 28, 1995: B1–B2.

Bowering, Marilyn. "Peter Rabbit Sex Poem." *Sleeping with Lambs*. Online. Available at URL: http://www.swifty.com/SW/cone/MBsleeping/sleepingl.html February 2, 1996.

Bradford Exchange. "Join Peter Rabbit on his exciting adventures with this musical three-dimensional collector's plate." Advertisement. *Canadian Living*, April 1995: n.p.

Brown, Craig. "Having a Jolly Rotten Time." Review of *The World of Peter Rabbit and Friends*, produced by John Coates. *Sunday Times*, December 27, 1992: 4.4–4.5.

Bruner, Jerome. *Acts of Meaning*. Cambridge, MA: Harvard University Press, 1990.

Buckingham, Lisa and Roger Cowe. "Capitalism Faces Consumer Backlash." *Guardian Weekly*, July 2, 1995: 15.

Buss, Robin. "Rabbit and Pork about Peter." *Times Educational Supplement*, December 11, 1992: 33.

Carpenter, Humphrey. "Excessively Impertinent Bunnies: The Subversive Element in Beatrix Potter." *Children and their Books: A Celebration of the Work of Iona and Peter Opie*. Ed. Gillian Avery and Julia Briggs. Oxford: Clarendon Press, 1989.

Carpenter, Humphrey and Mari Prichard. *The Oxford Companion to Children's Literature*. Oxford: Oxford University Press, 1984.

Carter, Erica, trans. *Female Sexualization: A Collective Work of Memory*. By Frigga Haug and Others, 1983. London: Verso, 1987.

Chambers, Aidan. "The Difference of Literature: Writing Now for the Future of Young Readers." *Celebrating Children's Literature in Education*, ed. Geoff Fox. London: Hodder & Stoughton, 1995.

Chatman, Seymour. *Coming to Terms: The Rhetoric of Narrative in Fiction and Film*. Ithaca: Cornell University Press, 1990.

Collins, David R. *The Country Artist: A Story About Beatrix Potter*. Illus. Karen Ritz. Minneapolis: Carolrhoda Books, 1989.

Cox, Roger. "Audio Versions of Children's Stories." Conference paper. "Celebrating *Children's Literature in Education*" Conference, Devon, U.K., 1995.

Darnton, John. "The Japanese, Lots of Them, Call on Peter Rabbit." *New York Times International*, September 7, 1995: A4.

Diller, Barry. "Don't Repackage—Redefine!" *Wired*, February 1995: 82–84.

Dyson, Esther. "Intellectual Value." *Wired*, July 1995: 136–141, 182–184.

Enchin, Harvey. "CanWest Bid Fails in Britain: Pearson PLC Wins Channel 5 Licence." *Globe and Mail*, October 28, 1995: B2.

Engelhardt, Tom. "Reading May Be Harmful to Your Kids." *Harper's Magazine*, June 1991: 55–62.

Epstein, Jacob. "'Good Bunnies Always Obey': Books for American Children." 1963. *Only Connect: Readings on Children's Literature*, ed. Sheila Egoff, G.T. Stubbs and L.F. Ashley. Toronto: Oxford University Press, 1969.

Extel Financial Companies Service. *Pearson plc*. Company Report. London: Extel Financial Limited, June 23, 1995.

Fakih, Kimberley Olson. "Brightening Up Beatrix." *Publishers Weekly*, September 25, 1987: 25–26.

"Financial—Pearson: Pearson plc Preliminary Results (unaudited), Year ended 31 December 1996." *Pearson plc Website*. Online. Available at URL: http://www.pearson-plc.com/finance/pearson.htm March 19, 1997.

Find Out About Beatrix Potter: Projects, Presents and Puzzles. London: Frederick Warne with the National Trust, 1987.

Foucault, Michel. "What is an Author?" *The Foucault Reader*, ed. Paul Rabinow. New York: Pantheon, 1984.

Gass, William H. *Fiction and the Figures of Life*. Boston: David R. Godine, 1979.

Godden, Rumer. "An Imaginary Correspondence." 1963. *Only Connect: Readings on Children's Literature*. Ed. Sheila Egoff, G.T. Stubbs and L.F. Ashley. Toronto: Oxford University Press, 1969.

———. *The Tale of the Tales: The Beatrix Potter Ballet*. London: Frederick Warne, 1971.

Goldthwaite, John. "Sis Beatrix (Part One)." *Signal* 53, May 1987: 117–137.

Graham, Judith. "Trouble for Arthur's Teacher? A Closer Look at Reading CD ROMS." *English and Media Magazine* 31, Autumn 1994: 15–17.

Gray, John. "Why Irony Can't Be Superior: The Contradictions of Richard Rorty's Postmodernism." *Times Literary Supplement*, November 3, 1995: 4–5.

Hale, Robert D. "Musings." *Horn Book Magazine* LXIV(1). January/February 1988: 100–101.

Hamilton, Alan. "Rabbit Tale Takes on a New Look." *Times*, September 16, 1987: 5.

The History of The Tale of Peter Rabbit. Taken mainly from Leslie Linder's *A History of the Writings of Beatrix Potter Together with the Text and*

Illustrations from the First Privately Printed Edition. London: Frederick Warne, 1976.

Hollindale, Peter. "Ideology and the Children's Book." *Signal* 55, November 1988: 3–22.

Howlett, Karen and Susan Bourette. "Pension, Mutual Funds Dominate TSE Trading." *Globe and Mail*, July 21, 1995: B1–B6.

Iser, Wolfgang. *The Act of Reading: A Theory of Aesthetic Response*. Trans. of *Der Akt des Lesens*, 1976. Baltimore: Johns Hopkins University Press, 1978.

Kinder, Marsha. *Playing with Power in Movies, Television and Video Games: From Muppet Babies to Teenage Mutant Ninja Turtles*. Berkeley: University of California Press, 1991.

Klein, Norman M. *Seven Minutes: The Life and Death of the American Animated Cartoon*. London: Verso, 1993.

Kline, Stephen. *Out of the Garden: Toys and Children's Culture in the Age of TV Marketing*. Culture and Communication in Canada Series. Toronto: Garamond, 1993.

Kreuger, Lesley. "Can't Sneak Creationism In by the Back Door." *Globe and Mail*, June 30, 1995: A20.

Ladybird. Catalogue. Toronto: Penguin Canada, Fall 1995.

Lane, Margaret. *The Tale of Beatrix Potter: A Biography*, 1946. Revised edition. London: Frederick Warne, 1968.

Lees, Janet. "Licensed to Sell." *Bookseller*, 11 December 1992: 1764–1766.

Letterbox Presents. Catalogue. Truro, Cornwall: Letterbox, 1995–1996.

Lewis, David. "The Picture Book: A Form Awaiting Its History." *Signal* 77, May 1995: 99–112.

———. "The Jolly Postman's Long Ride, or, Sketching a Picture-Book History." *Signal* 78, September 1995: 178–192.

Linder, Leslie. *A History of the Writings of Beatrix Potter, Including Unpublished Work*. London: Frederick Warne, 1971.

Lowry, Malcolm. *Under the Volcano*. Penguin Modern Classics, 1947. Harmondsworth, Middlesex: Penguin Books in association with Jonathan Cape, 1963.

Macaulay, David. *Black and White*. Boston: Houghton Mifflin, 1990.

Mackey, Margaret. "Communities of Fictions: Story, Format and *Thomas the Tank Engine*." *Children's Literature in Education* 26(1), 1995: 39–51.

Meek, Margaret. "Protocols of Reading: The Little Books of Beatrix Potter." *Books for Keeps* No. 92, May 1995: 4–5.

————. "What Counts as Evidence in Theories of Children's Literature?" *Children's Literature: The Development of Criticism*. Ed. Peter Hunt. London: Routledge, 1990.

"Michael Lynton to Join Pearson plc." *Pearson plc Website*, August 5, 1996. Online. Available at URL: http://www.pearson-plc.com/news/contents/headline/current/pengceo.htm March 5, 1997.

Mitchard, Jacquelyn. "Peter Rabbit: Just How Fuzzy Was He?" *TV Guide*, March 27, 1993: 26–27.

Morash, Gordon. "Bridges Spins Gold for Mawkish Waller." *Edmonton Journal*, July 16, 1995: E5.

Munro, C. et al. "Pearson—Company Report." Hoare Govett Securities, July 12, 1994. Thomson Financial Networks. *Investext*. Online. InfoTrac. May 26, 1995.

O'Connor, John J. "Such a Mischievous Bunny Boy." Review of *The World of Peter Rabbit and Friends*, produced John Coates. *New York Times*, March 29, 1993: B10.

National Trust Centenary Beatrix Potter Competition. Advertising leaflet. 1995.

Paige, Robin. *Death at Gallows Green*. New York: Avon Books, 1995.

Parrinder, Patrick. "The 70 Year Hitch." *Times Higher Education Supplement*, December 10, 1993: 19.

Paterson, Richard and Belinda Richards. "Is There a Peter Rabbit in the House?" *Bookseller*, November 16, 1990: 1468–1470.

"Peter Rabbit Comes to Life." *Bookseller*, April 9, 1993: 32.

Pope, Kyle. "Pearson Shareholders Getting Anxious." *Globe and Mail*, May 21, 1996: B10.

Potter, Beatrix. *Letters to Children*. New York: Harvard College Library Department of Printing and Graphic Arts and Walker and Company, 1966.

Potter, Beatrix. *The Tale of Benjamin Bunny*. London: Frederick Warne, 1904.

Reuter news item. No title. Online. June 14, 1996.

Review of *The Tale of Peter Rabbit and Benjamin Bunny*, produced John Coates. *Publishers Weekly*, March 15 1993: 31.

Rose, Sue. "The Tale of Beatrix Potter." *In Britain: The Magazine of the British Tourist Authority*, April 1993: 6–10.

Salvio, Paula M. "On the Forbidden Pleasures and Hidden Dangers of Covert Reading." *English Quarterly* 27(3), Spring 1995: 8–15.

Savy, Nicole and Diana Syrat. *Beatrix Potter and Peter Rabbit*. London: Frederick Warne, 1993.

Schultz, Charles. *Peanuts*. Syndicated comic strip. *Edmonton Journal*, August 1, 1995: C6.

Sefton-Green, Julian. "From Real Books to Play Books to Un-Books: Developments in Digital Publishing." *English and Media Magazine* 30: Summer 1994: 32–37.

Shatz-Akin, Jim with Connie Guglielmo, Rik Myslewski and Joseph Schorr. "The Ultimate Guide to Children's Software." *MacUser*, December 1994: 97–104.

Shreiner, David F. "The Way of the Flesh." *Amorous Poems*. Online. Available at URL: http://www.webcom.com/~orpheus/amor.html
February 2, 1996.

Strassel, Kimberley A. "Pearson to Launch U.S. Edition of Financial Times." *Globe and Mail*, March 18, 1997: B8.

Susina, Jan. "Editor's Note: Kiddie Lit(e): The Dumbing Down of Children's Literature." *The Lion and the Unicorn* 17(1), June 1993: v–ix.

"Switch On to an Animated Autumn." *Bookseller*, September 4, 1992: 675.

Talbot, Bryan. *The Tale of One Bad Rat*. Milwaukie, OR: Dark Horse Books, 1995.

Taylor, Jennifer. "Updated Beatrix Potter Brews a Storm in Britain." *Publishers Weekly*, October 30, 1987: 26.

Taylor, Judy. Letter. *Bookseller*, October 9, 1987: 1517.

———. *Beatrix Potter: Artist, Storyteller and Countrywoman*. Harmondsworth, Middlesex: Frederick Warne- Penguin, 1986.

———. *Beatrix Potter: Artist, Storyteller and Countrywoman*. Revised edition. London: Frederick Warne-Penguin, 1996.

"The Revised Peter Rabbit." Editorial. *Guardian*, September 16, 1987: 14.

The V&A Treasury. The Victoria and Albert Museum Mail Order Catalogue. Christmas 1995.

"The Year of the Rabbit." *Bookseller*, 4 December 1992: 1710.

Thwaite, Ann. *The Brilliant Career of Winnie-the-Pooh: The Story of A.A. Milne and his Writing for Children*, 1992. London: Methuen, 1994.

Trousdale, Ann. *"Who's Afraid of the Big, Bad Wolf."* Children's Literature in Education 20(2), June 1989: 69–79.

Tucker, Nicholas. "From Fairy Tales to Barbie Dolls." *Times Educational Supplement*, May 2, 1997: 25.

Walker, Tim. "How Peter Rabbit Got into a Stew." *Observer*, September 20, 1987: 7.

Warne, Frederick. Advertisement. *Bookseller*, October 9, 1992, front cover and verso.

Warne, Frederick. Advertisement. *Bookseller*, September 11, 1987, front cover.

Warne, Frederick. Catalogue. Toronto: Penguin Canada, Fall 1995.

Warner, Marina. *From the Beast to the Blonde: On Fairy Tales and their Tellers*. 1994. London: Vintage, 1995.

Winner, Ellen. *Invented Worlds: The Psychology of the Arts*. Cambridge MA: Harvard University Press, 1982.

Wolf, Shelby Anne and Shirley Brice Heath. *The Braid of Literature: Children's Worlds of Reading*. Cambridge MA: Harvard University Press, 1992.

VERSIONS OF *THE TALE OF PETER RABBIT*

Original work

Potter, Beatrix. *The Tale of Peter Rabbit*. 1902. New reproductions. London: Frederick Warne-Penguin, 1987.

———. *The Tale of Peter Rabbit*. London: Frederick Warne, n.d.

———. *The Tale of Peter Rabbit*. New York: Dover, 1972.

Adaptations

Story books

The New Adventures of Peter Rabbit. Adapted from the Golden Films Production of *The New Adventures of Peter Rabbit*. Adaptation by Bonnie Trachtenberg. Enchanted Tales series. New York: Sony Wonder, 1995.

Potter, Beatrix. *The Complete Adventures of Peter Rabbit*, 1982. London: Puffin-Penguin, 1984.

———. *The Complete Tales of Peter Rabbit and Other Favorite Stories*. Illus. Charles Santore. Philadelphia: Courage-Running Press, 1986.

———. *Peter Rabbit and Eleven Other Favorite Tales*. Illus. Pat Stewart. Dover Children's Thrift Classics. New York: Dover, 1994.

———. *The Tale of Peter Rabbit*. London: Puffin-Penguin, in association with Frederick Warne, 1991.

———. *The Tale of Peter Rabbit*. Beatrix Potter Jumbo Storybooks. Madison Jumbo Books-Ottenheimer Publishers, 1993.

———. *The Tale of Peter Rabbit*. The Original Peter Rabbit Miniature Collection. London: Frederick Warne, 1986.

———. *The Tale of Peter Rabbit*. [Some pictures omitted] Ashland, OH: Landoll's-Ottenheimer, 1993.

———. *The Tale of Peter Rabbit.* [Some rewording] Illus. Florence Graham. New York: Grosset & Dunlap, 1990.

———. *The Tale of Peter Rabbit.* Illus. David Jorgensen. New York: Golden Book-Western, 1988.

———. *The Tale of Peter Rabbit.* Illus. David McPhail. New York: Scholastic, 1986.

———. *The Tale of Peter Rabbit.* Illus. David McPhail. Favourite Tales from David McPhail. New York: Scholastic-Cartwheel Books, 1986.

———. *The Tale of Peter Rabbit.* Illus. Adriana Mazza Saviozzi. 1958. New York: Little Golden Book-Western, 1970.

———. *The Tale of Peter Rabbit.* Illus. Adriana Mazza Saviozzi. 1958. New York: Little Little Golden Book- Western, 1993.

———. *The Tale of Peter Rabbit.* Illus. Cyndy Szekeres. New York: Golden Book-Western, 1993.

———. *The Tale of Peter Rabbit Big Golden Book.* Illus. Cyndy Szekeres. New York: Golden Book-Western, 1993.

———. *The Tale of Peter Rabbit and Other Stories.* Illus. Lulu Delacre. New York: Julian Messner, 1985.

———. *Tales of Peter Rabbit.* Illus. Charles Santore. Philadelphia: Running Press, 1991.

———. *The Tales of Peter Rabbit and The Flopsy Bunnies.* London: Frederick Warne, 1995.

———. *The World of Beatrix Potter(TM): 13 Original Peter Rabbit(TM) Tales.* London: Frederick Warne, 1993.

The Tale of Peter Rabbit. Based on the original and authorized story by Beatrix Potter. Loughborough, Leicestershire: Ladybird Books in association with Frederick Warne, 1992.

The Tale of Peter Rabbit. Based on the original and authorized story by Beatrix Potter. Adapted David Hately. Lewiston ME: Ladybird Books in association with Frederick Warne, 1988.

The Tale of Peter Rabbit. Based on the original and authorized story by Beatrix Potter. Adapted David Hately. Loughborough, Leicestershire: Ladybird Books in association with Frederick Warne, 1987.

The Tale of Peter Rabbit. Based on the original story by Beatrix Potter. Retold Sarah Toast. Illus. Pat Schoonover. Lincolnwood, IL: Little Rainbow-Publications International, 1995.

The Tale of Peter Rabbit and Benjamin Bunny. From the authorized animated series based on the original tales by Beatrix Potter. London: Frederick Warne, 1992.

The Tale of Peter Rabbit. Gallery Gold (TM) Little Classics. Noel MO: Gallery Graphics, 1993.

Board books

Dinner Time. Beatrix Potter First Board Books. Harmondsworth, Middlesex: Frederick Warne-Penguin, 1991.

Peter Rabbit. Based on the original story by Beatrix Potter with all new illustrations. Illus. Wendy Edelson. Leap Frog Lift-a-Flap. Lincolnwood, IL: Publications International, 1996.

Peter Rabbit and his Friends. Beatrix Potter (TM) Mini Board Books. London: Frederick Warne, 1993.

The Peter Rabbit Peek-Through Board Books: Bunnies. London: Frederick Warne, 1995.

The Peter Rabbit Peek-Through Board Books: Mice. London: Frederick Warne, 1995.

Potter, Beatrix. *Meet Peter Rabbit.* Harmondsworth, Middlesex: Frederick Warne-Penguin, 1986.

The Tale of Peter Rabbit. Illus. Florence Graham. Pudgy Pal Board Book. New York: Grosset and Dunlap, 1994.

The Tale of Peter Rabbit. Retold Maida Silverman. Illus. Jody Wheeler. A Golden Take-a-Look Book. Racine, WI: Golden Book-Western Publishing, 1995.

A Tiny Tale of Peter Rabbit. Illus. David Carlson. A Chubby Board Book. New York: Little Simon/Simon & Schuster, 1982.

Pop-up books and movables

Dear Peter Rabbit. A story featuring the letters written for children by Beatrix Potter (TM). London: Frederick Warne, 1995.

The Original Pop-Up Peter Rabbit. London: Frederick Warne, 1996.

The Peter Rabbit Spectacular: A Giant Pop-Up-and-Play Book. Based on the original tales by Beatrix Potter. London: Frederick Warne, 1994.

Potter, Beatrix. *The Tale of Peter Rabbit Animated!* Illus. Julian Wehr. New York: Grosset and Dunlop, 1943.

———. *The Tale of Peter Rabbit: A Pop-Up Book.* Retold Elsa Knight Bruno. N.p.: Smithbooks-Ottenheimer, 1991.

Scenes from The Tale of Peter Rabbit. Adapted from The Tale of Peter Rabbit by Beatrix Potter. London: Frederick Warne, 1989.

Where's Peter Rabbit?: A Lift-the-Flap Book. From *The Tale of Peter Rabbit* by Beatrix Potter. Design and illustrations, Colin Twinn, 1988. London: Picture Puffin-Penguin, 1993.

Instructional books

Bray-Moffatt, Naia. *The Peter Rabbit and Friends(TM) Cook Book*. Illustrations from the authorized animated series based on the original tales by Beatrix Potter(TM). London: Frederick Warne, 1994.

Dobrin, Arnold. *Peter Rabbit's Natural Foods Cookbook*. Illus. Beatrix Potter. New York: Frederick Warne, 1977.

Menchini, Pat. *The Beatrix Potter Knitting Book*. London: Frederick Warne, 1987.

Potter, Beatrix. *Peter Rabbit's ABC*. With new reproductions from the original illustrations. London: Frederick Warne, 1987.

———. *Peter Rabbit's (TM) ABC and 123*. London: Frederick Warne-Penguin, 1995.

Smith, Debbie. *The Peter Rabbit(TM) Craft Book*. From the original and authorized stories by Beatrix Potter(TM). London: Bloomsbury Books in association with Frederick Warne, 1987.

Miscellaneous

Beatrix Potter(TM) Posters. London: Frederick Warne, 1988.

Beatrix Potter(TM) Miniature Nursery Library. Boxed set of three books: *A First Peter Rabbit Book* (1996, *Peter Rabbit's ABC 123* (1995), *Beatrix Potter's Nursery Rhyme Book* (1995). London: Frederick Warne, 1997.

Dear Ivy, Dear June: Letters from Beatrix Potter. Published for the Friends of the Osborne and Lillian H. Smith Collections, Toronto Public Library by Other Press, 1977.

Audiovisual materials

Audiotapes

The Beatrix Potter Book and Storytape Collection. London: Frederick Warne, 1989.

The Beatrix Potter(TM) Soundbook(TM). Reader Claire Bloom. Audiocassettes and program booklet. New York: Caedmon, 1974.

Meryl Streep Reads The Tale of Peter Rabbit. Story Beatrix Potter. Music Lyle Mays. Audiocassette. Rowayton, CT: Western-Rabbit Ears, 1988.

The New Adventures of Peter Rabbit. Adaptation Bonnie Trachtenberg. Music Guy Moon. Narrator Corey Burton. Enchanted Tales series. Audiocassette. New York: Sony Wonder, 1995.

Potter, Beatrix. The Tale of Peter Rabbit and The Tale of Benjamin Bunny. "Follow the Reader," FTR 69. Audiocassette, book and study guide. Old Greenwich, CT: Listening Library, 1983.

———. The Tale of Peter Rabbit. "Look, Listen and Read" Filmstrips. Filmstrip, audiocassette and study guide. Old Greenwich, CT: Listening Library, 1977.

———. The Tale of Peter Rabbit and The Tale of Benjamin Bunny. The World of Peter Rabbit and Friends. Audiocassette. BBC Young Collection, 1993.

———. The Tale of Peter Rabbit and The Tale of the Flopsy Bunnies. Reader Rosemary Leach. Music Carl Davis. Audiocassette. Helen Nicoll Productions for Frederick Warne, 1987.

Videotapes

Beatrix Potter (TM): Artist, Storyteller and Countrywoman. Narrated by Lynn Redgrave. Produced in cooperation with Frederick Warne & Co. Based on the book by Judy Taylor. Videocassette,. CT: Weston Woods, n.d.

The New Adventures of Peter Rabbit. Producer Diane Dskenazi. Enchanted Tales series. Videocassette. New York: Golden Films-Sony Wonder, 1995.

The Parables of Peter Rabbit: Friends. Producer/director Ricky Blair. Videocassette. Brentwood, TN: Brentwood Music, 1994.

The Parables of Peter Rabbit: Faith over Fear. Dir. Michelle Weigle Brown. Producer Ricky Blair Videocassette. Brentwood, TN: Brentwood Music, 1995.

The Tale of Mr. Jeremy Fisher and *The Tale of Peter Rabbit.* Reader Meryl Streep. Illus. David Jorgensen. Story Beatrix Potter. Music Lyle Mays. Produced Mark Sottnick. Videocassette. Rabbit Ears Storybook Classics, 1988. Children's Classics from the Stars.

The Tale of Peter Rabbit and Benjamin Bunny by Beatrix Potter. Dir. Geoff Dunbar and produced Ginger Gibbons for Grand Slamm Partnership. Based on the Original Peter Rabbit Books (TM) by Beatrix Potter. *The World of Peter Rabbit and Friends* (TM) series produced by TVC London for Frederick Warne and Co. Series dir. Dianne Jackson. Series producer John Coates. Frederick Warne and Co., 1993. Videocassette. Pickering, ON: HGV Video Productions Inc.

Tales of Beatrix Potter. Dancers of The Royal Ballet in association with The Royal Opera House, Covent Garden. Dir. Reginald Mills. Choreography Frederick Ashton. Designed Christine Edzard. Music John Lanchbery. Produced Richard Goodwin. Executive producer John Brabourne. EMI Film Productions Limited, 1971. Videocassette. HBO Video.

Tales of Beatrix Potter. Narrator Sydney Walker. Producer/Director Brian McNamara. Illustrator/Animator Penny Yrigoyen, Mark Escott, Robert Burke Sound On-Tape Productions, Motion Control Video. Videocassette. Coffee Table Videos, 1986.

CD-ROMs and computer texts

"Peter Rabbit's Math Garden." *CD-ROM Today: The Disc*. Disc #18, December 1995.

Potter, Beatrix. *The Adventures of Peter Rabbit and Benjamin Bunny (TM)*. CD-ROM. Peter Rabbit's Interactive World. Novato, CA: Mindscape, 1995.

———. *The Tale of Peter Rabbit*. CD-ROM. Text and illustrations, London: Frederick Warne, 1902. Background audio, text and pictures and Discis Book software, Buffalo, NY: Discis Knowledge Research, 1994.

The Tale of Peter Rabbit. Interactive Books. Illus. Lonnie Sue Johnson. Diskette. La Crescenta, CA: Knowledge Adventure, 1993.

Activity books

Beatrix Potter Scrapbook and Scraps. Licensed by Copyrights. Bury St. Edmunds: Mamelok Press-Frederick Warne. 1993.

LaBelle, Susan Whited. *Little Peter Rabbit Paper Dolls*. New York: Dover, 1985.

Peter Rabbit: A Beatrix Potter Story to Color. Based on the original story by Beatrix Potter. Auburn, ME: Ladybird Books, 1988.

Peter Rabbit and Friends(TM), No. 17. Fun to Learn Series. Illus. and text based on *The World of Peter Rabbit and Friends(TM)*, produced for Frederick Warne, 1992, 1993, 1994. London: Redan, June 1995.

Peter Rabbit's Puzzle Book. Based on the original and authorized stories by Beatrix Potter. Devised and illustrated by Colin Twinn. London: Frederick Warne, 1987.

Potter, Beatrix. *The Little Tale of Peter Rabbit: A Coloring Book*. Rendered for coloring by Anna Pomaska. New York: Dover, 1986.

———. *Peter Rabbit(TM): A Puzzle Play Book*. New York: Seafarer Books-Penguin, 1993.

————. *Peter Rabbit Colouring Book.* Paignton, Devon: Ladybird Books, 1992.

————. *Peter Rabbit Sticker Book.* London: Ladybird Books-Frederick Warne, 1992.

————. *The Tale of Peter Rabbit: A Coloring Book.* Rendered for coloring by Nancy Perkins. New York: Dover, 1971.

————. *The Tale of Peter Rabbit Coloring Book.* Adapted by Howard L. Roy into Signed English. Illus. Ralph R. Miller. Washington, DC: Kendall Green-Gallaudet UP, n.d.

The Peter Rabbit and Friends(TM) Poster Activity Book. From the authorized animated series based on the original tales by Beatrix Potter(TM). Harmondsworth, Middlesex: Frederick Warne-Penguin, 1995.

The Peter Rabbit Theatre: Starring Peter Rabbit and Benjamin Bunny. Based on the original and authorized stories by Beatrix Potter(TM). Theater created and illus. Colin Twinn, 1983. London: Frederick Warne-Penguin, 1992.

The Tale of Peter Rabbit: A Rebus Sticker Storybook. Based on the original authorized edition by Beatrix Potter(TM). Created and manufactured by arrangement with Ottenheimer Publisher, Inc. under license from Frederick Warne. Toronto: Stewart House, 1996.

The World of Peter Rabbit Sticker Book. From the original and authorized stories by Beatrix Potter. Illustrations by Colin Twinn. London: Frederick Warne, 1990.

The World of Peter Rabbit(TM) Treasury. From the authorized animated series based on the original tales by Beatrix Potter(TM). London: Bloomsbury Books in association with Frederick Warne-Penguin, 1994.

APPENDIX

Categories of Peter Rabbit Commodities*

apron (adult)
advent calendar
alphabet book
audiotape
baby "brag book"
baby china
baby clothes
baby day book for first year
baby mirror
"baby sleeping" sign
bib
big book
birthday party invitation
board book
board game
bookmark
cake
calendar
CD-ROM
change-purse
checkers/draughts game
china bookend
china figurine
china/music-box collectible
chocolate eggs
christening mug

clock
cloth book
cloth rattle
coasters
coloring book
computer program
cook book
counting book
crayons
cutlery
decorative egg
decorative storage pot
diary
eraser
facecloth/face flannel
finger puppet
framed découpage picture
glass rondel
greeting card
growth chart
hooded towel set
jam
jigsaw
mask book
miniature book
mobile

monthly activity magazine
musical mobile
notebook
nursery frieze
pacifier/dummy
pencil holder
photograph album
picture frame
pill box
placemat
plaster casting mold
plastic bath book
pop-up book
porcelain bookends
postcard
poster
poster activity book
printed cotton fabric
puzzle-play book
soap

socks
stationery
stencils
stick puppet
stick-on wall decoration
sticker book
stuffed toy
stuffed toy with music box
sweater
T-shirt
tea
toothbrush
towel
two-handled training beaker
video
waterball
wooden bookends

plus a special promotion on Kellogg's cereal boxes

*these are category headings only; some entries on this list represent dozens of different items

Index